HOW TO GO COLLECTING MODEL SOLDIERS

HOW TO GO COLLECTING MODEL SOLDIERS

Henry Harris

With a chapter on wargames
by Donald F. Featherstone

Foreword by
Brigadier Peter Young, DSO, MC, MA, FSA, FRHistS

PSL

PATRICK STEPHENS
LONDON

SBN 85059 036 1

1st edition—August 1969

Set in 9 on 10pt Juliana Roman type.
Printed on M6 Cartridge 36×46 110/500 for
Patrick Stephens Limited, 9 Ely Place,
London EC1. Printed and bound by
Hazell Watson & Viney Ltd., Aylesbury, Bucks.

Foreword

by Brigadier Peter Young, DSO, MC

FIFTY YEARS have passed since, during the closing months of the First World War, someone presented me with my first model soldier. My interest in the Wargame, though more recent, goes back at least to 1935 when I was first initiated into its mysteries by the late Captain J. C. Sachs, whose armies were geared to the 1912 period, and Dr P. B. Cornwall, an exponent of Napoleonic warfare. Since those days the number of devotees of miniature violence have multiplied so that the founder members of the British Model Soldiers Society, some of whom, happily, are still with us, must be truly astonished at the success of their efforts to pass on the expertise of the craft.

Thirty years ago it was difficult, at any rate in England, to find soldiers in anything but the full-dress uniform of the period just prior to the Great War. Nor can it be said that such figures as were obtainable were remarkable for their animation. Thanks to the efforts of Carman, Stadden, Surén, Hinton, Hunt, Russell Gammage and a host of others, both amateur and professional, all that has changed.

Henry Harris, soldier and historian as well as collector, is one of those who has contributed to the forward march of these model armies. But his book is not just another book about model soldiers. Within the limits of 200 pages he traces the origin and development of the arms and corps of the fighting forces, giving the collector the background of each, and emphasising that his hobby can be a valuable stimulus to the study of military history.

The author is alive to the technical problems, and at the end of each section and chapter gives the would-be model maker practical yet imaginative suggestions for converting models normally available in the main stores. He gives the beginner his ideas as to the general lines, the 'Order of Battle', on which a collection may be built up, but here, in the nature of things, no two collectors will agree—and perish the thought that they should!

I am not one of those that believes in making my own soldiers. I have neither the skill nor the patience. It is possible, however, to derive much pleasure from designing dioramas, or building up units and formations, without wielding the scalpel and the paint brush oneself. This book, however, caters for the collector—the more normal collector perhaps—who derives real satisfaction from making his own figures. He will find fascination in the chapters, 'The Sinews of Model War', and 'Hints and Tips on Making-up Models'.

The range of interest in this book is wide and, with an attention to detail which I find wholly admirable, we are even offered an appendix detailing the martial music which should be played as metal heroes or plastic hordes join battle. The pictures show the great variety of ways in which models can be displayed, as well as illustrating their use in wargames.

There are those who believe that it is wicked to encourage wargaming and to collect model soldiers. They argue that these activities glorify war and by doing so bring World War III imperceptibly nearer. It is a point of view, but one can also make a case for saying that it is better to work out one's aggressions on the table-top rather than on the battlefield. If you ignore war it will not necessarily go away. To those who regret the redcoat age, when soldiers fought with muskets and sabre, without the covering fire of poison gas or atom bomb, a step into the past is positively attractive.

To the collector, then, I commend the book in which Henry Harris tells us of his own collection and how and why he has built it up. And in parting I offer him the maxim that 'The best is good enough'. I am confident that it is an attitude which has inspired Major Harris in building up the collection, which he describes in these pages, and that the work will give pleasure to a multitude of readers, both young and old, here and abroad, for many years to come.

Contents

Illustrations

Diagrams in text

Front end paper shows part of the author's permanent display case combined with bookshelves and materials storage cupboards.

Rear end paper illustrates the author's display at the Empire Cancer Campaign Exhibition 1961. It comprised nearly 1,000 1:32 scale models—staff, cavalry and artillery in a free-standing layout.

Dust jacket illustration is of a Historex 1:30 scale (54 mm) Trumpeter of the Imperial Guard. Dust jacket design by John Barber.

Introduction

COLLECTING MODEL SOLDIERS today is a rapidly expanding pastime in most countries. No one knows for sure how many people possess collections; from my enquiries I estimate the number could be half a million. It may, of course, be twice that number. This book is an attempt to tell you how to go about collecting model soldiers in a knowledgeable way. There are, of course, a number of other books on the subject and also countless books on the art of war itself. But when I was looking at the literature on the subject recently it struck me that whilst there were these good books on buying or making the models themselves on the one hand, and the vast bibliography of war on the other, there did not appear to be any one book that brought the two aspects together—a book which said, 'The Duke of York had 10,000 men. They were dressed and armed as follows, etc. . . . Now, here is where you can buy such figures or (alternatively) this is how you can make them yourself'.

This book is based mainly upon my own collection and how I went about building it up; but, as I realize my interests may not be those of everyone, I have sought the comments and advice of other collectors and these are included to fill the gaps. The book does not attempt to be a history of war—in such terms it can only be considered the shortest of reviews—and for reasons of size it also stops short of strategy and tactics. I appreciate that the serious student of the hobby will want to know something of these and the most obvious way is by reference to wargames. Now I am not a wargamer myself but my friend Donald Featherstone is among the experts and we have therefore included a chapter on the subject from him.

Readers may wonder what model soldiers are and what sort of people collect them today.

Taking the second point first, collectors include men, women and children of all ages and backgrounds. Some may only have the slenderest reason for doing so, or may pursue it as a serious intellectual interest. Some see it as an extension of separate interests; others follow it because they think there might be money in it. Advertisers are using model soldiers increasingly to catch the public eye. They march across the pages of magazines and newspapers often for products not even remotely connected with them. Together with military prints and uniforms they figure in announcements about interior decorating, deodorants, clothes, cigarettes and drink. Currently known collectors include Royal

Princes, learned men, actors, dress designers, military (including naval) men, professors, lawyers, scientists, engineers and administrators. An American society which conducted an occupational survey of its members classified 57 activities from artist to attorney; psychiatrist to postman, salesman to student. Collectors of the past, some of whose items are now highly prized exhibits in museums, included (not unnaturally) Kings and other rulers, and many eminent men of peace such as Goethe, Anatole France, R. L. Stevenson, G. K. Chesterton and H. G. Wells.

It is only fair to say that the hobby has its critics. From time to time it comes under attack from well meaning people who see toy and model soldiers and other 'war toys' as a means of encouraging violence. They therefore wish to see them banned. But in the context of them being bad for the young or immature to have access to, what is a war toy? If we are to take a woman politician's recent definition of war toys they include almost every form of plaything there is, including the rubber dagger and tomahawk, garden archery sets, cowboy pistols, all the Bond armoury and the Batman and Thunderbird paraphernalia.

It has yet to be proved that playing with 'war toys' has the sort of effect on young minds that their critics allege. In fact, there is a large body of belief, both scientific and lay, that it has precisely the opposite effect by providing safe outlets for the primeval instincts in all savage young breasts. Military playthings form part of the culture of all civilizations as museums and libraries throughout the world testify and the most un-warlike people have played with or approved of them, as the names mentioned above will show. There was also Hans Christian Andersen, whose delightful story of the lost love of the steadfast tin soldiers must be one of the peaceful romances of the young world.

On the other hand, we have no information that Napoleon, Hitler, Stalin, Presidents Nasser and Castro or Chairman Mao played with toy soldiers in their youth. Perhaps they would have got all their war-like urges out of their systems if they had?

What are model (and toy) soldiers? To begin with, the line between a model and a toy is hard to draw. Some 'Jouets de luxe' were not really intended for children to play with at all. Dictionary definitions of models—'a representation of the designed or actual object'—are not of great help and the modern use of the word in mathematics and statistics if anything misleads. The silver army the Dauphin played with were exquisite little works of art, if not to scale at least in great accuracy. Early hand-made figures of soldiers, whilst clearly inaccurate in military detail, are praised as rare works of art of that particular period. Factory production made toys available to the masses and inevitably some were crude and ugly. Many toy soldiers of the past lacked accuracy, both anatomical as well as military, but this cannot be said today of the mass production of a firm like Britains or the 'give aways' of the Belgian and French coffee firms.

Until very recently most people identified the toy or model soldier with metal—the 'tin' or 'lead' soldier—but there is, of course, no material exclusive to the making of miniature soldiers. Throughout their history they have been made from a great variety of materials, clay, mud, wood, paper, gingerbread, cloth, wood and bone as well as base and precious metals. It is because that up to the early 20th century mass producers turned them out in lead and tin in their millions that the popular notion arose that a toy soldier *had* to be of metal and by sheer weight of numbers these have dominated the collecting scene up to now. But today the volume production of toy soldiers is entirely of one or other plastic composition. The making of custom-built models in metal continues at present in the UK and the USA, mainly I feel out of deference to collector conservatism, but the logical French have broken out of this unnecessary restraint and at least two model makers are producing superb figures and accessories in 'la plastique'. But collectors are still shy of them, some saying because they are not so easy to alter as those of lead. Before I wrote this book I was not so sure; but thanks to the generosity of the firms that supplied me with samples I was able to carry out a lot of conversion work on plastic figures (sometimes with only the heat of a candle or hot water), and I have found, once you acquire one or two little skills, that they are, if anything, easier to mess about with than metal figures.

What about size? When does a toy or model cease to be such on grounds of size? Here again there is no precise definition but the answer lies in custom and usage. For nearly 150 years the mass production of metal soldier figures led to several sizes for both round figures and flats. We have to thank the founder of the firm of Britains for trying to standardise the former. When he began output the great nursery floor game was toy trains and the most popular size was in what we now call O gauge. William Britain made his soldiers the same size, which meant an average infantry man of 5 ft 9 in plus head-dress came out at 2⅛ in high. People later began to worry about this and regularise it and we were then told it was 1:32 scale. (This may be so for men of 5 ft 9 in high but who has seen or heard of whole armies or nations in which every man was the same height?) Many, but not all, toy makers followed, chiefly because of the trades' great proclivity for copying one another's successes.

The battle of the scales continues. The increased popularity of wargaming has created a demand for smaller figures and so the sizes variously called 'one inch', '1:72', '20mm', '30mm', 'HO' and 'OO' have gradually appeared improving in design as well as widening in range available. The trend in scale, if there is one, does seem to be towards miniaturisation which is understandable on many grounds, cost and space being the more obvious. On the other hand, Airfix find a continuing demand for their 6 in high military figures and Palitoys' Action Man (see photograph No. 2) at nearly twice the size appears in an increasingly wide variety of fighting outfits of many nations.

In the chapters which follow I have tried to arouse the interest of the reader in having a collection of soldiers of any nation in an interesting period, and I leave the choice of scale to him. My own collection happens to be in 1:32 scale because this was the most readily available when I began. I have taken each type of soldier, the Staff Officer, the Cavalryman, the Infantryman, the Gunner, the Sailor and the Airman and given an outline of how they began. In this way I hope to get the reader collecting along satisfying lines. He does *not* have to follow my ideas entirely though I hope he may find my methods and thought processes helpful. But there are other subjects for collection which, as far as I know, have not been attempted by any other collector and which would be very worth while, such as the following:

(a) Police of the world, mounted, dismounted and mechanised;
(b) United Nations Peace-keeping Forces;
(c) Foreign Legions—men of one nationality serving in the armies of others.
(d) Women at War—From the Amazons to Odette.
(e) Odd men out—unconventional and unorthodox warriors, eg, Wingate, Lawrence.
(f) Guerilla, resistance and underground forces.
(g) Mini-armies in full strength ie, Monaco, Vatican City, San Marino.
(h) l'Armée Bizarre—the unusual from all armies.
(i) Soldiers of the Bible—from Joshua to the Zealots.

I would like to thank the firms of Airfix, Britains, Charben, Hales (Monogram-Merite, H-R Products Inc, Humbrol, Mini-Models, Palitoy, Scalecraft and Timpo for providing me with generous samples of their products to use for conversion.

I also want to thank the following for assistance—Brigadier Peter Young of Sandhurst for general helpful advice and for consenting to write the foreword; Bob Bard of the USA for his friendly correspondence and permission to quote from his books; my old friend Roy Dilley for jogging my memory about many matters and reading a large part of the script and for his contribution thereto; Donald Featherstone for his valuable and lucid chapter on wargames; John Fowles for his interesting contribution on military music; Alan Cleaver for his assistance with many conversions, especially in the building of tanks and vehicles; Madame Simone Gayda of Paris for her feminine graciousness and Gallic courtesy in helping me with French research; Max Hundleby for his valuable piece on AFV developments; another old friend Harry Middleton for much information and for whose enthusiasm I have a great admiration; my friend Glenn Thompson of Dublin for whose work I have a great respect; and Edward Walker of Liverpool, who is typical of the average collector and who sent me examples of his own castings.

The majority of the photographs in this book have been taken by Dick Kingshott, of the Windlesham and Camberley Camera Club. I found his enthusiasm and interest in table-top photography a great stimulus. Other photographs have been taken for me from time to time by Alan Meek. I would also like to thank the following for supplying other pictures which appear: The Army Department Public Relations Directorate; Mr W. Y. Carman, of the National Army Museum; Messrs A. A. Hales; Captain Roy Dilley; Major A. Donald, Royal Marines, Eastney; Mr D. Featherstone, of Southampton; Mr Russell Gammage (Rose Miniatures); M Heitschel, Paris; Mr Max Hundleby, Stockport; Editor, Oldham Chronicle; The Salvation Army International HQ, London; Curator, United States Marine Corps Museum, Quantico, Va; and Mr E. Walker, of Liverpool.

August 1969 HENRY HARRIS

CHAPTER ONE

Planning a Model Army

WHAT SORT OF AN ARMY do you want? There is a story told of the great philosopher and intellectual, R. B. Haldane, when he became War Minister in the Liberal Government in 1905 and held his first meeting of the recently created Army Council of top War Office generals and civilians. The re-organisation of the whole Army—regular and reserve—was urgently necessary and Haldane's career had had nothing to do with military matters, so they were curious to learn his views. What sort of an Army did he envisage? he was asked. 'A Hegelian Army,' he replied, 'whereupon,' recorded someone who had been present, 'the discussion fell away.'

But it remains a good question, which all collectors should ask themselves without trying to answer it in metaphysical terms. It is easy enough (providing you have the money) to buy models which catch the eye, the 'pretties', but if one collects solely on this basis the result will be to end up with a lot of figures though not a balanced *collection*, based on conscious decisions. This is, of course, understood well enough by intelligent collectors in all fields so need not be stressed. What may be helpful is to suggest the aids and disciplines which will help the collector of model soldiers to achieve this aim.

There are a number of good reasons for a model collection. It seems to me that one of the most satisfying is to attempt to reflect some part and period of a real army. It is impracticable (unless one has the Army of the Prince of Monaco or the Papal Forces in mind) to attempt to reproduce any real army in actual numbers. Selection has to be made and this is very much a personal choice. Most collectors have personal interests in some army of a national, family, sentimental or intellectual sort and so a decision based on one or more of these can be reached. Is it to be one Regiment only, depicted throughout its long history? Is it to be of a type of soldier, say, artillerymen or musicians in different Regiments or Armies? Is it to be perhaps just one battalion of your (or your Dad's) old regiment, 800 or 1,000 figures all alike on parade on one particular moment of the past? Or is it perhaps a fantasy army that you want to create to fulfil some Walter Mitty dream? (An acquaintance of mine had such a model army—all the figures wore shakos with green plumes but he always stoutly denied they were meant to be Irish. I regret to say that I think it was my continually questioning *why* he had this shako army that caused him to lose interest in it and eventually break it up.)

The decisions should not be rushed into; the subject is vast, and if the collector is to get the intellectual pleasure and relaxation from it that a good hobby should bring all the aspects should be gone over carefully. In my case a factor which played a big part in shaping my collection was that I had the residue of a boyhood set of lead toy soldiers and these formed the nucleus of the collection. These had been given to me by my father who was a professional soldier and so even in a battered state of imbalance they bore some resemblance in proportion to the real thing. As a regular soldier I eyed them professionally and saw their potential—as the *cadre* of a *model army of cadres*, which would depict the real British Army in the period which appealed to me most—1890 to 1918.

It will be seen that I have used a number of military terms in describing these thought processes which should lead up to the decision of 'What sort of an Army?', 'regiment', 'cadre' and such. I have done so deliberately because I think these military expressions can very profitably be applied to the collection of military models if one wants to acquire a meaningful collection. So, the thinking we have been doing above would in military jargon (or 'Staff Language') be called an 'Appreciation' and the result of the Appreciation, your idea of what your collection is to depict, would be known as the 'Aim'. I would hasten to add that this thought process, together with the use of the magic words, is not one which can *only* be done successfully by soldiers or ex-soldiers. With so much interest in military affairs as there is today and so many books on military subjects, ranging from 'How to be your own Field Marshal' to 'Systems of Inspecting Swill Bins in Mixed Billets', a sufficient smattering can soon be acquired by an enthusiast.

Deciding on The Aim is fine, but it will not get you very far without working out how to achieve it. If you are going to depict a regiment, or a historical period, or a type of soldier, *how many of what sort doing what* are you going to finally have? Again, some thought is required, or otherwise your collection of musicians, say, may have an undue predominance of piccolo players. (A friend of mine often hints that my collection suffers from imbalance in having too large a proportion of my father's Regiment and of Irish regiments included. This is, of course, quite untrue and in fact it is *his* otherwise excellent collection which is spoilt by an undue preponderance of one particular Guards Regiment.)

Once again, I suggest we turn to the real life Army to see how they deal with this question of structure—How many units, HQs, generals, colonels, trumpeters, riflemen, ADCs on the Staff, chaplains, horses, guns and wagons are needed to achieve the Aim? We work this out by drawing up a list or table which is called an Order of Battle but which chaps who have been to Staff College (and others who imitate them) call an 'Orbat'.

It will pay you to take time over drawing up your Order of Battle; it is, in tabular form, your blueprint of arms and services, ranks and numbers. It can be intellectually a very stimulating exercise because you will be able to work out the proportions of each type and argue out with yourself (or preferably with a kindred spirit) the reasons why you want so many of a particular regiment or type. In my case it took me over two years; I had called a halt to what I now regard as my 'squirrel' or 'magpie' period because I saw I had no plan, no means of master-minding the build-up of a balanced collection. So I started with a blank sheet of foolscap, an old Army List and an Official War History, and ended up two years later with what is summarised in Appendix 1. The kindred spirit helped; he, too, thought along military lines and gave me much help in annotating my drafts (except when a small child or domestic pet with which his house seemed to be infested at that time caused an accident to the document before he returned it).

At the same time as this master-minding tool is being hammered out comes the need to acquire a store of knowledge about the soldiers your models are going to represent. This knowledge must not be sketchy, it *must* be precise—exact—as sooner or later you are going to make or paint or buy a figure which will claim to be a faithful replica of the real thing, in so far as the scale and the media employed permit. This brings us to 'research'. Research is the process of discovering facts by study or investigation and it is probably the most painful process of all the preliminaries to actual collecting.

Obviously existing knowledge will reduce the amount of research, but even so I recommend checking all such details as dates, rows of buttons, if worn on the left or right, etc, especially if they are matters one has had personal knowledge of for years. I must admit that a number of things I was adamant about, having 'worn them' or 'been there' 20 or more years ago, turned out to be rather different when I referred to the record. Memory plays all sorts of tricks; it may be a slight slip that can be put right by a brush stroke after some candid friend has pointed it out, but equally it may be a Homeric Nod of such proportion as to make a large number of models valueless.

The field to be researched can be as big as the collector likes to make it and has the time and energy to devote; but there are certain basic sources always to be checked. In my case the field is moderately large and I have over the years built up a personal library of books I need for continual reference (see Appendix 2), plus collections of regimental journals, press cuttings, cigarette cards and postcards. Inevitably one gets drawn into correspondence with editors, authors, curators, librarians, fellow collectors, makers of models and toys, old soldiers, old soldiers' widows, schoolchildren and the occasional crank. It must be faced that if these go to the trouble of writing to you you must at least acknowledge their letters, particularly if they have supplied information. I resort to the Shavian habit of replying by postcard whenever possible. A filing system is very necessary for all the paper which will accrue as a result of this but as everyone will have his own pet ideas of how to index, etc, I will say no more on this aspect.

Finally, how to control the build-up of the collection, be it 50, 500 or 5,000 figures? The former can be looked after reasonably well in one's head or on the back of an envelope, 500 needs a little more attention, and for the last some form of programme is essential. Here again we can turn to the real military world, for 'build-up' is a well-used phrase especially in such operations as amphibious warfare. Look up any good book on, say, the Sicily, Salerno, Anzio or Normandy landings and at the back you will find an appendix on the build-up of the force by D+1 or D+10 or D+30. There is probably also a chapter on why the build-up was planned the way it was, which will also provide the modeller with food for thought. At first, its infantry, followed closely by some tanks and artillery, then an intermediate HQ, then some administrative and supply services. The planned follow-up may be upset by bad weather, or unexpected enemy resistance, so, after delays, the build-up has to be changed —more infantry or maybe tanks—but as soon as possible the balanced programme is resumed until the whole force is built-up.

So, I suggest this is the way for the modeller to tackle it. Divide the Orbat up into annual programmes of some predetermined timetable—three, five, seven, ten years. You won't stick to them, of course, but it helps to clear your mind. In my case I programmed my build-up over ten years to make maximum use of my battered toys first. I then decided to 'specialise' for the next three years—first cavalry, next infantry and then artillery at the rate of 500 pieces a year; 40–50 a month was not impossible as, when specialising, a 'run' on one general type of figure can be obtained. Nevertheless, in real terms my build-up was out of balance for the next three years and it was not until year five that I could claim to have a proper representation in models of the British Army pre-1914.

CHAPTER TWO

The Sinews of Model War

IT WAS LORD KITCHENER, the first soldier since Monck to become War Minister, who in 1914 spoke of the 'sinews of war—Men, Money and Materials'. A national hero for his work in Egypt, South Africa and India, he was a lonely mysterious bachelor, with a formidable appearance, slightly boss-eyed and with a great reputation for thoroughness and drive. He did not share the general opinion that 'it would all be over by Christmas' but, on the contrary, made plans for a world war of three years duration and for a new army of one million men. His stern, unsmiling, resolute face looked down from thousands of posters and the caption 'Kitchener wants you' brought them in faster than the military machine then could cope. He has had many detractors, chiefly political enemies, but he built Britain up into a world fighting power and when he disappeared in a sunken ship at sea two years later his work had been completed.

Happily for the model soldier collector, his plans do not have such grim purpose; unless he is eccentric, his armies, once carefully and lovingly built up, will not be smashed by miniature shells in some ferocious wargame but will last, barring accidents, as long as he desires them to; they will, if he has chosen wisely, increase in value much more than they will cost, especially if he has modelled them himself. But like the armies of real life they, too, need sinews—three 'Ms' also but in this case they are 'Money, Materials, and Making-up'.

Few readers of this will be fortunate enough to be able to purchase outright the full complement of their proposed collection. For many it will need to be a carefully worked out budgetary operation over a number of years, geared to the 'Orbat' suggested in the last chapter. This is only right and the discipline so enforced by financial considerations adds to the eventual pleasure of acquisition. In doing his sums the collector will immediately be struck by the high prices of completed models produced by professional modellers and firms making for the collectors' market. This is not to say these prices are extortionate. A quality finished, scale model on display in an 'arty' shop in an arcade or some continental-type boutique, represents many hours of research, design, toolmaking, moulding, assembling, painting, inspection checks for accuracy plus packing and transport. The professional modeller must, of course, get some return on his (or his backer's) capital employed and also make a profit. The retailer—the suave young man or soignée woman who serves you in the boutique—must eat as well as pay the overheads for the premises, which are always in a 'smart' district. However, having allowed for all this, there is also a tendency for these models to be priced-up, like mink or jewellery or a drink on the Golden Arrow, to 'what the market will stand'.

Now a point to be stressed here for the collector to ponder is that these prices do *not* bring him a 'personalised' or 'one-off' model but a production model as the catalogue or the boutique shelves will show. The figures he buys off the shelves will be the same as many other collectors may acquire and if they fit into his plan of collection—the Order of Battle of a balanced model army—it is a matter of luck.

I experienced this when I began collecting—it really boiled down to basing my collection on what was available to be collected. Now, my Order of Battle is fairly large—5,500 figures—and so at first there was some compatibility between the figures specified in my lists and those in the model makers' catalogues. But I found this lacked satisfaction, so my next step was to ask the model makers to make, or at least paint, some of their figures to my specification. The results were not very happy; because these were special figures I was charged 'special' (ie extra) prices. This made me expect rather too much and I was inclined to be over-critical of the finished models, which was possibly unfair as I'd asked for somewhat esoteric items such as 'Officer of the Mummerset Yeomanry in dismounted undress order, circa 1902'.

There are, of course, one or two model makers who will execute special commissions for the exacting collector, charging accordingly say £15–£25 for a single piece, but here again my type of collector remains dissatisfied. For, despite it being to *your* specification, it remains the *creation* of the artist, it is his brainchild and his handiwork and, whilst it will fit into a definite place in the collection, one feels that somehow it doesn't belong.

What then is the discriminating collector to do? He wants to build up a balanced, accurate, collection which will reflect his interest in a particular section of military history; most of all, if it means much to him, he wants to infuse into it a definite personality or ethos, not necessarily a reflection of his own but a distinctive one which his knowledge, experience *and skill* will help to develop. If he has come to admire or be amused by human types or individuals he has met or read about—the Colonel Chinstraps, the Captain Foresights, the Mulvaneys and the Snooks of fact or fiction, he will want to include them in the collection, in the right dress, in the right attitude, doing the right job.

So *skill*, that is some handicraft skill, is the next requirement to emerge in our review of how to start collecting. Some collectors become attracted to the hobby because of an already well developed dexterity—woodwork, metalwork or do-it-yourself skill of a wide sort. Others, who perhaps have never done anything more technical than mend a fuse or wield a screwdriver (a category in which I include myself) are initially drawn to collecting by the intellectual appeal. When I began collecting I doubt if I was even capable of cutting the head off a lead figure or painting a simple wide straight line down a model trouser leg. But, bit by bit, I began to be 'useful'—I overcame my feelings of inadequacy in handling tools and, urged on by a desire to create a figure which would represent one of my admired military types, I began to do my own alterations. The aforementioned kindred spirit, whose skill at this work (when he's feeling like it) borders on genius, helped. There was a period, when we produced a large quantity of models from lead toys, in which he was the master craftsman and I the apprentice-cum-labourer. In these sessions I acquired enough knowledge of the technique to overcome my inhibitions and which, allied to my desire to have a large collection, drove me on.

As shown above, *material* in the form of completed model figures is reasonably plentiful. But, as pointed out, the collector has little power to influence the output of these makers and the prices make a large collection beyond the reach of many. However, some of these makers do sell their figures in an unpainted (some even in an un-assembled) state at reductions in price of about half of what they ask for the fully finished figure. But the collector, assembling and painting such figures, is really only gaining a price advantage and some choice of difference in painting, if the design permits this. He is still stuck with figures *created* by the professional maker and not by himself.

What material is available to the enterprising do-it-yourself collector today? As suggested in Chapter 1 the collector who aims to build up a miniature army very much his own creation has to consider a number of factors; the choice (the Order of Battle) and the period of time over which he proposes to do it (the Programme). These two aspects must be somewhat provisional (or even a pipe dream, until the cost and the availability of models, or materials for them, has been examined. This situation is well known in commercial life and is reduced to formulae, such as the Make-or-Buy and the Economic Batch Quantity and other theories of production control.

On the subject of conversions, whilst I mention particular toy and model makers' products, it does not follow they are the only ones available. I prefer *not* to openly advocate one maker in preference to another, this being very much a matter of how far their products fit your proposed collection, but I include in Appendix 6 a table of makers and retailers which may assist in the thought processes I suggest necessary when deciding on a model army.

There are two alternatives to purchasing model figures, one is to cast for yourself, and the other is to convert an ordinary 'toy' soldier and other associated military miniatures to the model standard required. There are various degrees of casting as well as converting, but the following are the basic steps of each:

Casting

(1) Design generally. This includes usually a little draughtsmanship for the figure required; the decision whether to cast in one or in parts for assembly. Mould design must be considered for such aspects as economy of material and whether single or multiple figure moulds, or separate moulds for accessories, etc, are to be used. See photo No 69.

(2) Construction of a well-cut master figure. This must be in some hard material from which to make the mould. Attention must be given to engraving of dress details, facial expressions, and general anatomical requirements (eg, a Life Guard should not be given the slight figure typical of a Hussar).

(3) Materials. Buying of lead or lead alloy and other materials required.

(4) Making of the mould. This must be either in Plaster of Paris or vulcanized rubber. This depends on the quantity of figures required, ie, the number to be cast from the master mould.

(5) Casting. The heating of the metal, or melting down of scrap lead, pouring it into the mould, and turning out the rough casting.

(6) Finishing process. This includes cleaning off flash from the casting, trimming, sub assembly and assembly, including the fixing of heads, limbs and stands if the figure has been cast in parts. Some light soldering, filing and polishing is almost invariably required.

(7) Painting. Undercoating the casting, applying the main colours, eg, tunic, trousers, flesh. Finally needed is the detail painting such as buttons, braiding, rank badges, and accoutrements, followed by shading and lining-in.

Converting

(1) Design generally. Some design work is also required but need not be as elaborate, or as precise, as for the casting process. In its place one wants a knowledge of the most suitable toy figure or figures for the model required. This may, of course, involve several cutting and soldering processes over one or more toys. The 'design thinking' is intended to eliminate unnecessary cutting up, especially of lead figures which are becoming increasingly scarce. The end product of the 'think' stage could be a make-up list as given in Chapter 15.

(2) Cutting and soldering. These are really a combined operation. The change is obtained by cutting with a hacksaw and the variation or replacement is annealed by soldering and filing and polishing off. When changing heads of soldiers it is best, particularly with metal, to form a spigot on the neck and fit it into the collar. For types of cutting and soldering and tools for the job see also Chapter 15.

(3) Plastic figures. In the case of plastic figures similar cuts and joins can be done, except that the joining up has to be done by a fixative of the sort recommended for the type of plastic, ie, PVC adhesive, epoxy cement, etc. The fixatives recommended by some toy makers for their products are usually shown in their catalogues or lists or stated on the boxes holding the kit. Changing the shape or bending limbs, etc, of plastic figures is achieved surprisingly easily by warming them over a candle flame or immersing briefly in very hot water. The French Model Soldier Society has given the following advice for working on plastic figures:

'We recommend that for the conversion of figures in either of the plastic materials, the purchase of an *appareil de pyrogramme*, which is something like a little soldering iron fitted with a thermometer and which can have different tips.

'When heated to the required temperature, this iron enables the plastic to be moulded rather as moulding sealing wax or modelling clay (do not warm it too much in case the plastic burns and becomes brittle). It is in fact easier to work than lead, and the figures can be varied *ad infinitum*. As with metal, matters of detail can be added by moulding with the iron. These figures can be 'clothed' as in lead, with a sheet of laminated lead which you inlay when it is warm, with plastic or more simply with paper which you stick on the plastic.

'Lead details can also be inlaid on the plastic figures, such as sabres, guns and even heads.

'Figurines in cellulose acetate soften when heated. To modify the position of a body, bend an arm or leg, turn a head or even twist a body a little, soak the figure in very warm water for ten to twenty seconds and make the change. It will harden again when it cools.

'Acetate dissolves in acetone. If some pieces of acetate are put in a hermetically sealed vessel with acetone, in a few hours a paste will be obtained. The thickness will depend on the amount of acetone used. This paste is an ideal glue to join the different parts of the figures, it fills any gaps and, smoothing it with the finger, you can get a solid and invisible weld. It can be equally well used as a solder.

'If, as mentioned above, you clothe your figures with paper, soak the paper first in water to avoid little wrinkles. When you have finished, smear the paper with a layer of fairly thin acetate and when it has dried, you will have a figure covered with a plastic-like coat, more resistant to wear and retaining its appearance and rigidity.

'Figures made of polystyrene do not soften in warm water and thus must be worked like lead. Polystyrene dissolves in trichlorethylene, it can be stuck together with adhesive used for modelling clay.

'The usual ways to add little details to figures can be employed using fine leather for bridles, and buckles for stirrups. Pipe cleaners make excellent feathers and plumes.'

(4) Detailing. This covers the adding of, say, head ropes to horses, shoulder belts to men, accoutrements, and equipment according to type of figure. Fuse wire, thin sheet lead and plastic metal and wood are some of the materials which can be used to represent these items.

(5) Painting. This is generally the same as for cast figures (step 7 in the previous section), with variations for plastic as mentioned in the section on painting at the end of this chapter.

(6) Spare parts. As a result of conversion, a stock of sawn off heads, torsos, legs, horse parts and spare arms with and without weapons, etc, will accrue. Do not throw these away, they should be kept, roughly segregated, and looked over every time a conversion job is needed. Over a period it will be found that many needs can be fulfilled from these spare pieces without the necessity of cutting up new figures.

The basic tools and implements required for the process are given in Chapter 15. A fairly high scrap rate should be expected to begin with.

The way to maximise converting is to know what is available in the toy market. This knowledge is acquired by building up, as part of your reference library, a list of all makers and retailers and obtaining copies of their catalogues. In writing this book I carried out a survey of toy makers at the 1968 and 1969 Brighton Toy Fairs and the results are summarised in Appendix 6.

To the great majority of collectors this will not be a new idea; like myself some of them may have toy soldiers as part of a collection, either in their original 'toy' state or converted into models. Some readers may well know more about the toy market than I do, but nevertheless the following general remarks may be of help in bringing their thoughts or knowledge into focus.

The 'Toy' Market

The toy industry is highly competitive and very vogue conscious. Financially it is speculative and on the whole made up of a number of small firms. For every popular item which 'catches on' there are several which don't, and smaller manufacturers are constantly facing difficulties and going into liquidation. Piracy is widespread and the aim is to get in and out of a new idea as quickly as possible, with the knowledge that as soon as it becomes popular competitors will copy it at a lower price. One effect of this is to have batch quantities of toy figures produced, the majority being quickly dropped and those marketed being dispersed in small toy and fancy good shops all over the country. The output is avowedly directed at the young, which for our purpose means that the model collector has no influence and if some toys are found to be what he wants this is completely fortuitous. For many years I have had strong personal contacts with the leading British manufacturers of toy soldiers and associated figures, and often attempted to influence the choice of a new line. Whilst always polite and interested they would consider what I proposed but the final decision was always based on a hard-headed assessment of the 'play-value' of the item in the hands of a particular age group.

Modern methods of communication greatly influence the demands of children and it is therefore not surprising that current output of toy soldiers reflects the recent past rather than battles of long ago. One or two of the larger manufacturers attempt to turn the juvenile demand into a continuous one, on which their production can depend, by producing a whole range of one *type* of toy whereby the acquisition of one leads to a need for another; and a good example of this is to be seen in some of the items in the Airfix range. By this method a large firm can keep its production high (and so keep cost down) and at the same time combine an element of educational, as well as play, value into its products.

For many years the firm of Britains dominated the toy soldier market; the pre-1939 catalogue contained types of almost all British Army regiments, bands, colour parties, vehicles and guns. Within the limits of toy making economics most of their lines were remarkably accurate, particularly in the details of the casting, and as they stood made the acquisition of a large army an easy matter for the unsophisticated collector. The annual output was literally millions of castings and, as a result, Britains' figures (and products by a few lesser rivals) have come to be the basic standard figures for many long-established collections. My collection was begun by my father bringing me boxes of horse, foot and artillery whenever he came home on leave in the Great War. Model Soldier Societies and informal groups of collectors have built up histories of the firms' products and earnestly write and croon over the merits and attributes of 'Early Britains' and other types of yesteryear.

But times change and whilst a large manufacturer's range as shown in a bright catalogue may stimulate and sustain demand up to a point (as well as giving collectors some vicarious pleasure), the realistic toy maker looks at the annual sales of each individual item and where a downward trend persists the line is dropped, to be replaced by a new one. Or sometimes, even, the range contracts. For 15 years now collectors like myself who looked to Britains for our basic raw material for model soldiers have watched anxiously as this trend developed and tried to do what we could to anticipate.

'I see you've dropped the Argentine Horse Grenadiers and US Cavalry from the new catalogue, Mr Thake.'

'Yes, I'm afraid we have Major; you see their sales no longer justified continuing production.'

'Are there any other lines likely to suffer the same fate? So I can buy my requirement before they go off the market.'

'I'm afraid I can't tell you that at this stage Major.'

'Well what about, say, Infantry of the Line, Full-Dress, Marching-at-the-Slope and the Egyptian Camel Corps?'

The reply to this inferred that Infantry-of-the-Line were, saleswise, in no immediate danger but that the Egyptian Camel Corps set were only being retained because the head of the firm had decided to give them a reprieve.

Anyone writing on the subject of toy soldiers ten or more years ago would have hardly thought it worth while to mention what they were made of; he and his readers would have taken it for granted that they were cast of some metal composition loosely referred to as lead or tin. For over 150 years the great bulk of toy soldier production in Germany, France and England had been in such material, with a very small amount in wood, papier maché, cardboard and, rarer still, in silver (for young princes). But soon after the end of the 1939–45 War, with the continuing shortage (and high price) of lead, a few firms began to make soldiers in that characteristic 20th century medium, plastics.

One of the earliest pioneers of plastic soldiers was a friend of mine, the late Fred Winkler, a German refugee, who came to Britain in the 1930s and began model ship and toy soldier manufacture in South Wales. In 1940 he was one of many foreigners to be interned, but when seen to be harmless was released and employed on war work in the Midlands. He was a great model soldier enthusiast, full of ideas, many of which were impracticable in business, but in one he was ahead of his time. In 1946 he brought out a range of plastic toy soldiers in 54 mm (1 : 32) scale, mounted and dismounted. The latter were the best and, pressed in component parts, they were sold assembled and painted. Poor sales promotion and a surprisingly strong resistance to platics, both as toys and models in Britain, forced Winkler to stop production and drop his plans for extending the range. About the same time the French firm Segom began to market plastic soldiers of good design. This firm is one of several which has aimed deliberately at collectors and, as a result, in France the plastic figurine won earlier acceptance as a *model* than elsewhere.

But other early plastic toy and model soldiers were not of high quality and collectors' fears that they would supersede lead were allayed. Inevitably, however, the quality of design improved and the leading firms began to introduce them into their catalogues whilst curtailing the range of lead figures. Britains, because of their premier position in the 54 mm size range, must be cited with their 'Eyes Right' or 'Swoppet' range. Trunks and limbs are interchangeable, being joined by nipples and spigot heads, while some figures have 'attachable' items such as equipment and head-dress. Musicians' arms are integrated with beautifully plated instruments which eliminate one minor difficulty for collectors who do their own painting, the problem of obtaining a polished metallic smooth surface.

In this plastics field Britains have been followed by all firms who continue to produce toy soldiers, and the overall position is a greatly reduced volume of the conventional types of toy soldiers by pre-war standards. As a commercially produced toy, the metal cast soldier is a thing of the past.

The other uncertain factor in the toy soldier world is the variety of scales in which they are now being produced. Before 1914 there was a 'battle of the scales', but for the round (solid or hollow-cast) figure the 54 (or 55) mm size (1 : 32 scale) became the accepted 'standard' size. This gave a dismounted soldier some 5 ft 9 in high, with horses, vehicles and other accessories in proportion. Flat figures were an exception, as were also wooden, cardboard and a few special composition types. But these variations were known and a would-be collector could decide in advance which genre he was going for and could there expect to find a wide range in the one scale.

The position today is that, whilst most of the model makers of castings work more or less to the old 55 mm scale (apart from wargame figures which are mostly 30 mm), there is a wide variety of sizes and scales in plastics at the 'toy' end of the market. Biggest are the Palitoy Action Man figures, about 12 inches high, made of durable plastic and so constructed that they can assume the positions of real soldiers. These doll-like figures have a large number of kits and equipment sets with which they can be converted into US Combat Infantry, Australian Jungle Fighters or British Infantry. The kits, all available separately, include boots, respirators, grenades, entrenching tools, first aid packs and mountain warfare items. At the 1968 Brighton Toy Fair horses, vehicles and heavy weapons were displayed as additions to the range.

At the mini size end of the scale are the 'OO' series made mostly by Airfix. Some 36 sets are available, each of approximately 40 figures, ranging from Ancient Britons and Romans, through Robin Hood and the American Civil War to First and Second World War soldiers. The sets include vehicles and guns and are excellent value for a remarkably low price per set. They are unpainted and some slight cleaning and paring is required if you are going to make collectors' pieces out of them. Personally I find this size rather too 'fiddly' to lavish a lot of detail on, but a number of other collectors have, with high results. These little figures have a high conversion potential, as the articles contributed to 'Airfix Magazine' testify, and they are, of course, just the job for wargamers.

Whilst a multiplicity of scales does create a difficulty for collectors it is not insuperable, and it chiefly applies to the collector who intends to convert from toys. It means he has to spend a little longer working out his Order of Battle, allowing for scale as well as prices, timetable and quantities. There is no reason why a collection cannot be two, three or multi-tier where scale is concerned and, indeed, some collectors cheerfully ignore scale altogether, but I do not think this makes for a good collection. Some toys, especially gun, vehicle and tank kits, also seem to fall between scale sizes but after a bit of experience a modeller can, say, use an oversize light tank kit by modifying it into a heavy pattern of his own scale. I have had some success in this area by 'up-wheeling' guns or conversely 'down-wheeling' limbers to provide me with the required model. My friend Captain Roy Dilley has done it to great effect with plastic vehicle kits.

For out-of-production toys the collector has to turn to the small toy shops still carrying old stocks, or to the few dealers who buy up toy collections for re-sale. I never pass a toy, antique or 'junk' shop without a quick inspection, even though my collection is almost complete, for there is always a chance that the shop may have just the sort of scarce toy soldier I can use or convert.

Painting

This is the most difficult of all the modelling processes to give advice on; like the others, practice, of course, brings improvement, but quite a number of modellers admit that they are least proficient with the brush, particularly with painting faces on figures. But there are a few general hints which may save the beginner time and trouble.

The type and size of the figures are two prime aspects. The larger or fewer, the more detailed and lavish one can be; the smaller and greater the quantity (eg 'OO' size wargame figures of several hundreds) have of necessity to receive more rapid treatment. Until recently there were two rival schools of finish—the 'shiny' and the 'matt', but with the end of commercial production of metal figures the former is disappearing and it is now accepted that a matt finish is the correct one for plastics. I know of a couple of collectors who still paint their metal figures in shiny paints and there is no doubt that this finish is more resistant to dust and stands up to a lot of handling. But spray varnishes to give a matt (or glossy) effect are now available which are colourless and give the figures a thin barrier which protects them against discolouration and blemishing.

In passing I should perhaps mention for anyone who acquires secondhand metal figures that their old paint should be removed, either by one of the well-known paint strippers, or by boiling in caustic soda water. Both processes are messy and the figures must be thoroughly washed and dried out afterwards to avoid blistering of the new paint later on.

Choice of make and type of paints is a matter of personal preference and there are many on the market easily available to be tried out. Many converter-collectors buy their paints either from the custom modellers who supply unpainted figures or from the hobby shops which stock types primarily for plastic kit painting but which are ideal for model soldiers, especially those made of plastic. One large manufacturer of modelling paints, Humbrol, now also produces ready mixed 'authentic shade' paints for RAF, British 8th Army, Jungle Green, Full Dress, and other uniforms (as well as a wide range of adhesives, fixatives, cement and flatting agents). All the hobby paints are quick drying nowadays, some being firm in three to five minutes.

Brushes are probably the only tool in the modeller's kit bag which are worth buying only the best. Sable hair are the best and you should acquire a set, including the finest. Do not try to trim a large brush down by pulling out some of the hairs. It doesn't work. After use, clean the brushes by wiping the tip with a piece of clean cloth. There is no need to have different brushes for each colour, but some modellers have found it a good idea to keep a separate one for white work. Paints come either in tubes or small pots; it is best not to paint straight from these but to put a little out on a saucer, jar lid, or a make-shift palette. You do not really need a 'Rembrandt'-type palette; most modellers find that an odd bit of hardboard or glass is sufficient.

Like other forms of painting the basic steps are the same; the work should be rubbed down smooth, all blemishes must be removed, and the surface must be clean. Some modellers affix their figures to a holder, say a block of wood or a clothes peg, so as to prevent spoiling them by fingering. An undercoat of matt white, cream or other light shade should be applied all over as the first covering.

Not surprisingly, women are good painters and an American collector, Mrs Beatrice A. Hurd, of Baltimore, said, 'I doubt if there is anyone who has painted their first model soldier as well as expected—but each figure you paint will be better than the last. . . . After experimenting with model railway "quick drying" paint (this dried too quickly !), silk screen and others, I finally came round to casine paints obtainable in tubes. These can be thinned by either oil or water . . . water colours came off too easily and the work became a vicious circle of touching-up the touched-up parts . . .' On faces, Mrs Hurd says, 'I once used red and yellow in small amounts mixed with white. This gave a delicate complexion suitable for a lady under a parasol but definitely not that of a soldier !' She now mixes brown and yellow, plus a little of red or orange in white mixed with a deep beige. Orange-beige cheeks, nose and chin give a tanned, weathered look. 'An unshaven effect can be obtained with a blue-grey paint and the lips almost brown.'

A well-known UK collector suggests that to avoid the extremes of (1) over expressive and (2) doll-like faces it is best to hold the model at a distance of 6 to 8 inches from your eyes and compare with the actual size of a man in the street at a distance where he appears the same size. What do *you* see? The whites of his eyes? The full outline of the mouth? This painter makes up his flesh colour by mixing red into white with a touch of yellow and brown and tries it out on the back of his hand until it is barely distinguishable from his own flesh. When he has got it right he makes up a small bottle of this and keeps it tightly sealed for future use.

A few final tips on face painting:

(a) Use the same colour to pick up ears and neck.

(b) Avoid the 'painted doll' look by 'easing' out the hard lines with a brush dipped in thinners.

(c) Avoid the 'lipstick' or 'sword cut' effect on the mouth by giving the bottom lips fullness in the centre and making the upper lips thinner—this is a job for a single-hair brush and a steady hand.

(d) Paint the eyes last of all, again with a single-hair brush—putting in the whites first if you decide these ought to be seen. The centres should be directly over the corners of the mouth; paint the irises last. A very, very thin grey line at the bottom of the eye will give the necessary shadow effect.

(e) Eyebrows, moustaches, beards and hair should be done at the same time and be of the same shade.

Another of my modeller friends obtains very realistic relief effects for buttons, badges, lace, etc, by building these up with repeated layers of *thick* paint before giving the final coat of the finishing colour. He squeezes the 'building' paint (his choice is black) on to a palette and only wets it enough to make it workable. A fine O or OO brush is loaded with the thick paint and applied to the figure as required, ie, tiny blobs for buttons, or in lines for lacing. Drying is rapid so he proceeds to apply further layers until he has the desired relief effect. Then the finishing colour (say gold) is applied but not brushed completely to the edge of the relief portion. In this way a very fine surrounding line of the underlying colour gives the raised detail further effect.

Shading of creases, folds and openings of garments can be obtained with darker tints of the colour being used, applied while this is still wet. To avoid hard lines the colouring should be 'watered out' until it fades into the rest of the garment. Chevrons, badges and equipment, etc, throw shadows on their bases; a study of photographs of the troops concerned (but not of models of them) will show how this appears.

CHAPTER THREE

Headquarters Staffs

'Came there a certain lord, neat, trimly dress'd,
fresh as a bridegroom; and his chin new reap'd . . .
and as the soldiers bore dead bodies by
he call'd them untaught knaves, unmannerly . . .
he question'd me; among the rest demanded
my prisoners in your majesty's behalf.
I, then all smarting with my wounds being cold,
to be so pester'd with a popinjay.
Out of my grief and my impatience,
answered neglectingly, I know not what . . .
. . . for he made me mad
to see him shine so brisk, and smell so sweet
and talk so like a waiting—gentlewoman
of guns, and drums, and wounds—God save the mark.'
(Henry IV, Part I, Act 1, Sc 3)

TO THE MODELLER the exciting thing about including staff figures in his collection is that it permits him to introduce many types and styles of figures which would be out of place in the units or regimental groups. And staff officers *are* different, whoever they are and whatever the army—the donning of an aigulette, wearing a brassard or adding a particular coloured stripe to the breeches seems to effect a metamorphosis in otherwise normal men. To capture and portray this 'staff attitude' either by stance, tilt of head, dress distinction or facial expression is to mark the modeller as a man that knows his army.

Hotspur's outburst to the King quoted above expresses a feeling existing between the fighting man and the staff which is as old as the history of fighting. The late Field Marshal Wavell, probably the most cultured and civilised as well as brilliant military leader of the 20th century, selected this passage to depict the grudge between them. He recalled he had been a regimental officer in two wars and 'realised what a poor hand the staff made of things and what a safe luxurious life they led'.

But he was also a staff officer in the Great War and 'realised that the staff were worked to the bone trying to keep the regimental officer on the rails'. There is no doubt that dislike of the 'gilded staff' reached its height in that war. This was exacerbated not only by the contrast between the grim life of the fighting man in the trenches and that of the staff in Chateaux and pleasant towns only a few miles away but in safety. A further factor was that all officers on the staff, from Lieutenant upwards, wore the distinctive red cap bands and gorget patches.

In 1940 I served with a re-employed infantry officer who told me he had once seen a young officious staff officer shot by another infantry officer. The latter was the sole officer survivor of a battalion and had been leading the remnants of his unit back from an attack when the staff officer had come up and upbraided his unit for not sending in a return of empty bread sacks.

When I first joined a Divisional HQ Staff in the late war it was firmly implanted into me by the GSO1 (a brilliant Irish Guardsman) that all our thinking and activities had to be devoted to reversing this unhappy relationship, and that the rôle of the staff was to *serve* the fighting man and to help him do his supreme job of fighting. Yet, with the best will in the world, this is often hard to demonstrate. Good staff work often leads to toil and drudgery on the ground, both for the fighting men and the men behind him. If it all goes off well the Staff like to take the credit. If it becomes what our American friends call a 'SNAFU' the tendency is to let the troops take the blame!

The concept of a staff has existed since the earliest days of organised fighting, so the collector is not limited to a particular nation or army. Whilst we lack exact details, it is obvious that commanders such as Alexander, Hannibal and Caesar could not have controlled their armies without the help of subordinates who deserve to be called staff officers. In the Roman army, two legions (approximately 12,000 men) were commanded by a Consul who had a staff of military tribunes, usually six to a legion.

Medieval and Crusading forces often had what can be described as a 'Chief of Staff' to take military detail off the leader who was almost always the Head of State. Staff work, such as it was, was done by the members of the Court of the Pro-Consul, Prince, King or Emperor—such functionaries as the Lords of the Chamber, the Treasury, the Horse, and the Wardrobe. Many of the modern staff functions, now well established in military departments of today, can be traced back to the few high personages that stood close to the rulers of early times. Lengthy periods of peace made such Court Officials lose touch with the military aspects of their posts and then the fighting men suffered much from the effect of confusion and muddle. When the Civil War broke out in England neither King nor Parliament had military staffs. The first battle of that war, Edgehill, was indecisive, chiefly due to neither of the opposing commanders having adequate trained staffs by which to control the course of the fighting.

In the Napoleonic Wars the Prussian and Austrian staffs made great progress in precision and objective thinking, and Scharnhorst, Gneisenau and Radetzky were outstanding Chiefs of Staff. Whilst Napoleon created large staffs, he is rightly criticised with allowing them little scope because of his passion for keeping everything in his own hands. Yet his Aides-de-Camp General were in fact high-grade staff officers. Bold and experienced, hard riders and well mounted they could be relied on to transmit the spirit as well as the letter of verbal orders. On occasions they could issue orders in the Emperor's name based on their knowledge of his thinking.

Wellington's staff was, by comparison, fewer and less colourful, yet contemporary accounts of his headquarters portray a high degree of organisation. Tragically for Britain, staff and staff services were all broken up after Waterloo so that when Britain became involved in war with Russia in 1854 there was no staff machinery in existence. It all had to be built up again whilst the fighting men suffered. Fortunately for the British Army, the lesson was learned and a basic staff organisation has continued ever since.

In truth the 19th century demanded a more thorough system of control. The coming of railways and steam ships increased the size and mobility of armies and permitted wide frontages. Large armies were based on reservists and these were recalled by the process of Mobilisation. It became a prime task of staffs in peace time to work all this out, because the quicker it was done the sooner the army took the field and seized the initiative. The German General Staff have become identified as the experts in this type of precise, methodical, arithmetical staff work and the creation of special staffs for planning, operations, administration, intelligence, discipline and training. This fully developed staff system was imitated by most other countries as the need to control movement of mass armies developed. It will no doubt strike the collector at this point that, if he is going in for a large and diverse model army, he is going to need a large number of staff figures. There is no real yardstick or proportion, except that it would be considered somewhat bizarre to have more staff figures than regimental models. But the provision of staffs offers legitimate scope to add personality, unusual or even eccentric figures, which all collectors have the urge to introduce (many of which will be based on personal and sometimes painful experience!).

As to how many *separate* headquarters staff there should be in the collection, this obviously depends on its size and the way the owner has organised it, ie, the Order of Battle.

Once the collector has rationalised his ideas, more or less based on military principles of command and control, the number of HQ and the figures to appear on each will follow in profusion. (In fact, the collector will find himself experiencing the conflict, so well known in armies, of large HQ staffs swelling continuously at the expense of the fighting troops!)

To be of intellectual satisfaction to the collector each HQ must reflect the organisational pattern of the real-life army on which it is modelled. But new or would-be collectors need not shy away from this 'must' bit; a knowledge of a particular army or nation has probably motivated your desire to collect model soldiers and this knowledge will either include or provide signposts for easy reference to organisational handbooks and the like. In my case my army staff organisation reflects the three British branches, ie, General Staff (G), Adjutant General (A) and Quartermaster General (Q). I have to remember that where a lower HQ depicts pre-1905 organisation to *omit* 'G' Branch as it was not formed before the Esher Committee's recommendations as a result of our troubles in the South African War.

1. *Captain Roy Dilley, one of the most brilliant amateur convertors, 'passing it on' to his son Anthony. Many of the author's pieces are the product of joint thought and work with Dilley père over 25 years.*

2. *Examples of extremes of scales—Palitoy's 'Action Man', 11½ inches high (right), directs a wargame of Airfix OO/HO figures.*

3. *The 'Gilded Staff'. Author's models of pre-1914 Staff Ride Conference. 54 mm metal figures conversions.*

4. *George Washington, first C-in-C US Forces, circa 1775. Author's conversion using Britains' Civil War Cavalryman's legs and horse with body and head of War of Independence infantryman—55 mm plastic.*

5. *French Grenadier à Cheval circa 1815, from Timpo Waterloo infantry head and torso on Britains' Civil War Federal Cavalry Officer legs and saddlery, and cowboy horse. 55 mm.*

6. *Barbarian horseman, 5th century AD, from Britains' Medicine Man, built up with plastic wood, card, strip lead and wire on Charben's farm horse (plastic).*

7. *Norman Knight—example of easy plastic conversion of Britains' cowboy horse with legs astride catapult attendant. Card shield, etc.*

8. *British cavalryman circa 1740, from Britains' Confederate Cavalry Officer legs and horse with War of Independence body.*

9. *British Household Cavalry in Egypt 1882. From Historex Napoleonic horse, Britains' CMP torso, show jumper's legs and Gammage head—all shown also as component parts. 55 mm.*

10. *British Cavalry 1914–18 War. Example of metal figure multiple conversions. 54 mm.*

11. *Bodyguard of President of India (also very like previous Viceroy's Guard). From Britains' Confederate Cavalry Officer, trooper's horse, CMP lance arm and head built up with plastic wood.*

12. *Egyptian Archer 13th century BC (above). Head and torso from Britains' Indian kneeling brave, legs from Timpo Roman charioteer. Headdress of paper.*

13. *Right: Old Testament Warrior of Joshua—made as for model above with necessary variations.*

14. *Improved and converted Britains' Papal Guards in metal.*

15. *Examples of quality model Roman figures by Rose Miniatures (in metal).*

16. *British Infantry, mid 18th century. Minor conversion of Britains' War of Independence figure.*

Visualising the rôle of each figure on the various HQs, the level of each, the rank of the model itself and the order of dress to be shown, will provide wide possibilities of postures and attitudes. The outline of staff duties I have given above may help to point the modellers' ideas but, of course, study and thought is a large factor in creating this type of model. The modeller can assist his thinking processes by asking himself:

Question	Answer
(a) What job or post is the model to portray?	Order of Battle should indicate.
(b) What are the characteristics of this job?	Research unto one's own source material or by reference to outside sources.
(c) What are the characteristics of the type of officer or soldier selected to fill the post (ie, his regiment, age group, etc)?	As above.
(d) What basic toy or model figure is there available to list/depict these?	(i) One's own stockpile. (ii) Toy and model makers' catalogues.

As we saw in Chapter 2 the collector-modeller will accumulate a stockpile of spare figures and parts, such as heads, torsos and limbs, (man and animal), either bought as such or left over from previous conversion surgery. From these the answer to (d) will be increasingly found and the exciting process of creating the 'one-off' staff figure carried out.

When my modelling collaborator, Captain Roy Dilley, and I were building up our Headquarters we spent many hours comparing notes and obtaining outside information on Staff Officers so as to have them as correctly representative as possible. Our collections have been worked out generally to complement each other but we overlap date-wise at one point, but not in actual battalions.

We both have a Supreme Headquarters which authorises us to introduce relevant court dress figures and the Monarch in one or more styles of military dress. In Roy Dilley's case this has enabled him to introduce such appointments as Gold and Silver Sticks-in-Waiting, Silver Stick Adjutants, Field-Officers-in-Brigade-Waiting and Equerries. My establishment allows me to have Royal Dukes, Field Marshals and Generals, and Foreign Royalty *dressed* as Colonels of particular regiments. In addition, my C-in-C appointments both on this and lower headquarters provide for 'personality' figures such as Field Marshal Roberts as Army C-in-C, Kitchener as his Chief or Staff, and a Prince Louis of Battenberg as Naval C-in-C. Roy Dilley provides for Field Marshal Alexander and some other well-known 'Very Senior' officers of the 1939–45 War. Neither of us has set a limit to our Supreme HQ establishments, feeling that, as in real life, there is a Royal prerogative in this allowing for any additions that may be willed.

We went to a lot of trouble to ensure that our Staff types looked typical of the period and, at the risk of being tediously repetitive, I would say here that this is what collecting model soldiers is *really* about. Almost anyone can, after mastering the casting, converting and painting skills, produce rows and rows of model soldiers all alike—the art, the satisfaction, lies in *creating* individual models which will typify the officer, the man, their animals, their personality, their period. This to my mind is *modelling*.

With us it is as important to depict this individuality as it is to have the uniform details correct. British General Staff posts (the G1s, G2s and G3s) seem to attract cavalry, guards and smart infantry officers. They must be depicted impeccably attired with slim and relaxed figures in characteristic poses. This type of officer tends to play down the working side of the job and this has to be conveyed. A and Q Staffs tend to attract RA and RE officers who have a reputation for being more methodical and scientifically minded than others, so models of these—Brigadiers, AQ, AQMGs and DAAGs—should give the impression of serious hard-working types. This impression can be heightened by giving them a fair amount of the appropriate impedimenta—message pads, map boards, binoculars, etc. Brigade Majors RA have to have that instant 'action front' look about them, an appearance which can be produced by giving both rider and horse a 'collected' appearance (see picture No 3).

These and other characteristic mannerisms can be embodied in both the conversion/assembly stage and also in the painting, as long as you know your man. He may be a character you feel strongly about and you will be able to work on him without much preliminary thought. You know exactly how you want to convey one part of his character—by a tilt to the head—so, if the head is integral to the figure you are using, off it must come, the collar and neck must be built up, and the head re-set. If you intend to use a different head, the change has to be made anyway and you embody the desired characteristic at the same time.

I had a number of pet types in mind when I was doing my full dress Army HQ but spent quite a while going through my own papers and in museums and libraries to get complete typicality for each. I needed an Honorary Bishop to the Forces. A picture in an old 'Army and Navy Illustrated' gave me the first idea; then I read up various accounts of senior chaplains in service publications and studied the names in the Chaplains section of the Army List. (Names are very important; they do help to crystallise one's mental picture. Read through Army Lists and regimental histories for yourself and you will see what I mean. Finally, I could visualise him—The Very Rev Marmaduke Le Poer ffrench-Crevasse, DD, DLitt (Hon), CVO. He looks a suitable mixture of worldliness and benignity, is dressed in shovel hat (chinstrap down), frock coat, pectoral cross, aind gaiters (which, after all, is episcopal mounted dress), and sits a handsome cob among the principal staff officers as good as any of them. An 'early Britain' village clergyman on an Indian silladar horse converted to the standing position were the main two components of this particular conversion.

With the Principal Ordnance Officer I had to convey a look of being sufficiently distinguished for the appointment and yet of being professional enough to have the trust of the rest of the Staff and the troops when it came to the matter of urgently wanting stores. A full dress, cocked hat figure, he emerged as grey-haired, well bronzed and business-like, with the 'right' mixture of campaign medals as well as decorations for administrative work. Similarly, the Director-General of Medical Services, (remember that in the British Army the medical officers are always one rank higher than their contemporaries on each HQ), had to look slightly more the surgeon than the general and his decorations were headed by the Order of St John of Jerusalem. (This was a bit of an anti-climax when it came to painting as its riband turned out to be black, which didn't show up on a dark blue tunic, but one is amply repaid when the knowledgeable observer peers close at the model and discovers it.)

The Provost-Marshal had to look as smart but somehow not quite as elegant as the cavalry Officer and convey the distinct impression of a very iron hand in a thin velvet glove. And, oh yes, remember that whenever you put Officers of Scottish regiments on to staff jobs that they are intensely proud of their national and regimental emblems and distinctions and insist on wearing them all the time (a cautionary word about Scottish dress will be found in Chapter 5—Infantry).

Now to consider what is available to the collector both in ready-made models and basic toys suitable for conversion to Staff figures. To the collector who is an enthusiast for the Napoleonic period, there is probably a greater selection than for anyone else. Not surprisingly, the largest range is in France, varying from the beautifully executed figures of Roger Berdou, through Madame Metayer to the volume producing firms of Mignot, Segom and Historex. Mignot still produces (December 1968) metal castings, but to my eye these tend to be stylised in posture and are open to some criticism on grounds of complete accuracy. Nevertheless, to the collector who still insists on metal, they fill a need.

The firm of SEGOM (Société d'Edition Generale d'Objet Moulés) include in their 1968 Catalogue all the principal figures for a Napoleonic headquarters staff, from the Emperor himself through Marmont, Murat, Ney and Soult to aides-de-camp, trumpeters and escorts for these and other staff personages. As noted in Appendix 4 the interesting thing about this firm is that the figures can be obtained either complete and painted, assembled but unpainted, or in a kit, ('en pochette cristal à assembler et à peindre'), with details for assembly and painting. In addition, the firm runs an accessories range from which it is possible to buy spare parts to achieve body and dress variations; this gives the collector some scope in assembling the figures in the style *he* wants and not as thrust on him by the vendors of completely finished figures. All SEGOM products at present are in 55 mm scale size and made in a good quality polystyrene.

The firm of Historex, a relative newcomer to the scene, also produces in 54 mm in polystyrene and include staff officers in their range. Their designs are supervised by M. Eugene Leliepvre, a distinguished French modeller and army painter. Their horse designs are some of the most exciting I have ever seen.

If collectors are also inordinately fond of coffee there is a French firm called Mokerex which gives away unpainted plastic historical figures with their product. These cover a number of epochs and the 1st Empire includes Napoleonic staff figures. The quality of the moulding is high but unfortunately the firm does not seem able to make up its mind as to what scale to use. Dismounted figures are about 70 mm high, but cavalry (detachable riders) about 50 mm.

To my knowledge no firm in England at present markets low-priced figures of Wellington and his HQ staff. The Belmont-Maitland/Norman Newton catalogue of metal figures illustrates several variations of Wellington and his chief subordinates, such as Combermere, Uxbridge and Ponsonby (as well as Napoleon and his staff). These are supplied to collectors either painted or unpainted. The firm's catalogue claims that all their 54 mm figures are 'individually made in every stage by hand and the collector can command whatever attitude or pose desired'. But the prices for any quantity of such figures may well be beyond most of us (they certainly are for me) so we must look at what can be converted more cheaply from existing toys.

Britains, Timpo and Charbens all currently produce plastic soldiers in 54 mm of the American War of Independence, Waterloo and the US Civil War period. They are all jointed on what Britains (so rightly for the collector) call the 'Swoppet' principle, which means they can be dis-assembled to varying extents. With the introduction of a very few heads, torso pieces and equipment items of Segom the enterprising collector will have no difficulty in making himself a Wellington and a Napoleon (personally, I would put them in this order of importance) plus staff officers exactly to his own requirement. It must be said that a number of toy pieces from Charben and some of Timpo will need considerable refining by hand to bring them to model standards. Photograph No 64 shows some conversions of Wellington and Staff by Mr W. Y. Carman, of the National Army Museum, Camberley. The basic figures for these are, alas, no longer available.

Turning from the distant to the recent past and following the same approach; if the collection is based on the 1939–45 War period it is well catered for by toy figures of fighting men. Timpo and Charbens produce British 8th Army and the latter do an Afrika Corps group. Britains' khaki infantry figures are basically English but can be easily modified to depict Americans. Here again, with some hand work, such HQ figures as Montgomery, Patton and Rommel can be produced.

Example of Staff Figure Conversions

(1) The Mounted Staff Officers in picture No 3 were all converted from Britain's metal castings (now only obtainable as secondhand items). The process was in general as described in Chapter 2.

(2) Illustration No 4, George Washington converted from:

Britains' American Civil War bugler/trooper horse.
Britains' American Civil War bugler/trooper legs.
Britains' War of Independence British Infantry body.
Britains' War of Independence British infantry head and periwig.
Britains' War of Independence British Infantry right-arm holding tricorne hat from head of same figure. This is a good example of the conversion possibilities offered by currently available plastic figures of the 'Swoppet' kind.

CHAPTER FOUR

Cavalry

MILITARILY, the term 'cavalry' is non-exact, but is taken to mean soldiers who fight assisted by some form of locomotion other than their own feet but, like most terms, it has had different meanings at different times. Broadly speaking, up to the end of the 1914–18 War it meant a soldier who fought mounted (almost always on a horse). From then on pundits and pedants have had to qualify it by such pronouns as 'horsed cavalry', 'mechanised cavalry' and, latterly in the US Army, 'air cavalry'.

Previously the broad division had been between light and heavy cavalry (which usually covered in their respective ages as well, the elephant, the camel and other unusual beasts). In this chapter we are considering the classical cavalry man—the soldier who fought mounted on a horse.

One of the pleasant things about a collection which includes mounted troops is that it allows the owner opportunity to possess models of the most beautiful animal ever tamed by man. The horse has now passed from the battlefield and this all true animal lovers must applaud, but we can include horsed figures in our collection because cavalry was a fact of military life in ages far less humane than our own.

The horse in war has a recorded history of more than 6,000 years, evidence of which we see in Egyptian and other ancient murals and potteries, etc. But before this it must have occurred to prehistoric men, once they had domesticated them, that the sure-footed, sturdy ponies of their times could provide them with advantages over their foes. Down the ages the employment of the horse in war has passed through a definable cycle, which in brief can be referred to as the light and heavy schools of usage. In some eras and peoples the horse was merely a means of transport to the place of battle. From this, man's quest for tactical advantage would lead him to including his mount in his scouting pre-battle duties, to using it as a firing platform for his bow (or pistol), and ultimately to riding up and engaging his adversary from the horse's back. From these activities gradually developed the armoured horseman, who was taught to regard his mount as a weapon—this was for long the philosophy of the 'arme blanche'—that cavalry were the shock arm which, launched at the right moment in the right place, would sweep the enemy away.

Unfortunately for the advocates of this school of thought the other side developed methods of resisting this—entrenchments, defensive fire, obstacles and such like, and after a series of defeats the shock type of cavalryman would fall into disfavour until there was stalemate and a thoughtful leader would see some new way of using the horse to help win battles.

The strength of the Persian Army was in its cavalry, assisted by archers; these latter would gall the enemy with arrows and then be followed by a well-timed cavalry charge. The Macedonian cavalry would not face up to war elephants and so these acquired a temporary prominence in battle until methods of dealing with them were evolved. At the classic battle of Cannae (216 BC) the Carthaginian cavalry, a mixture of light and heavy, were used by Hannibal at the right moment to annihilate a much larger force of Roman legions. But the tables were turned in North Africa when Scipio won the Battle of the Great Plain—the first victory of Roman Cavalry—which paved the way to the destruction of Carthage. Whilst the proportion of cavalry to infantry in the Roman Army gradually increased, it mostly used light horse, recruited from conquered peoples such as the Gauls or Spanish and North Africans. Romantic writers like to trace the descent of British Cavalry from the auxiliary horse that Celtic Britain provided. Legend has it that the Romanised Briton King Arthur won the Battle of Mount Badon by a cavalry charge against the Saxon invaders. The Eastern Roman Army of Byzantium under Belisarious had a long run of successes in battle through adopting the Parthian pattern of mixed cavalry, especially armoured archer-lancers.

There is very little in the way of good toy figures of the above early cavalrymen. I know of no maker of Persian horse soldiers. Britains include a horseman in their limited range of Trojan figures in their 'Herald' models series (Cat No 7599) but no Romans. On the other hand, Timpo and Crescent currently produce Romans. Of foreign firms, Elastolin of Germany produce excellent Roman figures, but not in 54 mm scale. All the above are of plastic composition. However, as I hope I have made clear in Chapter 3, this should not deter the determined collector. All the above firms include other kinds of figures which are basically suitable for conversion to Persian, Greek and Roman cavalry, in particular Red Indian figures. These can be judiciously cut up, and with various anatomical transplants from Greek and Roman foot soldiers, charioteers and gladiators, plus permutation of heads, etc, the 'Classical History' modeller can produce an original force of period cavalry.

The custom modellers also provide Greek and Roman figures. However, I do not think that they include a cavalryman as such in their current catalogues.

Horsemen of the Dark Ages, ie, the Goths, Vandals and lastly the mounted hordes of Genghis Khan do not seem to have much appeal to collectors at present and I am not aware of any toy or model maker producing them, so here is a new field for an enterprising manufacturer. Historically it is an important period as the habit of the barbarian aristocracies of fighting on horseback led to the deterioration, in size and quality, of infantry all over Europe and Asia. The general introduction of stirrups paved the way for the new order of armoured horsemen which ushered in the so-called age of chivalry.

Picture No 6 is an example of a Barbarian horse taken from a history book. For details of conversion see caption.

As the Bayeux Tapestry shows, the Normans brought the first war horse to England. (The Saxons had only used horses as a means of transport, considering it more manly to fight on foot.) Their armour was light so these were not the heavy weight-carrying horses of a later period. With the Normans came the mounted chivalry—a hierarchy of baron, knight, esquire, man-at-arms and page—organised in various Orders, and pledged to honour, charity, courtesy and justice, little of which, alas, were displayed by William or his followers.

Mailed and mounted knights could account for any number of half-naked Celtic kerns, as the Norman invasion of Ireland showed (and as, four centuries later, the handful of mounted Conquistadores were to demonstrate in Mexico and Peru), but Edward I raised a force of light cavalry from there—the hobelars—lightly armed for patrol work and mounted on animals similar to the Connemara pony of today. As the velocity of the arrow and the deadliness of hand weapons increased, so did the protective wearing apparel—firstly chain mail and then the heavy plate armour, chieflly as a result of Western experience against Turks and Saracens in the crusades. This led to a larger, heavier (and slower) type of war horse being introduced by King John from Flanders, from which the British Shire horse of today is descended. This is the type of cavalry we all think of as fighting such battles as Poitiers and Agincourt, though Edward III raised a body of horsed archers in 1336 which may be regarded as the first dragoons. The internecine Wars of the Roses so reduced the weight-carrying type of horse that Henry VIII passed a law which required 'prelates and nobles of a degree of wealth assessed by the richness of their wives' clothes (any French hood or bonnet of velvet) to maintain stallions of a given standard'. But by the end of the 16th century the heavy armoured horseman was on the way out and light cavalry was becoming 'heavy'.

The Age of Armour is reasonably well provided for in both toys and models. In the United Kingdom, Britains produce suitable figures in both 'Herald' and 'Swoppet' ranges; they are of the 15th century fully armoured horsemen, but the general design and method of manufacture permits change to earlier periods (eg Crusader) by fairly simple conversion, especially in the 'Swoppet' range. Timpo also have a mounted figure in each of their three groups of knights, Crusader (Cat No 015), Medieval (Cat No 016), and Silver (Cat No 08). These are also on the 'Swoppet' principle, so personal choice of figure is easily obtained even before you need consider more complicated conversions. Messrs Charbens also tell me they include medieval figures in their current production range. The main item missing in these products is a good Norman mounted figure with the characteristic pot helmet head and nose bar. However, Britains have recently come to the rescue here by including 11th century helmeted figures with their ancient Siege Engines (see picture No 7).

Before leaving medieval figures, a cautionary word should be said about an integral part of their study and that is on the subject of heraldry. Heraldry evolved from the need of men fully covered (including the face) with mail or armour to recognise and be recognised—very important in the medieval mêlée! This was done by painting a device on the shield (the coat of arms) and wearing something distinguishable on the top of the helmet (the crest). From this simple beginning has developed a most complicated subject with intricate laws and a special jargon (especially for colours) which I, for one, do not pretend to fully understand. I have, however, sufficient historical knowledge, to know better than to put King Arthur in 14th century heraldic armour (as in the 'Camelot' musical), or depict Robert the Bruce at Bannockburn in Milanese equipment which a most distinguished historical modeller once did. Collectors will need more than one book on Instant Heraldry before venturing into this subject, but it is a fascinating one and the making and painting of medieval models is an excellent projection of such studies. There are several inexpensive books on heraldry, including an 'Observer's Book'. Among the custom model makers Ping is probably the maker of the finest of such figures.

The British Civil War, in which leaders on both sides had had experience of contemporary Continental fighting, brought new ideas on the use of cavalry. Whilst the lance was discarded, the slow rate of musket and gun fire allowed unarmoured horsemen the chance of decisive action if they moved quickly enough. Prince Rupert and Cromwell were pioneers in these tactics which began a new era for cavalry. The British Regular Army dates officially from the Restoration. Kept very small by a suspicious Parliament, with only eight regiments, it included two regiments of Life or Horse Guards and one of Dragoons. (Dragoons were originally foot soldiers, so called because the firearm they used was nicknamed a 'Dragon' from its belching mouth; they were increasingly used as light cavalry and assumed the traditions and rôles of the horse soldier.)

That much misunderstood monarch James II is really entitled to be called the founder of the British Army, as it was during his short reign that the number of units were increased and foundations laid which have remained. Under him also, one of the most brilliant of British soldiers received his early training—John Churchill who, defecting to the Williamite side, went on to establish the value of British arms in Continental wars of the 18th century. As Duke of Marlborough he made brilliant use of British cavalry in the shock rôle at Blenheim, Ramilles, Oudenarde and Malplaquet. Following in this tradition, later leaders such as Ligonier and Granby (of 'going for it bald headed' fame) scored British victories by use of cavalry at Dettingen, Warburg, Beaumont and Willems.

It is somewhat remarkable that no British toy maker has models of this period. Yet in terms of 'play value' (words much in vogue in the toy trade) it has much to offer. Marlborough's cavalry wore large three-cornered hats, square-cut red coats, white breeches and long black riding boots. They were armed with swords, pistols and muskets and rode large strong horses. They opposed armies (including the French, then reckoned to be the finest in Europe) which nearly all wore the same general style of dress, if differently coloured, a style which remained almost unchanged for over a century. So a few basic models on the 'Swoppet' principle could provide representation of a great period in European military history.

Messrs Britains did produce English Civil War Cavalier and Parliamentarian horsemen in the 1950s but they are no longer in production, though the heads and torsos of their current American War of Independence infantry figures (Cat No 7385) can be transplanted on to US Civil War horsemen (Cat No 400 series) or on to most Herald horses. (See picture No 8.) Messrs Timpo and

Charbens also have War of Independence foot figures which, with some skilful trimming, can be converted, but the modeller will need to look outside their ranges for suitable horses. In the UK, Rose Miniatures have recently added a Waterloo Scots Grey and two mid-17th century mounted men (basically French but capable of conversion) and Norman Newton has one or two mounted figures of the period catalogued, but they are not cavalrymen as such.

The Peninsular and Waterloo periods have, in the model soldier world, come to mean little less than a glorification of Napoleon. This is perhaps understandable with the French, but the cult has spread in Britain and America also and, looking through the custom model makers' catalogues and model society magazines, it is sometimes difficult to remember who won the Battle of Waterloo. French cavalry certainly figured largely in the period. Although nearly bankrupt, Napoleon spent lavishly and widened its scope (he reintroduced the lance to Western cavalry) to move far and wide in reconnaissance as well as pursue with fury, as in the 1806 campaign. Their use on the battlefield was exceptional, and only occasionally did they appear, as at Waterloo, but under Kellerman they were used in the mass for pursuit. But by 1814 the Austrian cavalry, under the great Marshal Radetsky, was considered the best in Europe. The British cavalry of the period was well mounted and of great shock effect but lacked control. British cavalry leaders were so rash that Wellington was always nervous about launching it at the wrong moment.

There are no commercially produced cavalry of this period in Britain but, as I have indicated above, there are a wealth of Napoleonic items available from the specialist model makers. Conversions from other toys are not impossible (see picture No 5), but will need a fair amount of hard work, and the buying-in of the necessary heads for Cuirassiers, Lancers, cocked hats, etc, as well as the distinctive horse furniture. Messrs Britains' US Civil War Cavalry (the 400 Series) could be used as the basic figures but a fair amount of expenditure will be necessary on the bits and pieces. Rose Models are the best buy in UK in lead figures; the French Historex items in plastic are also available in Britain and are devoted entirely to the Napoleonic era. There are also the Segom products which can only be obtained from France. Converters using other figures, like the Britains' items mentioned, will be pleased to know that all individual parts of the Historex kits can now be bought separately, which thus gives a reasonable supply of pieces like heads and arms, all in plastic, at about 2s a time.

Little of note occurred in the cavalry world between Waterloo and the Crimean War, so as a result there were few changes in dress or equipment. To most people the conflict with Russia appears to mean the Charge of the Light Brigade. This episode has received attention out of all proportion to its importance in the campaign and I would advise any reader considering making Crimean cavalry to brief himself from two sources: the war correspondent Russell's despatches from the Crimea and the photographs of Fenton. The Crimea was the first war to be photographed and Fenton's work is very representative. In British cavalry terms the most important event was the *successful* charge of the Heavy Brigade of the Cavalry Division at the Battle of Balaclava.

Cavalry engagements were rare in the American Civil War, only one, Brandy Station (June 9 1863), being regarded by US authorities as 'the largest (and) first true cavalry combat of the war'.

Large numbers of horsemen were used on both sides, especially in raiding (eg Forrest and Stoneman's) but did not play the sole part in these. Shock tactics with the sword were rare, one authority quoting that out of 250,000 wounded treated in Union hospitals only 922 were due to saber (sic), 'And a large proportion of these were caused by private quarrels or inflicted by camp guards in course of duty'. Cavalry leaders or generals who employed cavalry include on the Federal side Sheridan, Torbet, Averall, Garrard, Merritt and Stoneman; on the Confederate side, Forrest (or 'Get there firstest with the mostest' fame), Fitzhugh Lee and 'Jeb' Stuart, the latter possibly the most attractive personality of all the many leaders thrown up by the war. Modellers are lucky here for reference material; the war was well photographed, the works of Brady and Alexander Gardner being especially valuable.

They are also lucky in that there is a comparative wealth of toy figures available. The three leading UK makers all produce cavalry of both sides, including officers, trumpeters and standard bearers. Naturally there is also a great wealth of US Civil War cavalry models in America, indicated in Appendix 4.

European cavalry played its part in the 19th century wars of that continent; in the West the victorious Prussian Army became known for its Uhlan lancers and Cuirassiers of the Garde du Corps; in the East the Austro-Hungarian Empire included a large body of Magyar cavalry, Hussars as well as Imperial Dragoons. Unhappy, divided Poland contributed its particular type of horseman, the lancer, with his individual flat-topped cap, to Germany, Austria and Russia. But the latter was best known for a type of horseman peculiar to that vast country, the very name of which was sufficient to strike a chill into the heart of neighbouring peoples—the Cossack.

In the Victorian British Army, cavalry took part in all the small wars in India and Africa, reaching its apogee in the South African War of 1899–1902. (See picture No 9.) During this period the light dragoon regiments were gradually converted into either hussars or lancers, adopting the accepted continental style of uniforms associated with these types. In dress the post-Waterloo lavishness of braid, plume and feather gave way to mid-Victorian dreariness in which the styles were based on French post-Crimea costume until 1870. Then, in an attempt to copy Germany, many national armies imitated their dress, particularly the spiked helmet. (Students of military dress will be struck by the fact that the campaign dress of a winning nation is nearly always taken up as a general costume by others, including the losers, in that post-war period.) But the improvement in fire-arms, particularly the introduction of the breech-loading rifle, began to reduce the scope of cavalry; colourful clothing, at one time an asset in overawing one's opponent, began to give way to dress of a neutral colour, such as 'khaki', (a Persian-Pushtu word meaning dust-coloured) evolved in India in the Mutiny period so as to avoid the eye of keen marksmen.

In this period the public imagination was caught by another unimportant cavalry action, that of the 21st Lancers at Omdurman, chiefly because a politically minded young officer, Winston Churchill, playing at war correspondent, had insinuated himself without permission into the regiment! In the Boer War there was one spectacular cavalry action when General French led his whole division between Boer positions at Klip Drift to relieve Kimberley. Mounted infantry was much employed in attempts to track down the elusive but fair fighting Boers. Some surplus artillerymen as well as Australians were used as mounted infantry and are said to have charged on horseback with fixed bayonets! Models of this unusual combination of weapons and movement would perplex less well informed students of the hobby. The 19th century was also the period of the volunteers, the part-time Yeomanry Cavalry which offer a rich field of uniform study, the general design and colouring being on the 'exception principle' in many instances.

Unfortunately for the collector there are now no commercially produced figures of British Empire or European cavalry of this period. Messrs Britains' metal range included every cavalry regiment of the British Army, as well as several Indian regiments, plus Prussian Hussars, French Cuirassiers, Austrian Dragoons and Russian Cossacks. In view of the enormous production (literally millions of pieces), large quantities must remain in private hands and do, in fact, appear with dealers, who tend to overcharge for them. Current plastic Household Cavalry can be converted to Dragoons and Cuirassiers and the Canadian Mounted Policeman is basically suitable for a conversion to a khaki service dress cavalry trooper. The specialist model makers produce some 19th-century full dress cavalry but these are very expensive.

The 1914–18 War spelled the end of the fighting horseman in battle against a modern enemy, although there were a large number of exceptions which misled many people into believing (some for sentimental reasons) that horsed cavalry had a future. There were certainly a number of important cavalry actions at the beginning and at the very end, ie, when the fighting was fluid. There was a great hand-to-hand cavalry fight between 15,000 Germans and 12,000 Belgian, French and British horsemen on the Lys in October 1914, during the race for the sea, and in the final advance of October 1918 the British Cavalry Corps came into its traditional own for a few days, the 5th Dragoon Guards actually charging and capturing a train at Harbonnieres, an incident afterwards painted by the great artist Matania. But the trench, barbed wire and, above all, the machine gun held them back in between. As part of each great offensive, horsed cavalry would be brought up in mass ready to ride through the gap but the real breakthrough never came because there were always stout-hearted German machine gunners to spray the 'no-man's-land' with hails of bullets. At times, the attempt would be made, as on the Somme in 1916, when horsed cavalry were sent up near High Wood. But Indian Lancers and British Dragoons were easy targets for unbroken German defenders and the dreams of great mounted actions ended in dismounted fights by the survivors.

In Palestine in 1918 British cavalry dominated the battlefield under the command of Allenby, himself a cavalryman and known as 'the Bull' for his energy and drive. He finally had a force of four mounted divisions made up of British Yeomanry, Indian, Australian, New Zealand and French regiments which certainly swept all before them. But it must be remembered that they were fighting an enemy much weaker than themselves, greatly demoralised and equipped only to mid-19th century standards.

In the 1920s and 1930s the place of the horse in battle received much study in an attempt to retain him. The British Army played with a mixed force of tanks and horses and umpires strained all the rules to prove the horse could get there quicker than the internal combustion engine. The United States Cavalry experimented with portee cavalry, moving horses and men in large motor loose boxes up to the scene of action, as is done for a peaceful point-to-point race meeting. But bit by bit reality prevailed and, after a long period of hesitation, British cavalry (except for four regiments) was mechanised by 1939. The BEF that crossed to France in September that year was, in fact, the only completely mechanised army in the world at that time.

The Germans and the Russians employed horsed cavalry on the Eastern Front throughout the 1939–45 War. The large horsed cavalry force of tragic Poland immolated itself against the German Panzers in 1939. A British Cavalry Division of three Regular and six Yeomanry Regiments was sent to Palestine and did mostly garrison duties but saw some action in the move into Vichy Syria in 1941. The units were then converted into mechanised armour and the fine hunters and riding horses brought out from the green fields of England were disposed of to Levantine horse dealers.

There are no figures produced by any maker, toy or model, that I know of, of horsed cavalry of either of the world wars, so would-be collectors must either carry out major conversions or ask the model firm to supply custom figures. (See picture No 10.) It must be admitted that the amount of material is limited and conversion complicated. For instance, when I made my 1916 Lancers it needed eight cuts and annealings to change the metal toy to the model desired. Britains' Canadian Mounted Policemen (Cat No 699) and their Military Show Jumpers (Cat No 2077) offer some possibility using show jumping horses 2078 and 2079 for variety, with, say, Rose Model heads and equipment, but the work involved is considerable.

So has passed the horse from the battlefield, on which for so long he played a noble part, often setting an example in patience and courage to the men he served. Man's conflicts with his fellows involved much slaughter of animals who had no part in these quarrels. In all armies, except for ceremonial duties, the garage now replaces the stall and the petrol pump the water trough and the haynet. The cavalry spirit, however, lives on, carefully cherished by the now mechanised dragoons, hussars and lancers. Whilst the nexus is a direct one, it is more practicable for modellers to leave them here and discuss armoured fighting vehicles and motor transport in separate chapters.

In conclusion I would offer the collector a valid collecting area in *modern* cavalry, in Escort and Guard Troops of Heads of State. We will all be aware of the British Household Cavalry, the French Garde Républicaine and the Italian Cuirassio. An Irish friend of mine, Glenn Thompson of Dublin, has specialised in this field for many years and his collection also includes examples of the bodyguards of Denmark, Sweden and Spain. There are also for inclusion in such a collection the Mounted Bodyguards of India and Pakistan (direct descendants of the old Indian Army), (see picture No 11), the Royal Canadian Mounted Police as well as such exotic bodyguards as that of the King of Morocco, the Argentine Horse Grenadiers and several other South American Republics.

And here a cautionary word about swopping the riders of one period to the other. Down the centuries riding postures have undergone changes; modellers not conversant with horses should make a slight study of these, otherwise some errors, especially with leg positions, may be perpetuated. Early riders,

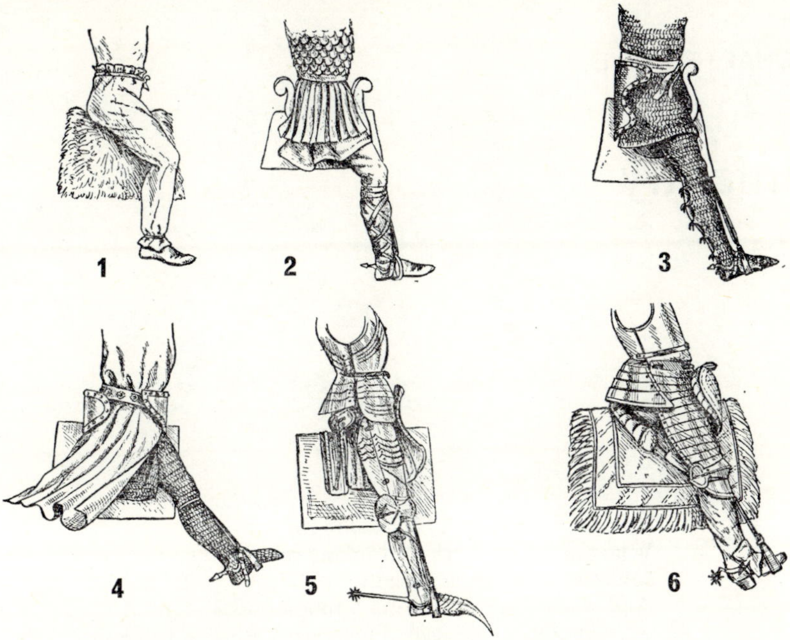

Key to riding positions: (1) Primitive, (2) Roman/Byzantine, (3) 12th century, (4) Middle Ages, (5) 15th century, (6) 17th century.

such as barbarian and Roman, had no stirrups and rode with a 'long' leg. The Romans gradually evolved a saddle but the cantle and bow only came about the 8th century. The Normans, with stirrups, rode mostly with a straight leg and the heel down. From the 13th century we have the 'well' saddle with low bow and rounded shape and curved corners to the cantle. The foot now was thrust more forward. By the 15th century the saddle was beginning to curve around the thighs and the leg was coming back to the vertical position. A feature of 16th century riding was the heel well depressed. The 17th century saw the bow pommel more developed and the ball of the heel on the stirrup thread. There are innumerable paintings of horsemen from then on until the age of the camera to give guidance, but it should be remembered that there were always exceptions by individuals who worked out and preferred their own postures.

And, lastly, a word about the horses. The horse is truly a noble animal; aim to turn out worthy models of him. Include at least one good horse book, with anatomical drawings and photos of gaits in it, in your source material. Whilst you should aim to put your men on the correct type of horses, remember that there are always exceptions, especially on active service. The US Marines actually did have a *mounted* detachment (at Peking pre-1941) mounted on stubby Tibetan ponies (see picture No 56); the Scottish Horse rode Highland garrons *not* troop horses and the Scots Greys have been known to ride bays and chestnuts in time of war.

CHAPTER FIVE

Infantry

'Here sleeps in peace a Hampshire Grenadier
Who caught his death by drinking cold small beer.
Soldiers be wise from his untimely fall.
And when you're hot drink Strong or none at all'
Epitaph on grave in Winchester Cathedral Graveyard, 1764.

THE BACKBONE OF AN ARMY is its infantry, the soldiers who form the battle line and fight on foot. Whilst success in battle depends on the right combination of all arms—cavalry (or armour), artillery, infantry and supporting services—the job of occupying and holding the ground can only be done by the foot soldier. In some places the fighting can only be done by him alone. We are not sure how the term *infantry* arose. One authority thinks it was a Staff expression to describe those who could only move at a foot's pace and were unable to carry their own heavy baggage any distance; in a legal-technical sense they were infants. Officers in the French Army used to address their men as 'Mes Enfants' which, if not strictly accurate when said to burly, heavily bearded poilus, was at least coincidental as well as being rather endearing.

Many collectors devote their work to infantry only, either in the form of the complete history of one regiment (usually their own) or a type of foot soldier which interests them, ie, Foot Guards, Grenadiers, Fusiliers, Light Infantry or Rifles. Despite what I have said earlier about balanced collections, the collecting of infantry figures on their own (in accordance with a conscious theme) is a valid form of pursuing the hobby. It also has some practical advantages; foot soldiers do not take up so much room as horse or guns, they are cheaper to buy, and the supply is larger and more varied both from toy and model makers in the UK and abroad.

The earliest reliable information we have of organised infantry is at the Battle of Kadesh, 1288 BC, between the Egyptians and the Hittites in Syria, shortly before the Exodus.* The Pharaoh's infantry was mostly archers or spearmen carrying shields. Contemporary models of these exist in Cairo Museum and are illustrated in another book by me on the hobby.† After a fight between the opposing chariot troops the Hittites fled for a river ford at which the Egyptian infantry poured a relentless fire of arrows. (See picture No 12.)

A thousand years later the Greek phalanx proved itself superior in the Graeco-Persian war. Greek city state forces were conscripted from freeborn citizens. (Socrates was called up to fight in one of these at the age of 47!) The backbone of the Greek army was the heavily armed pikeman or hoplite with a long spear and a short sword. Hoplites fought in the phalanx formation—a solid block of infantry up to 16 ranks deep in close order. The stiffened phalanx could crash through any thinner formation and in a charge was almost irresistible. It proved itself at Marathon (490 BC) and under Alexander the Great at Arbela (331 BC).

The next and probably best known of all ancient fighting men are the Roman Legionaries. Originally a part-time militia it was made into a paid (Soldati) force of long-service troops, which could move about and fight in all seasons. Beginning with the phalanx, experience led them to evolve the legion into three age groups of men, sub-divided into maniples or companies. The strength of the legion varied between 4,500 and 6,000. Legionaries were equipped with helmet, shield, cuirass, javelin and short sword. The chessboard formation of the maniples within the legion gave them greater flexibility than the phalanx; it did not break up when penetrated and, if part of the legion was overwhelmed, the remaining maniples (which, if necessary, also operated as independent units) could close up and carry on the fight. This is the formation which finally overcame Carthage and the later versions of the Grecian phalanx.

In the first century BC the cohort replaced the maniple, conditions of enlistment changed and tactics, especially hand-to-hand fighting, improved. This was the type of legion Caesar brought to Britain and which was severely handled by the chariot troops of Cassivellaunus. These Romans were strangers to this type of mobile warfare but the Britons found that the legions contained a hard core of resistance which was beyond the power of the chariots to break. In the ensuing centuries the Imperial legions became less and less offensive and more of an armed gendarmerie, manning police and custom posts and guarding natural obstacles such as river lines, and man-made defences like Hadrian's Wall. Progressive exposure of the legions to barbarians further weakened their efficiency, as tribal methods of fighting replaced the tactics of the cohort.

One of the few pagan lands to give precedence to infantry in this period was Ireland. The Fianna of the 2nd and 3rd centuries AD was a force maintained by the High Kings, 'to keep the peace among the men of Erin, to ensure rights and prevent wrongs, to check thieves and outlaws, enforce the payment of taxes and guard the harbours against foreigners'. Recruits to the Fianna had to pass some rather unusual tests, including the reciting of a lengthy amount of poetry, and also athletic exercises such as jumping over a tree branch forehead high and successfully warding off the spears of nine warriors with only a

* It surprises me that no collector appears to have gone in for collecting soldiers of the Bible. The Jews were (and are) a war-like race and the Old Testament is full of accounts of fighting. The late Otto Gottstein attempted a History of Jewish people in a series of large dioramas but their present whereabouts is unknown. (See picture No 13.)

† 'Model Soldiers' (Weidenfeld and Nicolson).

shield and staff. Other conditions were to swear 'Not to accept a wife for her fortune but for her moral conduct and accomplishments, never to insult a woman, never to refuse the poor or needy, and never to turn his back on overwhelming force.' Exceptionally for the time they did not use chariots for movement or battle but, lightly armed, moved over the country on foot at high speed. Later kings and chieftains continued the practice of keeping small bodies of fighting men under regular pay, the best known being the gallowglasses, fierce mail-clad Scottish foot soldiers of the 13th century.

In Saxon England the Fyrd or shire levies formed the majority of the army. They were the able-bodied peasantry who, under the law, could be called out for 40 days a year in defence of the realm.* Sheriffs of counties were responsible for organising the Fyrd and getting them to their assembly places. As they moved on their feet they disliked fighting too far from home. They had no special uniforms and carried a variety of weapons, including their farm implements. The shields were mostly improvised, including shutters. But they were not a rabble and fought very bravely. There were also the Housecarls, the regular household troops, who moved on horseback but fought on foot. Most wore helmets and chainmail surcoats. They were armed with heavy battle axes which, wielded with two hands or hurled at short range, could cleave a man in two. They carried large shields which formed a wall against arrows.

This type of infantry went down finally before the Norman cavalry and archers at Hastings. The Saxons had few if any archers, viewing them with disfavour as men who were afraid to come to blows with their adversaries. But their Anglo-Norman descendants changed from the Hastings short to the Welsh longbow which exceeded in rate of fire and accuracy any other weapon. It restored the prestige of English infantry until the coming of firearms, but oddly enough was not taken up by any other nation. Even as late as the time of Henry VIII (himself an expert archer who passed strict laws on archery practice) it was still preferred to firearms. The longbow remained a weapon of war until it was declared obsolete by the Privy Council in 1595.

There is quite a large variety of toys and models covering infantry types. There are Britains' Trojan foot soldiers (Cat No 4591) and two Norman archer types in Cat No 7402, both in the Herald series. Curiously, this firm has never produced any Romans, Vikings, Saxons or Normans, though I pressed the then Managing Director to make the latter two kinds at the time of the ninth centenary of 1066. Timpo and Charbens have each a range of Roman legionaries but nothing else in the period. Over the last few years I have picked up in various small shops some Viking and Saxon figures, marked 'Hong Kong' in minute letters on the base, as well as some Egyptian types, including a female reclining figure which bears a close resemblance to Miss Elizabeth Taylor. Airfix have also recently added very good Romans and Ancient Britons to their OO/HO range.

The leading model maker of 'ancients' in the UK is undoubtedly Rose Models, whose current catalogue includes Ancient Egypt, Greece and Rome. The Egyptian models include some delightful feminine figures such as priestesses, girl musicians and slaves, an acrobatic dancer and two goddesses. The student of Egyptology will find plenty to interest him in this range, including

* The Fyrd was first raised by King Alfred and in one form or another, chiefly as Militia, has existed down to the present time. The Royal Monmouthshire Militia, Royal Engineers, TAVR, claims an unbroken descent as the last of them.

17. *Monogram 'Merite' figures, 55 mm, in metal.*

18. *4.5 howitzer gun and limber with team, etc. Author's multiple conversion from Britains' metal 54 mm figures.*

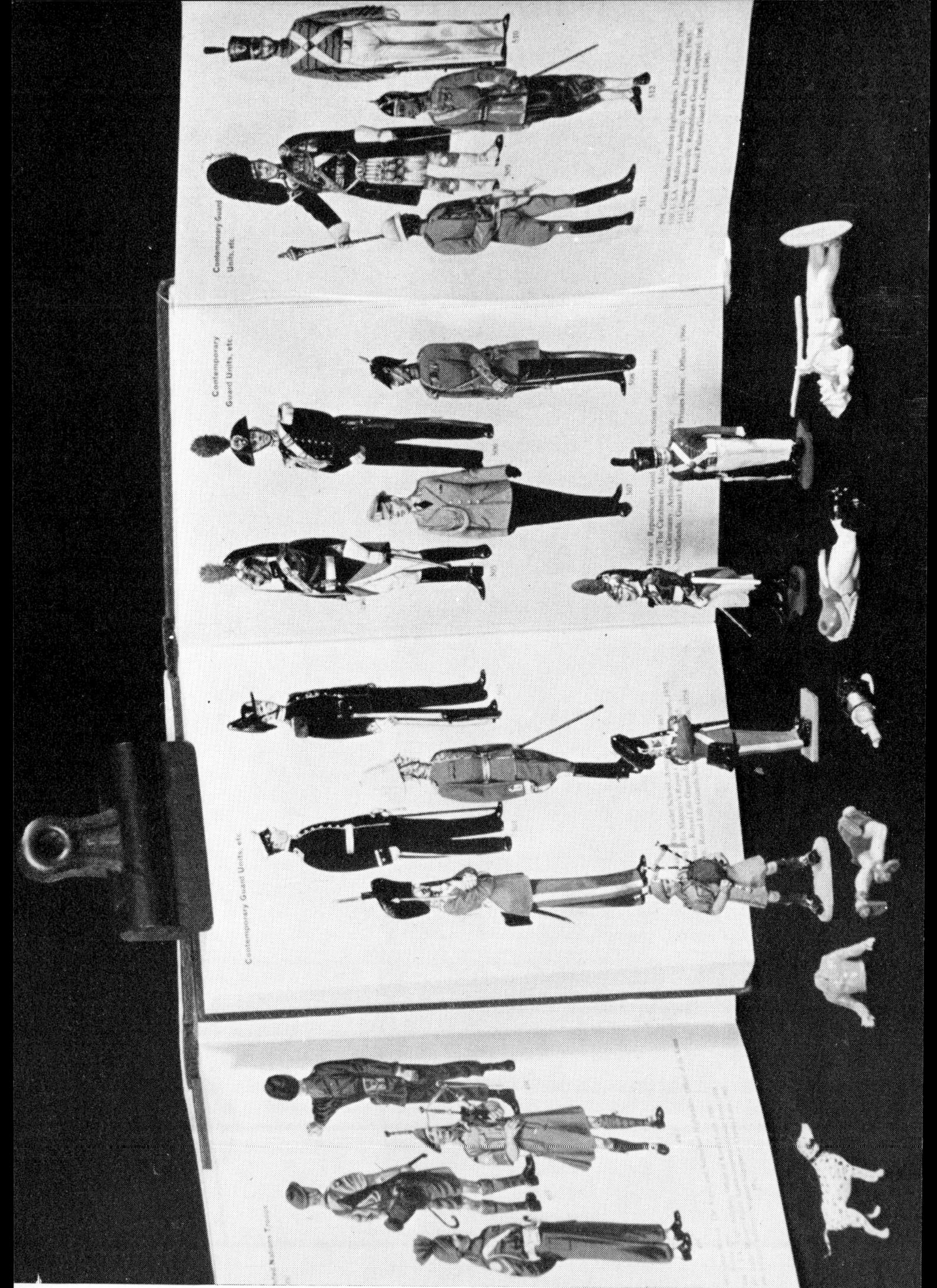

19. *Examples of easy conversions (from left to right): Britains' Indian torso and Timpo Roman legs; Britains' Guardsman and War of Independence Bearskin head and musket arms; Britains' War of Independence infantryman, with Civil War cavalry arms and SEGOM head; Timpo Waterloo figure with metal rifle arm.*

20. *Multiple conversion by Roy Dilley. Britains' field gun barrel built up and mounted on Airfix veteran car kit chassis.*

21. *'The Chaplain's place is with the fighting men.' Detail from author's diorama after a famous painting of 1914-18 War. 54 mm. Britains' metal figures, multiple conversions.*

22. *'The Casualties'—detail from author's group of wounded on Somme 1916. 54 mm multiple conversions, plastic and metal, all makes.*

some delicately designed accessories such as pitchers, dishes and ceremonial fans. Considering the research and the quality of the castings they are moderately priced when sold unpainted (ie, the 'C' Code prices in the Rose catalogue). The Greek figures are based on classical sources and include a Minoan woman in flounced skirt (which will delight followers of the distinguished archaeologist Sir Arthur Evans), as well as 6th and 5th century BC hoplites and a classical nude warrior. This latter, as the catalogue shows, can be easily converted into model statuary to give added realism to model buildings.

Six basic legionary figures of the Caeserian period are produced, including the centurion, which, for some reason, Rose's persist in making with his helmet plume across the helmet, instead of 'fore and aft' as I have always understood it to be. The definition in the castings is especially good and the tiny faces have those expressions of grimness and cruelty which were unpleasant characteristics of the Romans. The shields, helmets, spears and swords are interchangeable. (See picture No 15.)

Rose Models have also introduced some Celts, Franks and Gauls, chiefly, one suspects, to provide their Romans with prisoners and slaves! But they are also suitable for making into the types I have mentioned above, providing the collector has copies of the 'Annals of the Four Masters' and the 'Anglo-Saxon Chronicle' handy. The Rose Medieval foot soldiers are not of the 1066 but more of the 100 Years War period, but include a fine figure of the celebrated long-bowman.

There are various Continental producers of models of these periods, including another Coffee firm which gives them away with its product. This is the firm of Storme of Mouscron, near Menin, in Flanders. The range covers a couple of hundred figures and depicts the whole of Belgian history which is a reflection of all of Europe's. These fine models run from Roman, through Goth to Frankish (there is a splendid figure of Charlmagne) and from Norman to the Landsheckt. How to obtain them? Keep a sharp lookout when going to or through Belgium, which these days is not any further than going to Wales or Devon from, say, London. I found the firm very co-operative in supplying a sample range but we must remember their main object in offering them is to induce us to drink their coffee.

The golden age of infantry reaches from the Swiss pikemen into the era of the musket. The distinction of the Swiss infantry was that it could take the offensive, even against cavalry. On the defensive they formed large squares; in attack they advanced in broad deep columns, wheeling and changing formation without losing alignment. This ability was due to remorseless drilling. To relieve the monotony of all this and to improve march discipline, the Swiss introduced marching in step to the drums or some form of music. (See Chapter 8.) By these methods the Swiss gained a long line of brilliant victories in the 14th and 15th centuries, winning their independence from Austria and France. So celebrated did they become that Swiss mercenaries were enrolled in every important army in Europe. The Popes employed them and the modern Swiss Guard at the Vatican commemorates this by wearing the Medici costume of that period. (See picture No 14.) This was the age of the condottieri—traders in soldiers, the Middle Ages' equivalent to 'Have gun, will travel'. The condottieri had private armies for sale. They fought well but their main interest was to remain alive in order to get booty or ransom for wealthy captives. They were organised in companies which had a commercial meaning somewhat akin to that in present-day civilian life.

The Spaniards pioneered the use of small firearms. With the arquebus, or hand gun, they began to dominate the battlefield. In trenches or behind palisades, cavalry and pikemen charged them in vain. In the open they were vulnerable so pikemen were mixed with the arquebusiers (and musketeers) for mutual defence. The problem of the 'correct mix' of pikemen and hand gunners was the military question of the 16th and 17th century. (It was not until some French soldiers providently stuffed the hilts of their dagger-swords into the muzzles of their muskets at a place called Bayonne in SW France that the problem was solved and pikemen could be dispensed with.) It was with these troops that the Spaniards held large parts of Europe, ruled their Main and conquered Mexico and South America. It was against (or with) these that Tudor soldiers learned their business; when Sir Phillip Sidney made his act of sacrifice, when Shakespeare served and learned the art of war, so vividly portrayed in his plays, and from where British adventurers brought back some knowledge with which to lick the English civil war amateurs into shape.*

I hope I have not aroused too much interest in this exciting period of infantry, because I regret to say that there are almost no toys or models representing these types of soldiers. Before they ceased the production of metal castings, Britains had a Papal Swiss Guard which was suitable for conversion; likewise Mr W. Y. Carman's 'Carbago' models included a pikeman and musketeer but are now out of production. Up to recently I saw some early 17th century infantry in fencing postures on sale in the chain stores which were made by Crescent, but there is nothing else on the market in the UK. In Germany there is the well-known 'Elastolin' range which includes all these types, as do the Belgian 'Storme' Coffee 'give aways'. The Spanish Almirall brand includes some and that is about all.

The late 17th and almost all the 18th century saw infantry develop as part of standing or regular armies, dressed uniformly (Red for England, White for France, Blue for Prussia, Green for Russia) and organised in groups of companies called regiments (from the Latin *regimen*, a rule or system of order). Firearms (and tactics) now began to vary and some infantry began to specialise in one or other. Grenadiers were tall musketeers who received special training in handling and throwing grenades; picked men who came to be regarded as the elite of a regiment. So they could easily sling their muskets in order to throw the grenades, their tricorne hats were replaced by some caps rather like those of sailors in musical comedies. But this was unacceptable to the rigid formal school of discipline then prevailing, and the floppy ends of these caps were straightened up and stiffened and made to look like bishops' mitres. (Napoleon, to be different, put his Grenadiers in round fur caps—bearskins [see picture No 5]—and when the British First Foot Guards defeated them at Waterloo, as a distinction they were permitted to adopt their type of headdress.) Some British grenadiers wore fur caps but the traditional Grenadier mitre headdress remained in most armies, especially the German, which retained the tall mitre cap for grenadiers in full dress up to 1914.

Fusiliers were infantry armed with the fusil, a superior type of musket with

* The now internationally popular 'Flamenco' dance is named from the Spanish word for Flemish, which was given to the type of dances popularised in Flanders by Andalusian soldiers stationed there in the 16th century.

a flint- instead of a match-lock. Fusiliers were originally raised to escort the train of artillery, to protect the guns from attack and also to deter the hired civilian drivers from running away from the scene of battle. When all artillery personnel became militarised these duties ceased and fusilier regiments took their place in the line. They retained their titles of fusiliers long after being equipped with these weapons, and this became a sort of honour title for other infantry in due course, though I can't really see why.

The British campaigns in North America against the French, Indians and certain colonists revealed that stiff lines of red-coated musketeers were sitting ducks against loose formations of sharpshooters firing from behind cover, and lying down to do so, too! After a lot of painful experience, 'Light Infantry' were formed of hand-picked men who could scout and skirmish and move about quickly and quietly using individual initiative and without words of command. Later, Sir John Moore trained a special brigade (three regiments) which expanded into the famous Light Division under Wellington. 'Rifle' regiments were a further development of light infantry armed with muzzle loading rifles (a system of grooving the musket barrel which gave the bullet spin and so increased its velocity) and dressed in dark green uniforms as an early attempt at camouflage. These practices spread to other armies; the Austrians and Germans had their Jagers and the French their Chasseurs and Voltigeurs. These distinctions in tactics persisted until the end of the 19th century and whilst now all infantry is the same, except airborne, they have left their traces in the titles of certain regiments.

Apart from these distinctions, which are common to many armies, other countries developed types of infantry peculiarly their own. The British (and latterly, Commonwealth) Highland units are probably the most unusual. The original Highland dress consisted apparently of a shirt and a rug only, which must have called for exceptional hardiness in the wearers. The main reasons for this scantiness were poverty and an absence of indigenous sheep to provide wool. About 1600 a heavy belted and pleated kilt with a shoulder cape began to be worn but they were very heavy and hot, and in a battle in the Civil War the Royalist leader told his Highland levies to take them off and tie the long tails of their shirts between their legs. These heavy kilts and plaids (filleadh mor) were worn by Mackay's Regiment serving under Gustavus Adolphus in the 30 Years War. About 100 years later the filleadh beg or little kilt, the lower part of the garment with the pleats permanently sewn in, replaced it. The upper part was worn as a loose plaid and this is fundamentally the national dress of Scotland as known today.

Following the 'Forty Five' Rising, all Highland Dress was proscribed, including trews, with severe penalties for wearing. (Even the bagpipes were banned, 'the Duke of Cumberland having decided on firsthand evidence that they were instruments of war'.) The only place Highland dress could be legally worn was in the Army and this was no doubt a potent recruiting factor when the Highland regiments were first formed. But before this six independent companies of Highlanders were raised to police the land and keep an eye out for Jacobites. As they came from more than one clan the Government had an entirely new 'tartan' (an established arrangement of colours woven in the cloth to identify wearers as belonging to one tribe) devised. This became known as the Government or Black Watch pattern, the latter name coming from the dark colouring of the cloth, though Jacobite sympathisers say it was more to describe the character and behaviour of the wearers.

This may be the place to give a word of warning about Highland dress and tartans in general. Strictly speaking, only those who have historic claim to a tartan may wear it. This means the clans and the regiments entitled to a particular clan sett. Many clans have more than one tartan and the subtle distinctions over these are varied. It is another form of heraldry and, in fact, the Court of Lyon King of Arms still exists to determine questions affecting clanship. Most modellers find the making of Scottish figures irresistible but they would be well advised to study the regiment's dress regulations very carefully. Any cases of doubt should be referred to the Regimental Headquarters concerned, who are always pleased to answer serious requests for such information.

Apart from the Greek Royal Guards (the Evzones), some Indian pipers and the Fijians, no other nation has soldiers in a special kilted dress. The Irish Army and Irish Regiments of the British Army dress their pipers in kilts, but experts on Irish dress tell us that this style of kilt is not the original national dress of Old Ireland, which was a liene or shirt-tunic (also worn by the Scots *before* the kilt).

Converting kilted figures I have found to be comparatively easy. I have a preference for standing figures but all the kilted toys are at a smart walk. So, to provide myself with the stationary type, I found the best way was to cut off the bases from the feet and then the legs from the kilts. I then built up the heels where necessary, and re-fixed the feet in positions of 'attention' or 'at ease' back on the bases. It is then a simple job to trim the tops of the legs (one can heighten or shorten figures this way, so adding realism to a group of one sort), smooth off the kilts' under surfaces and re-affix on to the legs. I have done this with several Scottish groups but my *tour de force* was the recent conversion of some Britains' marching Evzones (now, alas, unobtainable) into a band playing at the halt, plus a colour party at the salute (see picture No 26).

But to return to our study of the ordinary infantryman. Frederick the Great evolved a new type of foot soldier, a highly drilled automaton, who could shoot three times as fast as any others. Frederick also introduced new tactics, including the oblique order of attack, which for a period made him master of the field. In these periods British infantry surprised everyone when six regiments (plus some Hanoverians) advanced against a large force of 10,000 French cavalry. Extreme steadiness plus well disciplined volleys threw back six charges, after which the cavalry gave it up; this was the famous Battle of Minden, August 1 1759. Prussian successes led to copying in *two* ways. Most other armies initiated some of the drill, harsh discipline and dress of the Fredrician troops (I have already referred to this phenomena), but of particular interest to modellers is that the achievements of Frederick's troops led to the production of toy soldiers in quantities never known before and in a style always to be associated with Germany—the tin 'flat' soldier. These were the products of the Nuremberg toy makers, from Hilpert to Heinrichsen, now all long ceased. Such figures as survive are prized as collectors' pieces and, unless readers are very wealthy, I do not recommend trying to start collecting these. But the tradition lives on—immortalised in Andersen's 'Steadfast Tin Soldier'. German firms such as Staar still produce finely engraved flat figures and there are two magnificent museum collections of flats to be seen—at Plassenburg Castle, Külmbach, in Bavaria, and the Bayerisches National Museum, Munich.

French Revolutionary and Napoleonic mass armies (he introduced modern conscription and the big battalions), necessitated simpler manoeuvres for the unskilled conscripts. This was the column, which attacked on a narrow front, relying on weight and shock effect to crash through. The British infantry met these attacks in a line of three (Wellington preferred two) ranks, the front one kneeling, waiting until they 'could see the whites of their eyes' and then firing controlled volleys into the advancing mass. At the right moment they would make a bayonet charge which overthrew the column or caused it to pull back. The British infantry's defence against cavalry charges was to form regimental squares and keep the tide of horsemen outside them. It was these tactics that helped to win Waterloo.

In the 40 years of European peace which followed, the British infantrymen, neglected and ill paid, went on serving in Africa and India, his deeds rarely coming to public notice. But the behaviour of two drafts of infantry on a sinking troopship, when the officers and men stood fast so as not to capsize the already overloaded boats of women and children, fired the imagination of the world. Not a man moved until the ship sank under them. Out of 638 on board 454 were drowned but all the women and children were saved. The King of Prussia was so impressed by this example of self discipline that he had it read out to every unit in his army.

The Crimean infantryman was a trench fighter. 'If you please, Sir, the Russians relieved the –th, and we relieved the Russians' explained an NCO, in the rifle pits before Sebastopol. Ill-supplied, not very well led from the top, Russell's Despatches, Fenton's stiff photographs and Lady Butler's romantic paintings tell what he was like—ragged, bearded and emaciated. To recognise the troops' endurance the Victoria Cross was instituted. Paradoxically, the first recipient was a brave sailor, but other early awards included an Irish sergeant serving in a Welsh regiment who carried the regiment's colour all one day in battle, there being no officers left. He afterwards rose to be a general in the British Army.

The American Civil War introduced modern total war but few recognised this at the time. Improvements in firearms—rifling, breech loading, brass cartridges, magazine feeding, machine feeding (the Gatling Gun)—combined to make killing quicker and more accurate. Battles began at longer range, concealment was vital for infantry not on the move. At first the slaughter was great, but they eventually learned how to lie down, and advance in short rushes followed by supports spread out chessboard fashion in what became known as artillery formation. Where co-ordination was not good or circumstances prevented it, such as at Gettysburg, the casualties were enormous. Long, bloody and mechanical, all natural resources were mobilised, and also attacked on both sides, General Sherman's march to the sea resembling that of Attila the Hun's.

The collector who wants to acquire 18th and 19th century infantry has a reasonably large market available. Britains, Timpo and Charbens all catalogue foot fighters of the period. Britains including Daniel Boone-type figures among the uniformed colonists. The musketeers of both sides are basically suitable for altering into Prussian and Seven Years War infantry by careful trimming and some additional equipment. (See picture No 16). Only Timpo produce Waterloo infantry figures at present, but as imitation (and piracy) is a feature of the toy trade we may expect these to be copied or added to by other firms. There are no Crimean-type toy soldiers (not even anything of Miss Nightingale with her celebrated lamp) but we are well served with infantry of both sides for the American Civil War in various positions, including lying down. It will probably strike most alert collectors that many cowboy figures of the above and many other firms can be altered to fit in with and enhance Civil War groups, and the following personnel changes are a few suggestions:

From	**Into**
Britains' series:	
509 Camp fire	Army camp fire
511 Wigwam	Army tent
608 Wounded cowboy	Wounded soldier
607 Cowboy on guard	Soldier on guard
658 „ resting	Soldier resting
661 „ firing behind barrel	Soldier firing behind barrel
Stage coach male passenger	Lincoln, also various general and other Officers seated
„ „ female „	Mrs Julia Ward Howe, writer of the lyrics of 'The Battle Hymn of the Republic', better known as 'John Brown's Body . . .'
Timpo series: Ref 2—Standing cowboys Charben series: 'Straight Eight' cowboys	Army cooks, CSA irregulars, medical workers, camp followers

The lessons of the American Civil War were largely lost on Europe's armies, who had to learn the hard way. The Prussians got the message at Köinggrätz and passed it on to the French at Sedan. The British had to be taught theirs by the Boers in South Africa at the turn of the century. Up to then large squares had been good enough to beat off primitively armed Dervishes and 'Fuzzy Wuzzies' but the Boers were all keen-eyed hunters, crack riflemen, who fought in loose irregular formations—commandos—which got around and behind the British lines and just melted away when things got too much for them. British infantry marched hundreds of miles to get to blows with them; one old officer of the Connaught Rangers told me he had marched 4,774 miles with his unit in the campaign. Though they were often baffled, the infantry spirit shone through. The Boers once captured a train, the last four guards of which, surrounded and without cover, continued to fire until three were killed and the fourth wounded. They asked this survivor why they had not surrendered. 'Why man,' he replied, 'we are the Gordon Highlanders.' So the infantry had to be mounted and made a part of little mixed forces, flying columns, which drove the larger Boer bodies off the field but were never able to pin down or round the remainder up.

The martyred infantryman, as depicted in steel helmet, battle order and muddied puttees on so many town and village war memorials, is the symbol of the Great War. Nearly ten million troops on both sides were killed or died, the majority of which were infantry. (On the Somme in 1916, 20,000 British were killed in one day, see picture No 22.) The British regular infantry had learned their painful lesson from 'Brother Boer' well; the rate of rifle fire at Mons was so high that the Germans thought they were all armed with machine guns. (Though there were only two of the latter per 1,000 men.)

The huge armies deployed put an end to movement and in the four years of trench warfare on the Western Front the machine gun became the dominant weapon. It increased the power of the defence 1,000-fold, and in the hands of specially picked elite troops, like the German machine-gun corps, held up whole armies. Infantrymen died horrible deaths in 1914–18 by poison gas, flame-throwers, pulverising shellfire and crushing tanks. They fought and died on the scorched hills of Gallipoli, the snowy mountains of Serbia, the malarial swamps of Salonika, the chalky slopes of Picardy, the slimy mud of Passchendaele, the frozen wastes of Poland. On the Eastern Front hundreds of thousands of poorly equipped Russian infantry perished, no one really knows how many. The Germans afterwards said the Third Battle of Ypres (Passchendaele) was 'their greatest martyrdom of the war'; to the French, Verdun is the epitome of infantry valour—'Ils ne passeront pas'; to the British, it was perhaps the 1918 retreats, when Haig issued his famous message, 'There is no other course open to us but to fight it out. Every position must be held to the last man . . . there must be no retirement . . . *with our backs to the wall* and believing in the justice of our cause each one of us must fight to the end'.

In the Second World War infantry played a more complementary rôle, depending very much on the terrain. Well roaded country, deserts or open plains gave the advantage to tanks and mechanised troops. Mountainous country, jungle and primitive islands still needed the patient, well trained, well led infantryman, whether he be Briton, American or Pole in North Africa and Italy, Japanese, Indian or British in Burma, or American in the Pacific, to penetrate and hold them. The infantryman had to specialise more in the 1939–45 War—to move about in light armoured vehicles called carriers, to accompany tanks in special lorries, to operate anti-tank guns, to fly to battle in aeroplanes, to jump out of them by parachute, to crash land on his enemy's head in flimsy gliders and to assault a fortified coastal position as a Commando. They did all these things superbly and in the course of the War came new elites of the world's infantry—the German and British airborne forces, the mechanised and panzer grenadier troops of both sides, the Japanese light divisions, the US Marines and Rangers, the Russian Guards infantry and the British Commandos.

For modelling purposes these three rather different periods, pre-1914, 1914–18 and 1939–45, overlap. Taking the last first, there is a considerable amount of material about for the Second World War produced by Messrs Airfix, Britains, Timpo, Crescent and Charben, as well as small amounts of unidentified production. More individual models can be made from other toys; eg, the slightly sceptical but elegant looking officer with arms folded listening to Field Marshal Montgomery expound in picture No 41 is made from the upper part of an Airfix bus passenger, Renwall motor kit polo player and Rose Models head. Apart from Britains', which is consistently high, the quality of the remainder tends to vary. All include European-style British–US soldiers, and what are referred to as Eighth Army and Fourteenth Army soldiers. The only firm I know of which brought out types of all main 1939–45 fighting men is Mark (GB), in the unusual size of 110 mm. Their Japanese fighting figures were especially good reproductions of the real thing.

The custom modellers cover the last century fairly well, especially Rose Miniatures, whose 1914–1918 models typify the officers and men of that long struggle. Expensive though they are, a few of these merit a place in any collection of 1914–18 (see picture No 17), as do their products of the 1939–45 War.

The Infantry of today is, in operational terms, a Vietnam or UN style soldier. The former US, Australian, South Korean and, of course, South Vietnamese. Their dress is jungle kit as Palitoy's Action Man is clad; their weapons are the automatic rifle, the mortar and the grenade. Their general-purpose vehicle is the helicopter. Neither these nor the fighting men of yesteryear—the 15 nations of the Allied Forces in the UN Korean War—have been produced by the toy makers. It is a strange paradox that, whereas current events such as pop personalities, motor cars and aircraft are usually rushed out by the next annual Toy Fair, the soldiers of the current conflict are ignored by toy manufacturers, at least in Britain. Writing in January 1969 I know of no toy maker who has made or proposed to make United Nations in blue berets, Vietnam war or even NATO infantry contingents. Yet here are topical, interesting and group-type figures that by most sales criterion should be steady production line items. To the modeller wishing to collect soldiers of today one can only indicate other products of the toy makers with varying conversion potential, viz:

	Model	Basic Material	References
1.	1944–45 British and US Combat teams.	Britains' Herald Series; Britains' Infantry Swoppets; Crescent Commando and Red Beret figures.	Any illustrated war books and Imperial War Museum.
2.	1950–53 UN Forces Korea (in summer period).	As above.	Various, including press and Regimental journals.
3.	United Nations Infantry—1960–63 in Congo and 1966–69 in Cyprus (summer dress).	Britains' Cowboy shirted torso on Swoppet infantry legs. Beret from plastic wood.	As above.

Four easy conversions are shown in picture No 19. The book from which these are taken is Mr Carman's English translation of 'Uniforms in Colour' (Blandford Press).

CHAPTER SIX

Artillery

'The guns, the guns—
Thank Gawd the guns!'
(Kipling)

THE AGE OF THE GUN is only some 500-plus years in the history of warfare, though the word artillery, which is often synonymous, has a much older meaning, derived from the Greek root 'a', to join or fit together as applied to missile weapons generally. The word gun is also of respectable antiquity and was in use as a Saxon alternative for the ancient stone-throwing machines. Chaucer writes of a 'grete gonne, (which) hurtelen al attones, and from the top cometh the grete stones' which is a reference to the old ballista siege engine. Gonne or gun is a shortened form of the Scandinavian female name Gunnildr and was transferred to the cannon when it appeared performing the same task. The bestowing of female names on guns is not uncommon throughout history; ie, *Mons Meg, Queen Elizabeth's Pocket Pistol, Mother* and *Big Bertha.* In technical and official manuals guns are also referred to as 'Ordnance' and there are two schools of thought as to the origin of this. One is that it derives from an early ordinance (or decree) regulating the size, bore and bulk of early cannon; the other that it comes from the early English 'Thordinance'—a compound of Thor, the Scandinavian God of Thunder, and 'dunamis', the Greek for power. These were in due time corrupted into 'Thordynance' and finally to 'The Ordnance'.

Artillery in its ancient sense was well known to early man. The bow and arrow is a form of artillery, as was the sling by which David slew Goliath. The Assyrians are credited with the first large-scale missile machines, which the ingenious Greeks and Romans adapted and improved, the ballista, the catapulta and the mangonel. These were employed against walled defences and also troops in the open, the missiles including three-hundredweight stones, liquids or pebbles in containers, or blazing materials tied to armour-piercing javelins. The latter discharged from a ballista had a range of 400–500 yards. Ancient

Britons hurled blazing balls of clay into Caesar's invasion forces' camp and the Byzantines used 'Greek fire' against their enemies—an early form of flame-throwing equipment, the mixture being almost impossible to put out.

Gunpowder was probably invented by Roger Bacon in 1249 but he does not appear to have visualised its use as a weapon of war; nor did the Chinese, who had also developed it coincidentally on the other side of the world for use at weddings and funerals. As to who first thought of propelling a ball through a tube by exploding this new substance, opinions differ. Some believe it to be a German monk—Berthold Schwartz about 1313—others claim that cannons were mentioned in Arabic writings some ten years earlier. Be that as it may, one of the two earliest pictures of a cannon is contained in an illuminated manuscript (the de Millemete MSS) now in the British Museum. The cannon or gonne depicted is a vase-shaped vessel with a spear-like missile protruding from its mouth. There is a touch hole at the base and a mail-clad figure is gingerly leaning over to apply a light to it.

These early cannon or bombards were almost as dangerous to the gunners that manned them as to those at which they were aimed, but the work of early ordnance men was beset with other dangers as well. The church set its face against the new weapons (as it had also done with the cross-bow) and its use outraged the code of chivalry then in force. Palalins, such as Prospero Colonna and Gian Paola Vitelli lopped off the hands of captured cannoneers in an effort to deter them. But the new art of gunnery was not deterred and at a later date the church became reconciled to it and a Saint (Barbara) was appointed to look after the spiritual needs of ordnance men everywhere.

Whether or not cannon were used at the naval battle of Sluys in 1340 or at Crecy in 1346 is doubtful, although it is fairly certain that some were present at the latter. Edward III's 'Craykes of warre' taken to Scotland were primitive cannon, but these played only a minor part in his battles. Henry V certainly had some at the siege of Harfleur where he replied to the Dauphin's scornful gift of 'teneys balles' by bombarding the town with 'grete gonne stones for the doffyn to play with'. The French were quick to take up these new weapons and had large numbers (one authority said 300) to attack the English at Formigny and Castillon in 1453. In the same year the Turks used huge bombards or mortars to bring down the 1,000-year-old empire of Constantinople. The siege gun had arrived.

For the next 300 years the artillery story is mainly the story of the siege gun, and this influenced the design, weight and size of cannon. Their immense power of destruction was something that had to be controlled by the head of state, like nuclear weapons are today. Up to then power had been expressed in the form of the great castles in which a few determined and skilful men could hold out almost indefinitely in a hostile country. This is how the Anglo-Normans held down Wales and Ireland. Shrewd despots like Henry VIII saw this, and exercised a royal monopoly over cannon. A special department, the Board of Ordnance, was set up to store and control guns and ammunition of all types. Issues were only made on the authority of the Privy Council, ships of the emerging navy being supplied as well as the army.

Because guns were seen as mainly siege weapons their development was retarded in two respects. The confining of their use in this way led to heavy, cumbersome pieces which had to be transported in part loads and assembled on site. The men who looked after them in store, 'gentlemen of the ordnance', master gunners and matrosses also operated them in battle. When an expedition involving a siege was ordered the Master of the Ordnance got together a 'train of artillery'. The guns themselves were immobile so wagons, horses and drivers had to be hired (or impressed) to carry or tow guns, shot, powder and ancillary items. The rather venerable staff from the Tower and other fortresses (their ages in Tudor times being between 64 and 92) joined in, and the whole motley, *ad hoc* force went forth. When the campaign was over the train was disbanded and the ordnance personnel returned, one imagines rather thankfully, to the comparative quiet of the Tower. It was these methods which did so much to retard the development of British artillery. A 'cannon' (60 pound shot) weighed 3 tons and needed 20 horses; the culverin (16 pounds) weighed a ton and had a team of nine. There were no ammunition wagons as such in the field; munitions were carried in hand carts, wheelbarrows or on the gunners' backs.

Mobile or field artillery was developed first on the Continent. Gustavus Adolphus introduced the lightest—'leather'—cannon weighing only 88 lbs without their carriages. But they wore out too quickly and were replaced by heavier pieces with rates of fire faster than a musketeer could reload. In the meantime the French had discovered the principle of the limber and attached light guns to carts or mounted them on wagons. There was little use of field guns in the English Civil War; where they were employed, as at Edgehill, they were not significant to the result. It was William III's knowledge of artillery that led to the introduction of the howitzer, a high angle gun of Dutch origin.

Marlborough's experiences in Continental wars led him to press for permanent artillery for the British Army. The first two companies were raised in 1716 and the Royal Regiment of Artillery came into being in 1722. The first Commander was a Dane; he had ten officers, 180 men and the following guns:

24 pounders	— 4
9 pounders	— 4
1½ pounders	— 6
10 inch mortars	— 6
8 inch mortars	— 2
Other mortars	—42

The first three types were all on travelling carriages, with spare limbers and wheels. The ammunition included 9,800 round shot and 4,000 mortar shells. There were also two bomb vessels each carrying a 13 inch mortar. The little force's first action was at the siege of Vigo where their fire 'was so heavy and well directed' that the citadel capitulated.

Frederick the Great brought his field artillery to the same degree of high-speed precision as the rest of his army; he was also one of the first commanders to include a large proportion of howitzers, to mass his guns, and to harness the team horses in pairs. Once again the French saw the potentialities of these developments and adopted them, in the process adding such improvements as the 'coffres d'avant train' in which cannon balls with suitable charges were carried together.

Although an artilleryman, Napoleon was slow to see the possibilities of the mobile artillery he inherited from the Revolutionary army. At Eylau the Russians showed him what massed batteries could do and he then set about developing his own. From Wagram onwards he massed batteries against weak points in the enemy's lines and 'softened up' opposing infantry with a hail of case shot. At Waterloo a heavy bombardment preceded the first infantry attack and when this failed French artillery continued to pound the British infantry in their squares. (The British had to maintain these formations because of the cavalry attacks and as a result suffered heavily.) But, Napoleon had no howitzers to reach over the crest at the troops below it; if he had, perhaps history would have been different.

The guns of this period were still cast in brass, bronze or iron but of improved bores. Projectiles used included solid iron balls, grape-shot (a number of balls set round a wooden stem) and case-shot (cylinders filled with musket balls). About 1800 the British Colonel Shrapnel designed a shell holding leaden balls amid the bursting charge for use against troops in the open. Shrapnel shells were to remain in service for nearly 150 years. In sea defence forts, guns used heated shot for setting fire to wooden ships.

Whilst the US Civil War was primarily an infantryman's war, artillery played a significant part in all the major battles. The artillery 'work horse' was the smooth bore 12-pounder 'Napoleon' developed by US Army Ordnance experts following a study of European types of the 1840s. Unmatched for use in woods, defence of entrenchments and for short-range work, it remained a favourite with artillerymen and the High Command, despite the presence of a lot of rifled cannon. Foreign imports used by both sides included the British 12-pounder Whitworth, of which there were both muzzle and breech loading versions. Home produced rifled guns appeared in quantity in 1863; chiefly the Parrott family, which included 10- and 20-pounder field pieces. The Rodman 3-inch gun was a product preferred by horse artillery. There were howitzers, but guns were also used in the howitzer rôle by propping them up to fire at a high angle. Batteries seldom went unseen, although they made use of cover when available. Crews were much exposed, especially with the muzzle loaders, when the gunners had to run to the front to swab out, turning their backs on the advancing enemy. Black powder, crude sights and the unreliability of time fuses were limiting factors. Another was the increase in range of the rifle which, in the hands of trained infantry, often succeeded in keeping field guns beyond their optimum range.

Technologically there was a 'great leap forward' in missile weapons in the last part of the 19th century. Twisted rifling replaced grooving, which caused the projectiles to spin in the barrel and so improve trajectory. Guns were made first of wrought iron, instead of casting, and then finally of steel. To take increased charges, metal bands were added around the breech end. Breech loading (which had been known since the 16th century) was finally established, although British artillery took the astonishingly retrograde step of re-adopting muzzle loaders in this period. This was the era of enormous hydraulically and steam-power operated fortress guns, 100-ton monsters; some on disappearing mountings. Photographs of these have a peculiar period flavour about them and a special appeal to modellers; they are the military epitome of the Victorian technical age, huge, squat, cast cannon in sunken pits on special rail

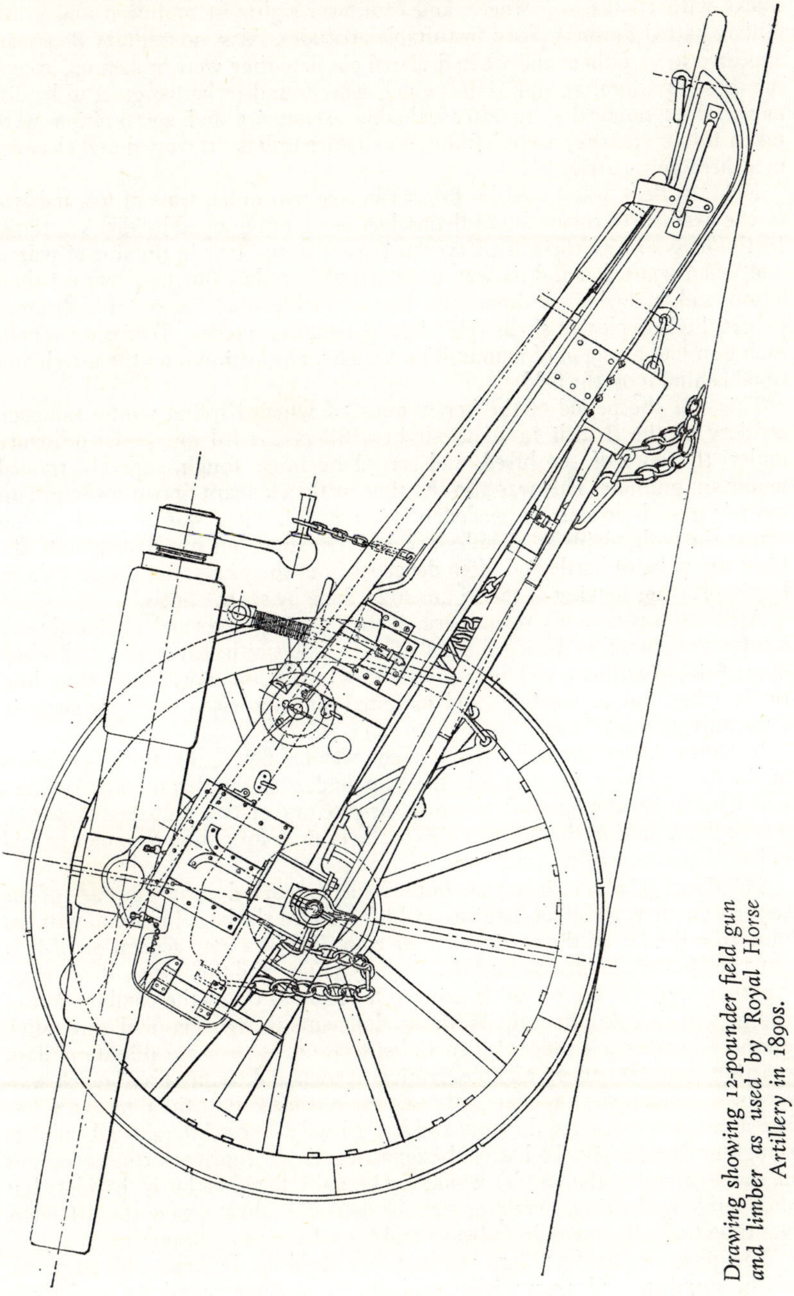

Drawing showing 12-pounder field gun and limber as used by Royal Horse Artillery in 1890s.

tracks with chains, cog wheels and counter weights in profusion and grave pillbox-hatted gunners posed in suitable attitudes. Alas, no military Betjeman appeared to save them and when declared obsolete they were broken up, except for those at Gibraltar and Malta which were found to be too gross to be dismounted economically, so after valuable accessories and ammunition were taken into store, they were left, on War Office orders, 'traversed and elevated in a threatening attitude'!

Field artillery was tested by Prussia in her two quick wars of '66 and '70. In the first the Germans found themselves being out-gunned by the Austrians. In the mass armies their artillery was too far to the rear in the line of march and when wanted found its way to the front impeded. But they learned their lesson and at Sedan, a three mile line of artillery at 2,000 yards distance poured high explosive shells (HE) into the massed French. To ensure supply each gun had a wagon of ammunition which went behind it on the march and stood behind it on the field.

This was the period of the 'screw guns' of which Kipling wrote; the pack artillery of the British in India—light artillery carried on special ordnance mules, the elite of the breed, and served by huge, tough, superbly trained mountain gunners. This was also the time of the elephant-drawn medium gun (40 pdr muzzle loader)—a modellers' piece if ever there was one—advancing across the wide plains at 12 miles per day. The huge but pacific elephants disliked the noise of battle and often departed from the scene after the first shots, leaving further moving of their guns to be done by spare camels.

Artillery was the only regular arm of the Boer Republics and, equipped with Krupp weapons, they besieged the British in Ladysmith, Kimberley and Mafeking. British artillery had no equivalent weapons, so naval guns were hurriedly taken out of warships and mounted on improvised carriages made in Cape railway workshops. (See Chapter 12.)

In South Africa the main requirement was for field guns, the 12-pounders of the Royal Horse Artillery and the 15-pounders of the Royal Field Artillery which were always handled gallantly, despite one or two disasters. However, due to the refusal of the Boers to give battle in mass formation it cannot be said to have been an artilleryman's war.

The Great War certainly was. Improvements worked out at the turn of the century, such as recoil mechanisms (which enabled the barrel to recoil without upsetting the lay of the carriage), were embodied in a new generation of field guns, the famous French 75 mm, the German 77 mm and the British 18-pounder. Another was the use of quick firing (QF) ammunition—the combination of charge and shell in one unit. With developments in sighting (dial and optic), gunnery became scientific with specialist techniques such as calibration, flash spotting, counter-battery and observation of own and enemy fire. Trench warfare was, in fact, siege warfare but few people realised it at the time and senseless assaults at trenches, dugouts and barbed wire fences brought only useless slaughter of infantry. To batter these barriers down enormous concentrations of guns (literally thousands) would be brought together by both sides; but their prolonged firing, heralding attacks as it did, always gave the defenders the time (even if they didn't always make good use of it) to prepare.

The gigantic use of artillery can best be gauged by the brief table (page 76) of the numbers and ammunition expenditure of some British guns. (This is

Drawing of team of Royal Horse Artillery showing collar harness in general use for draught animals in 1890s.

Drawing showing rear view of Royal Horse Artillery team, with gun and limber.

fairly representative of the other major combatants' growth except America who, entering the war late and with its munitions industry unprepared, used Allied equipments of smaller calibre.)

Gun	Qty in Aug 1914	Manu-factured by 1918	Range	Weight of round	Ammunition expenditure—rounds
13-pounder gun (RHA)	245	150	5,000 yds	13 lbs	5,500,000
13-pounder (converted RHA; 9-cwt) and 3-inch 20 cwt (AA)	—	1,221	up to 19,000 ft	13 lbs	3,200,000
18-pounder field gun (RFA)	1,126	9,239	6–8,000 yds	18 lbs	113,000,000
4·5-inch howitzer (RFA)	182	3,177	4–6,000 yds	25 lbs	29,200,000
60-pounder gun (RFA)	41	1,756	10–12,500 yds	60 lbs	10,250,000
6-inch gun (all marks)	—	700+	17,000 yds	100 lbs	1,200,000
6-inch howitzers (all marks)	100	3,633	10,000 yds	100 lbs	26,000,000
8-inch howitzers (all marks)	—	778	10–12,500 yds	200 lbs	5,000,000
9·2-inch howitzers (all marks)	—	512	10–12,700 yds	350 lbs	3,450,000
12-inch howitzer rail and road mountings (all marks)	—	138	11–14,500 yds	500 lbs	255,000
15-inch howitzer (ex-RN)	—	12	10,000 yds	1,450 lbs	26,600
12-inch and 14-inch guns (ex-RN) on rail mountings	—	6+	33–35,000 yds	850 and 1,400 lbs	5,250

The greater majority of these guns (and almost *all* the heavy ones) were employed on the Western Front. In all, 25,000 new guns were produced and nearly 10,000 overhauled. The type of warfare is reflected in the increase in howitzers, the weapons of indirect fire, as opposed to heavy guns. The stupendous concentrations of fire reduced large woods to scattered broken stumps, entirely obliterated buildings and changed roads and drainage systems into vast lunar-like landscapes of trackless pitted territory. (See picture No 18.)

War in the air led to the introduction of the anti-aircraft gun. The first were horse artillery guns propped up to achieve the up-to-then unheard-of elevations (although the resourceful Germans had experimented with high-angle fire in warships before 1914). These RHA guns were then fitted on suitable mountings on motor lorries with drop sides for all-round traversing and manning and with large jacks to act as shock absorbers for the recoil. (See picture No 20.)

The Second World War brought further advances in the design of artillery. The British 25-pounder, the standard weapon of the field artillery, was capable of direct and indirect fire and was considered the finest (and last) in the line of field guns. AA guns became more sophisticated to meet the increased speeds of aircraft, with such equipment as the predictor to work out height and speed of the target. The tank called for a new type of counter weapon and, as the

23. *Examples of custom-made female models in metal, 55 mm scale. Russell Gammages Greek Girl (left) and Cretan Snake Goddess.*

24. *Band of Royal Marines. Improved Britains' metal bandsmen. Similar details can be added to the current Britains' plastic equivalents.*

25. *55 mm metal models of US Marine Band with leader John Philip Sousa, by John Scheid. In US Marine Corps Museum, Quantico, Va, USA.*

26. *Band of Evzones, at halt. Multiple conversions by author from Britains' metal marching Evzone riflemen. Note variety of attitudes as well as instruments.*

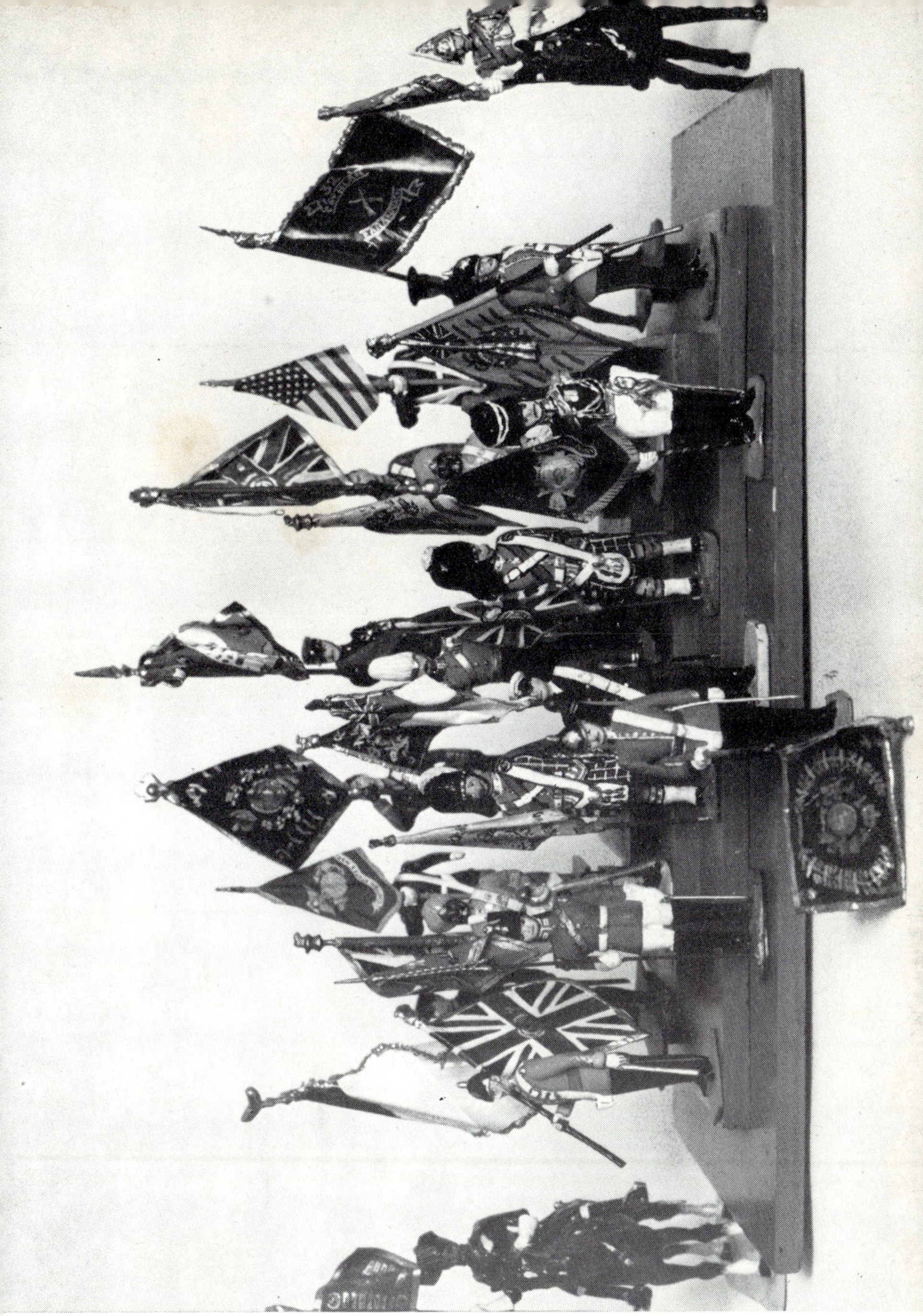

27. *Group of standards, guidons and colours from author's collection.*

28. *The other 'Army'—early Britains' metal Salvation Army figures brought up to model standard by the author.*

29. *'White man's burden'—African porters converted from Britains' metal running Zulus.*

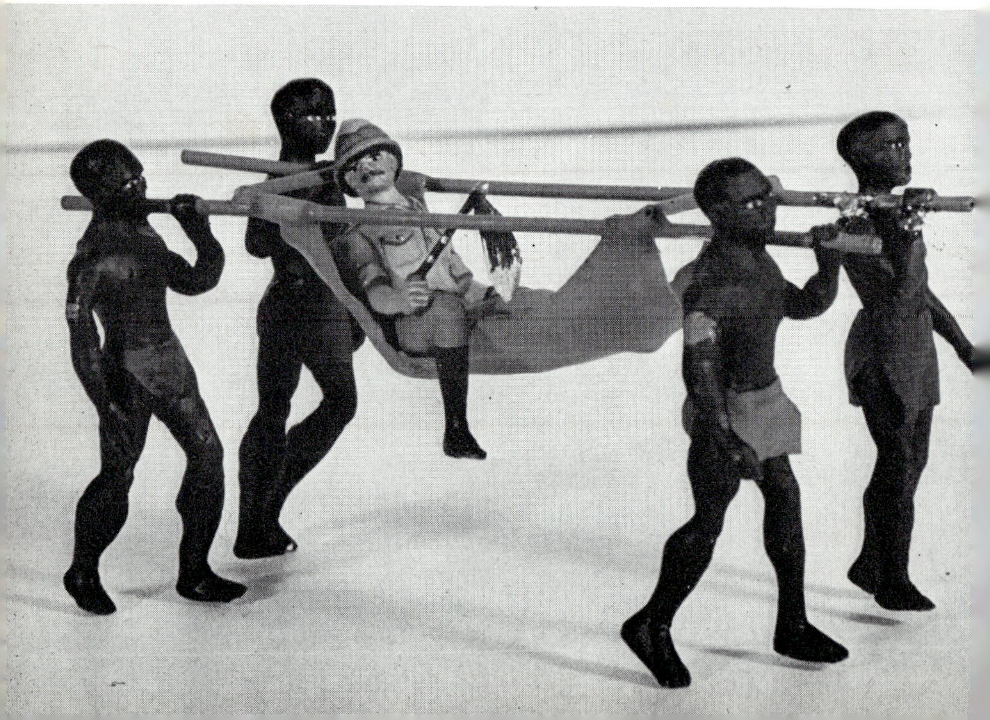

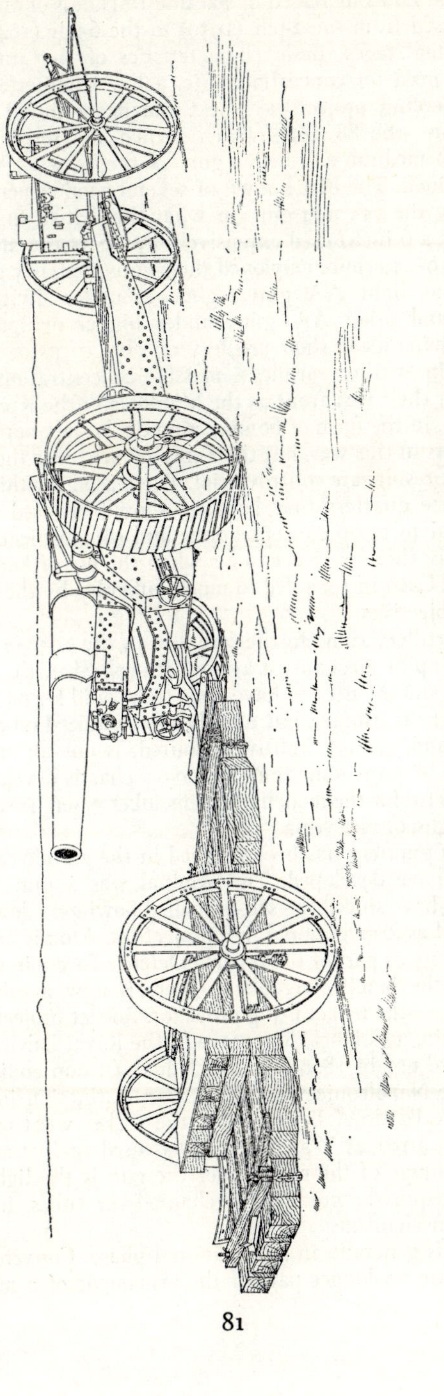

Drawing of 6-inch heavy gun showing limber for towing, and the firing platform in its travelling position.

war progressed and tanks increased in size and thickness of armour, so the anti-tank gun progressed from the 2-pdr (1939) to the 6-pdr (1940–42) and to the 17-pdr at the later stages. Basic characteristics of the anti-tank gun were its mobility, the need for concealment (ie, a low silhouette) and the use of special armour-piercing projectiles. The Germans produced a combined AA and anti-tank gun—the 88 mm—which earned the respect of their adversaries. The British medium and heavy guns of the 1939–45 War were the 5·5 inch and the 7·2 inch. The best known of several good American guns of this period is probably the 155 mm gun (or what the British in an earlier period would have called a 6 inch) used extensively by US troops and some Allies.

Most of the 1939–45 armies employed their guns similarly grouped—ie, field and anti-tank and light AA gun regiments under divisional command; medium, heavy and other AA guns under higher or specialist command control. The Russians made their artillery an elite corps of their vast armies and organised it in 'artillery armies'—massive concentrations of guns which were moved about their vast front as the Marshals in the Kremlin directed.

Flying artillery, in the form of bomber aircraft, largely supplemented heavy guns and howitzers in this war, but their employment was the subject of much argument and the results are controversial. The reason for this seems to be the belief held in some quarters that bombers should be used against strategic targets, as opposed to troop concentrations and communications. Even when employed tactically there were occasions when the use of bombers in an over-kill measure, as at Caen in 1944, led to much difficulty by the ground troops in occupying their objectives.

Self-propelled artillery came to the fore also in the 1939–45 War as part of the general speed-up of mechanised armies. It evolved in the open fighting in deserts and plains and the need to have guns that could keep up with armoured vehicles. SP artillery is usually, but not always, mounted on a tracked chassis. It is *not* a tank and, though lightly armoured, is not an armoured fighting vehicle. However, SP guns sometimes do have a chassis developed from a tank type and this is useful for the modeller to remember when he sets out to convert a tank into an SP gun or vice versa.

The ultimate in gunnery has been reached in the atomic cannon which the American forces have developed. The original was a gun, ie, a long-range weapon, but there have since been self-propelled howitzers designed which will fire nuclear as well as 'conventional' HE projectiles. Atomic artillery is mainly used in the US Army as part of the NATO Defence Forces in Germany.

Together with the bomber aeroplane, there is now another rival for the place of the cannon—the rocket firing projector. Rocket projectors are not new, of course. In Britain, a Colonel Congreave of the Royal Laboratory designed a rocket for offensive use in 1800. The RHA had a troop equipped with them for a while in the Napoleonic war which won distinction in being the only British unit at the Battle of Leipzig. But the rocket went out of favour for 150 years until the 1939–45 War, when it was used against and by tanks and aircraft. The advantage of the rocket over the gun is the lighter and simpler firing apparatus required: guide rails, channels or tubes, instead of barrel, breech and recoil mechanisms.

Artillery today is generally in a transitional phase. Conventional coast and air defence guns are no longer part of the armament of a modern state and such weapons are now museum pieces. In field weapons the following is the general situation in the British Army:

(a) Anti-tank

(i) 'Wombat' flat trajectory missile launcher used by infantry.
(ii) Some limited use of projectiles such as 'Malkara' and 'Vigilant' types mounted on Land-Rovers and armoured cars.

(b) Anti-tank and field rôle

(i) 105 mm howitzer (NATO standardised) towed by a one-ton truck.
(ii) 5·5-in field gun in limited use but is, in fact, obsolete.

(c) Medium and heavy rôle

Largely taken over by aircraft and ground-to-air missiles but a limited number of guns retained for mobile warfare in a battle area.

The organisation of these is not firm but in BAOR they are organised in Mixed Regiments, ie, one battery of 8-inch howitzers (either self-propelled or lorry-towed), one battery of light ground-to-air missiles, and one battery of the elderly Honest John missiles. Some of these weapons are, of course, capable of firing nuclear projectiles.

In the US Army the emphasis is on self-propelled medium guns although there is a 155 mm long-range gun which is a towed equipment; some of these are in use by other NATO armies. But the main strength lies in missilery, some of which is available to modellers in kit form of varying scales but a lot of which is still 'classified', ie secret.

The following toys are available in Britain to cover the last 100 years or so of artillery:

Period	Items available	Remarks
1860s; ie, US Civil War, Franco, Prussian, and British Colonial Wars up to 1900	Britains' American Civil War gun, Timpo American/Mexican gun, Britains' 4·7 Naval gun.	
1914–1918	Crescent 18-pdr QF gun.	Not to full 1:32 scale.
	Britains' '18-inch' heavy howitzer.	Is in fact 8-inch howitzer.
	Britains' 4·7 Naval gun.	Similar to 60-pdr Long Tom.
1939–45	Crescent 25-pdr gun and firing platform.	Good reproduction.
	Britains' 25-pdr gun.	Slightly below 1:32 scale.
	Crescent 5·5-inch medium gun.	
	Self-propelled 155 mm gun, M40, etc.	Various plastic kits.
Post 1945	Britains' 105-mm pack howitzer.	An excellent model.
	Britains' BAT A/T gun.	
	Britains' US 155-mm gun.	
	Frog Atomic cannon (kit).	
	Various kits of self-propelled guns.	Plastic kits.

The number of each gun to include in a collection must be a personal choice. As will be seen in Appendix 1, I work on the 'cadre principle' of one gun representing a battery. This means that my 1914 period Divisional Artillery consists of three guns with their limbers, horse teams and gunners plus a small HQ staff. If the guns are 'on parade' or on the move all personnel will be either mounted or seated on the guns and limbers. If a gun is to be modelled 'in action' the gunners would be dismounted around the gun as follows:

No 1. (Gun Layer)—rear of trail facing the front,
No 2. Close to and facing the breech on the right side,
No 3. Close to and facing the breech on the left side,
No 4. In line with eye of trail covering off right wheel.

If the collection includes ammunition limbers, one of these should be positioned along the gun on left side. The horses should be taken out. (The famous painting of 'L' Battery at Nery is a good example.)

CHAPTER SEVEN

Supporting Arms and Services

'A general must know how to get his men their rations and every other kind of stores needed for war . . .'

Socrates

THE INTERESTING THING about this pronouncement is that it precedes instructions on tactics and generalship in full. In the late Field Marshal Wavell's view this is the right order of importance, yet up to quite recently, logistics, to give these functions their 20th-century, American-inspired title, have rated low in Orders of Battle of most armies, and the units which performed them occupy a low place in the military order of pecking. This is not that the functions themselves were not done in the past or were unimportant, but because in general they were simple enough to be done by the fighting soldier or were performed by civilian agencies or extemporised for a particular battle or campaign.

As they exist today these functions are now generally recognised in the following shape:

(a) Military engineering. This covers assault, field, fortification and pioneer work. In the past some of these tasks overlapped with the artillery rôle and, as a result, in some armies artillery and engineers were at first in one body (the British Army is an example).

(b) Communications. These were carried by messenger, orally, written, then mechanical, electrical and finally electronically. In most modern armies this is done by a Signals Corps or Service.

(c) Personnel control. This is now generally identified as recruiting, educating, discipline, pay and welfare. Not all these functions are 'specialised' but most forces have, for example, a Provost Corps for disciplinary matters and a centralized Pay Corps or Department. Chaplains and teachers are also organised centrally and then sent to units for periods of attachment. (See picture No 21.)

(d) Medical, nursing and veterinary. These duties have existed at unit level from earliest times in all civilised forces. As mankind has become more humane and concerned for his fellowmen (and, paradoxically, as the destructive power of weaponry has increased) so care of wounded and sick has made centralised organisation more necessary. The coming of the Red Cross in the 1860s was a turning point in military medical organisation. Armies are supported in this by voluntary workers also, such as Red Cross bodies, St John's Brigades and the Society of Friends (Quakers).

(e) Rations. These are now generally taken to include food, water, forage for animals and also, in mechanised forces, petrol, oil and lubricants. Up to the 18th century many armies made a deliberate policy of living off the land they invaded or occupied. Food was obtained by sending out 'foraging parties' to take what was needed from towns and farms. Local inhabitants received short shrift from the foraging parties if they tried to hide animals or harvested crops. Napoleon, who ought to have known better, deliberately planned for his huge armies to live off the country. 'Requisitioning' was the quasi-legal term given to these activities, but it was a terrible visitation to fall on either friend or foe. Wellington went to great trouble to build up organised and disciplined supply systems, which the British Government most unwisely broke up after Waterloo. The Crimean supply scandal was the result, but happily since then supply in the field for the British Army has been on a permanent military basis. In World War Two the Royal Army Service Corps claimed to have made the British Army the best-fed army in the world. Even as late as the American Civil War, foraging took place on both sides when the organised ration scales fell short or failed. (It reached its nadir with Sherman's march through Georgia and the Carolinas in 1864–5, but his awoved purpose was more to impress on civilians the meaning of war and to weaken their desire to continue it.)

(f) Material supply and maintenance. These cover:

(i) Personal clothing and accoutrements.
(ii) Fighting items—small arms, guns, ammunition, signalling equipment.
(iii) Vehicles, both fighting and administrative (personnel and load carrying).
(iv) Camp and barrack furniture and equipment, ranging from flag poles to camp kettles, tentage to champagne glasses.
(v) The manufacture and repair of all the above, including the military aspects of research, experiment and user trials.

(g) Transportation and movement control. These are natural consequences of large well-equipped armies, and are tackled in various ways according to the national philosophy. It is somewhat an invisible service, ie, there is no tangible end product, but if the planners of transport and movement of troops and stores don't do their sums properly and have the right kind of conveyances (carts, rowing boats, sailing ships, pack mules, elephants or camels, railway trains, buses and taxis, lorries, aeroplanes or landing craft) in the right place at the right time the battle may (and has been) lost before it is begun.

(h) In modern war all sorts of other fringe activities create a passing demand which the Army in the interests of morale or law and order, has to deal with. Entertainment becomes a blanket term embracing all sorts of activities according to the culture of the nations concerned. In some of their colonial campaigns the French Army included all possible forms of welfare and comfort in their BMC for the troops.

All the above are sometimes referred to collectively as the 'tail' of an army, but in modern wars the sum of their personnel exceeds that of the fighting men. In the First World War it was calculated that four soldiers were needed to maintain one in the front line, and in 1939–45 the number, especially in undeveloped territory, could be as high as eight or nine to one. We have the record of Mr Churchill asking General Brooke, the CIGS, to explain about the 650,000 men on the strength of the Middle East Forces, of which only about 100,000 were available for combat.

Space does not allow any review of how these unglamorous but essential services have evolved or how they are grouped for performance in different armies. In most, however, they are the product of expediency (they are more prone to change and re-shuffle than the ancient arms of foot, horse and artillery), and national philosophies on organisation and method.

For many centuries, with few exceptions, campaigns and battles, especially the latter, were short (recall that, for the Hundred Years War, most school books only record *three* major battles). Armies raised from the people—the fyrd, the levies, militias—could only be deployed in between harvest time and spring sowing. When the men joined they brought a supply of corn or meal with them; for the rest they either foraged, or went hungry. It was the latter which often spurred invaders on to overcome the defenders and reap the spoils of war. But some leaders found they had to campaign in winter. The standing armies of Rome had to keep themselves going, (ie 'maintain' themselves) throughout the year. The ordinary legionary was a skilled pioneer and the officers were engineers; and under their supervision prisoners and slaves did the heavy manual work on roads, forts and other defence works. But the provision of weapons, equipment, food and accommodation was done centrally or contracted for under the supervision of the 'Tribunes Militum', the Legions' or Cohorts' Staff Officers. Their stores depots at places like York and Lancaster held stores for up to two years' reserves for their garrisons.

Typical figures to make from the toys readily available in the shops would be a group depicting a road or fort under construction. Workmen stoop under the weight of stones, others dig; an ox cart with driver waits to be unloaded; one or two legionary sentries stand watching, pikes at rest, as a centurion 'foreman of works' checks progress. To complete the scene, a high officer—perhaps Agricola, Governor of Britain in the First century AD. Inspiration for these and other Roman soldiers on domestic work can be had from any good illustrated school book.

The Bayeux Tapestry, and the many drawings copied of it, provide numerous examples of support and supply duties in the Norman armies. The master mind behind Duke William (a first-grade organiser himself) was the notorious Bishop Odo of Bayeux. Under him an expedition of 10,000 men and 3,600 horses was equipped, a fleet of 700 ships built and assembled and reserves of stores and supplies collected in six months. The tapestry shows hand carts designed to hold both weapons and rations and also depicts men carrying what are spare weapons, suits of mail, helmets,, barrels of wine and hams down to the ships. After the landing and before the Battle of Hastings food was obtained by raids on the Sussex Saxon settlements. Britains' Siege Engine attendants (Nos 4675/6) would be ideal figures for conversions into types of these men at work, and a suitable vehicle could be made from the engine.

Under the Feudal System barons and knights held their estates in return for a liability to bear arms when required by the King. This meant they also had to sustain themselves as well, but continental wars meant long absences from the land and the barons began to contract out by paying money in lieu, 'scutage' or shield tax. With this the Kings were able to hire mercenary soldiers, usually in companies under well-known soldier-adventurers. These were supplemented by militia or conscripts from the peasants who had no money to buy themselves out and, to provide for them, Kings were reluctantly compelled to introduce various forms of state and centralised reserves of weapons and equipment. In England this led to the Royal Wardrobe becoming the Office of Ordnance, which provided and accounted for weapons—bows and arrows, spears and sword, shields and siege items. In addition, Acts of Parliament were passed, such as the Assize of Arms in 1181 and the Statute of Winchester in 1285, whereby inspections and stock checks were done to see that these were in order.

Most equipment was held in the Tower of London and such other great castles, and sent out in the baggage train (which would include wagons of spare bows and arrows, axe heads, lances, etc, with blacksmiths' and armourers' repair kits), such as Edward I took with him to invade Scotland.

Food supplies remained for a long time a personal matter, the soldier being supposed to feed himself out of his pay, but peculation by the captains of companies and the conditions in places like the Netherlands and Ireland brought about some degree of organisation in Elizabeth I's armies.

The Parliamentary Army included a Commissary of Victuals and this office was continued through the Restoration, the cost of feeding the troops being held back from their pay as an 'off-reckoning', alas, another gross abuse of long standing.

Sutlers (and Sutleresses) played an important part in the feeding arrangements of the old armies. Fortesque states that in Hanoverian times the only ration supplied by the Commissariat was bread. Sutlers were officially recognised on a scale of one per company. They were one of several types of camp followers, which by custom were allowed to set up their booths or tents and carry out various services for the fighting men. They often took risks and were not compensated for loss of goods due to 'the extingencies of a campaign'. One of the most famous of these was Mother Ross, whose exploits included serving as a dragoon before her sex was discovered, the provision of good food for hungry staff officers and some careful plundering to replenish stock in trade. Her dress was a colourful mixture of petticoats and aprons, with soldiers' discarded coats and a waistcoat topped by a large hat edged with yellow lace. (Now, *there's* a model for you!) This practice of women who followed armies making use of cast-off uniforms was the origin of the fanciful military costumes worn by the Cantinieres and Vivandiares of the French Second Empire Army.

In the British Army after the Crimean scandals, the supply of food was done through a Commissariat Department, which was amalgamated with Transport (see Chapter 10) to become eventually the Royal Army Service Corps. The actual cooking of food was, of course, a regimental responsibility and over the years the selection of men for this work became one of the most hallowed subjects for wit in the army. Cooks certainly lend themselves to being modelled. Not much imagination is needed to produce good representations of scruffy, apron-clad, fed-up-looking soldiers ladling stew out of a camp kettle or carrying cans of liquid from cookhouse to dining room. Today in the British Army the work is done by Army Catering Corps men attached to regiments. These men enter for and win National contests for *Cordon Bleu* and *haute cuisine* efforts.

Recruiting has plenty of colourful stories attached to it down the ages which will provide modellers with good subjects. Shakespeare gives us a good account of how Falstaff enlisted men into his company (the Bard himself is generally thought to have joined up to avoid arrest for poaching!); and the recruiting posters of the Napoleonic wars appealing to 'Those who were fed up or with too much wife' evoke some excellent modelling situations. Farquhar's play 'The Recruiting Officer' is still performed as a faithful picture of the recruiting methods of this period. Lady Butler's famous painting of 'Listed for the Connaught Rangers' would make a wonderful small diorama and then there is the greatest recruiting drive of all—Kitchener's 1914 Posters 'Your King and Country Needs *You*', which brought in a million men—the flower of Britain—in under a year.

Curiously enough I have only known of one collector who included a recruiting group in his collection; the late Lester Hewett of Norfolk whose collection depicted the life of a soldier from the day he took the shilling to his military funeral. I regret to say I have neither in my collection.

At first soldiers' pay would seem to offer little scope for modelling but the story of the centuries-long swindles carried out by governments, officers, their agents, and contractors is one of the dark stains on the nations' treatment of its fighting men. The abuses were not finally checked until the 19th century, when regiments finally ceased to be their Colonel's private property. There must, of course, have been honest men among them but in almost every regimental history and story are recorded frauds against the simple, often illiterate, soldier. Modern pay corps, with their highly trained, bank-minded men and computerised systems, give the soldier a square deal and offer an unusual idea for a model group. My own favourite (yet to be done) is of an early 20th-century pay sergeant, pen behind ear, drooping moustache and ink-stained fingers, methodically entering sums on a large pay roll whilst an elegant frock-coated officer pays it out to a line of men. Included in the group must be two soldier witnesses, standing behind the table to see what is called out is paid out and written down! (No cheating of Queen Victoria's men.)

The supply of clothing and stores likewise seems to have little appeal unless the modeller is specially interested in these subjects. Yet to one who knows his army some recurrent types are well worth doing. QM Officers are nearly always promoted from the ranks; they are the business managers of a unit; they do all the ordering and accounting for the many items of stock. Yet they are also expected to be soldierly and come on parade occasionally. (In the Brigade of Guards they are the only officers to wear cocked hats in full dress.) Their assistants are also much of a type; the 'Q Sergeant'—substantial build, ponderous in manner, terse in speech to young soldiers, always armed with a list or ledger, taking over or handing over a consignment of stores. And the

'Q Storeman', an elderly somewhat bent private soldier, 'excused duties' but around whom the whole place seems to revolve. An attractive little group in this genre would be that depicting a recruit being fitted (yes! in the old peace-time armies, the uniform was altered to fit) by the regimental tailor (tape measure in hand) with the 'Q' Sergeant and an inspecting officer looking on.

Provost work in armies has altered much in the course of time. Barbaric conditions called for harsh discipline. Early provost marshals were empowered to execute summarily, and many enforcers of military law undoubtedly had streaks of sadism in them. (Some of Gardner's American Civil War pictures are very revealing.) Corporal punishments in units, the inflicting of hundreds of lashes, were carried out by senior drummers who 'doubled' as regimental police. In mass armies a large part of provost work was rounding up 'stragglers' and returning them to the front line. A US General of World War I stated that, during one of their offensives, out of a force of 650,000 there were 100,000 stragglers. In World War II, US truncheon swinging military police in polished steel helmets and whitened webbing constantly toured the Naples area in jeeps, seeking out the 30,000 US soldiers of Italian descent on the run there.

The British Army has made a conscious effort in modern times to model its military police on the traditional British bobby concept—keeping the soldier out of trouble, helping old ladies and school children across the road (in Aldershot today, this is a standing duty for a mounted red-cap) and traffic control. This latter is now big business for Provost units. Acutely aware of how traffic snarl-ups could affect troop movement, traffic problems of big cities are constantly studied and senior ranks trained in techniques of 'traffic engineering'.

Few modellers will need much advice on creating medical groups. The Romans had first aid centres at Legion posts, although their treatment of wounded was barbarous. One of the great orders of chivalry of the middle ages, the Order of St John of Jerusalem, was founded to look after sick and wounded. It survives today in the voluntary organisations of the St John's Ambulance Brigades. Whilst hospitals appeared early in most armies, the standards of surgery and nursing were appallingly low and hospitals were often the centres of epidemics. Surgeons attached to units and ships were too often incompetents and drunkards. Eighteenth-century playwrights' favourite characters were drunken, amorous surgeons (and chaplains!).

Whilst Miss Nightingale's nursing work has been greatly exaggerated, her administrative and organising qualities put British medical services on a sound footing. (Incidentally I have never seen a model of her with her celebrated lamp.) After her, it was no longer socially incorrect to nurse soldiers, and this new attitude was reflected in the South African War of 1899–1902 with the raising of the First Aid Nursing Yeomanry (the FANY), a body of young ladies trained in first aid who rode side-saddle on to the battlefield to minister to the wounded until the ambulance wagons came and galloped away with them across the rough veldt. Socially acceptable as it was, nevertheless these women did sterling work in driving ambulances in both the world wars. They still have an Old Girls' Association—in Chelsea!

Engineers are traditionally the technically brilliant, the innovators, the inventors, in armies. Generally nicknamed 'sappers', which gives an indication of their earlier rôles, in the British Army it used to be said (perhaps with some envy) that Engineer Officers were either 'mad, married or Methodist'. They seem to have pioneered or handled most of the technical developments since the Industrial Revolution—the use of steam, ('steam sapper' was the soldier's nickname for the road traction engines), electricity, submarine mining and military aviation. (See Chapter 12.)

No collection should omit appropriate women 'soldiers'. An Amazon model army would be a most original collection, but personally I prefer to see the gentle sex performing its traditional rôle of nursing and comforting. Apart from nurses from the Crimea onwards, there were auxiliary army corps in both World Wars—the WAAC in 1916–18 and the ATS from 1938 to 1947. The latter was then reorganised as a permanent part of the British Army called the Women's Royal Army Corps (I cannot say why it is not called the Royal Corps of Army Women or Royal Women's Army Corps). The British Army recruiting brochures for women's services provide some excellent illustrations of types to model. No commercial models of these are produced at present, but Britains' garden set woman suitably re-kitted can be made into an attractive little soldierette.

The landgirls of Crescent and Britains can be converted into various trouser-clad, operational-duty types, such as nurses at the Casualty Clearing Station, women drivers and female operators of telephones and radar equipment.

CHAPTER EIGHT

'With Drums Beating . . .'

'. . . the shrill trump,
The spirit stirring drum and the ear piercing fife,
The Royal banner and all quality,
Pride, pomp and circumstance . . .'

THERE IS NO DOUBT that in any type of collection, whether the most colourful or the most sombre, the inclusion of musicians and standard bearers gives a touch of blazonry to the other components. They are of, but not the same as, the rest of their groups, and it is these differences which delight the collector and arouse the admiration of well-informed viewers of his collection.

Throughout the ages music has formed part of the panoply of war. The sight and sound of a military band at the head of a parade or performing in a seaside bandstand is a familiar one, but the origin of military music lies in instruments 'ordained for men that fight, to cry and warn of the signs of battle, to fear and affray their enemies and to comfort their own men . . .' In 1750 one of the last of the German court trumpeters, Johann Ernst Attenburg, described the bugle calls of his day as 'nothing more than an artificially produced war cry'. The trumpet's blast gave the warning, the rattle of the drums and shrill notes of the fifes or pipes were meant to awe the enemy and control movement and the 'band of musick' brought comfort when the battle was over.

The ancient Greeks and Egyptians favoured flutes, while the Romans had a family of brass instruments ranging from a 'buccina' to the brass 'tuba'. The Roman brass 'band', if one can call it that, was mainly for signalling purposes but also figured in the triumphs (see two models included in picture No 15). Barbarians had animal and wood horns, less elaborate, but for similar purposes, as well as bagpipes, which some readers may query as being classed as musical instruments at all.

Feudal rulers abrogated to themselves the trumpet blast as a royal prerogative and bannered court trumpets became a recognised part of royal regalia. The flourishes at the beginning and end of a King's speech were the oral equivalent to the illuminated scroll work and the seal on a parchment. The use of the minstrels of war was considered a great privilege. On great occasions large numbers of minstrel trumpeters were used. When Isabella of Portugal arrived in Bruges in 1429 nearly 200 trumpeters greeted her and made the whole town resound.

The Crusader armies' instruments were little different from the Romans', but the opposing Saracens' brass, reeds, drums, cymbals and bells were new to them. This combination played for tactical purposes during the fighting and it so impressed the Crusaders that they brought them back to the West for use in similar fashion. Renaissance warfare led to the introduction of the Swiss drummer and fifer in each company of foot and a trumpeter to each troop of horse.

In the 17th century, Stuart England had drum and fife infantry bands and mounted trumpeters for the cavalry. The latter also had kettledrums which were granted to them as a special distinction or battle honour. In France, Louis XIV introduced oboe bands, derived from the Turkish, and this is really the birth of the first military 'bands'. These bandsmen were called 'hautboistes' from the word hautbois, the name for the oboe of that time. Trumpet bands developed in Germany and Italy about the same time, both as civil and military groups, with such composers as Monteverdi and Gabriele writing for them.

The ordinary military bands of fifes and oboes had a limited repertoire, though an increasing number of their marching tunes were based on folk songs. But then composers began to take an interest in these instruments, and to substitute the oboe by the horn, 'flat' trumpet (slide trumpets) and bassoon. This amalgamation led to the employment of civilians as bandsmen. Whilst actual fighting was strenuous, the ebb and flow of war allowed some time for relaxation and military music also became the music of the people. From this stems the long tradition of town (and factory) bands which have survived to this day.

The status of civilian musicians in army bands was a curious one: they were usually paid privately by the Officers of the regiment, (a meaningless 'credit' often seen on a band concert poster today 'By kind permission of Lt Col The Hon Gore-Blagh-Gore and Officers' is a survival of this); this and the upkeep of the instruments made Officers regard their regimental band as their own property. (The numbers were not large; 12 being the average strength of a band.) They would have it perform for their own personal delectation and let the drums and fifes do the more mundane military duties.

On active service, should a regiment have to surrender, it was not unusual for the 'musick' to be set free. Naturally these civilians were not overkeen to be at the sharp end; in one of Marlborough's campaigns when the oboes of a French regiment were called on to strike up a cheerful tune they could not be found. It appears that when the first shots were exchanged they had decided to make their exit! As Professor Farmer has put it—they were prepared for the pomp but not the circumstance of war. More often than not it was the drums and fifes of the regiments that felt the effect of war; these were the soldiers, many often mere boys, who had to combine the duties of battle signalling with morale boosting under fire and sight of the enemy. It was this kind of vital duty which Lady Butler immortalised in her painting of the 57th Foot (later the Middlesex Regt) at Albuera, 'Steady, the Drums and Fifes'.

Chiefly under French influence, military band instrumentation began to change. First they developed the oboe; then the oboe was fitted with a reed to hold in the lips instead of taking it into the mouth; the bassoon replaced the bombard; and then came the French horn, so called because the French altered the coiling of the tubing of the original horn. Numbers were still small, at the beginning of the 18th century usually no more than six woodwinds. In England and Prussia only, a trumpeter marched with this group; in 1731 the Honourable Artillery Company band was 'one curtall, three oboes and no more' and a German army band of the mid-century consisted of two oboes, two clarinets, two horns and two bassoons. In the 1770s a British cavalry band was four trumpets, three horns, and two bassoons. There were only five authorised bands in the British Army at this time, all the others were unofficial but tolerated.

Percussion instruments owe their origin to the Turks, who employed them in their Janissary bands. The Polish Army had a full Turkish military band transferred to it as a gift from the sultan, and soon after Russia, Prussia and Austria followed suit. Later copiers, including the British, dispensed with the actual Ottoman performers, using Negroes instead, already long-employed as trumpeters and drummers. By 1777 the 24th Foot (later the South Wales Borderers) had cymbals, the Royal Artillery bass drum and tambourine and the Coldstream Guards a Jingling Johnnie (a French corruption of the Turkish word '*chaghāna*') plus two tambourines. Negroes display great agility with these instruments, and with their fists! The famous story of the Negro drummer of the Grenadier Guards in about 1800 who, asked by a passer-by, 'Hello Darkie, how's the Devil?', replied 'He send you dat!' and knocked his questioner flat into the gutter! Dressed in outlandish Eastern robes they led a 'beat' craze of the day. The British War Office forbade these 'with-it' acrobatics to be used on parade but the new craze spread and did much to revitalise marching.

Negro drummers and drum majors were common sights in British bands up to the early part of the 19th century, when public opinion, becoming sensitive to the slavery question, led to their disappearance. But the animal skins (chiefly leopard and tiger) which they used to wear as drum aprons still remain as part of drummers' regalia today.

The French Revolutionaries used bands as a means of inculcating their new philosophies. Open-air national fêtes included large bands of 45 or more players, as in the famous band of the National Guard. These fêtes ceased with the coming of Napoleon who allowed infantry bands to remain, but suppressed those of the Cavalry for a time, saying he 'could raise another four regiments of horse with the animals he saved by sacking cavalry bandsmen'. But French bands came back bit by bit, and during the Empire a gala band consisted of:

10 flutes	2 tubas
30 clarinets	2 buccin
18 bassoons	12 horns
4 trumpets	3 trombones
8 serpents	12 percussionists

The serpent, a hybrid brass-reed instrument, owed its name not to its giving out a hissing sound but to its rather reptilian shape. It went out of British bands in the 1840s.

It will be seen that at this time most of the instruments of the band were fully chromatic reeds or woodwind which were the type on which most mechanical progress has been made. Up to then the brass, excepting the trombone, could only produce the harmonic series of a few notes, which limited them considerably. But in 1810, James Halliday, bandmaster of the Cavan (Irish) Militia, invented the keyed bugle. Five keys controlled holes in the tubing of the bugle and so allowed chromatic notes to be played. The then Duke of Kent took a royal interest in this, and soon after the bandmaster of the South Devon Militia devised an instrument with seven keys. A Frenchman developed a whole choir of brass instruments in this technique, whilst another, Adolphe Sax, invented the saxophone and saxhorns.

Developments in Germany brought about the introduction of cornets and tubas. Many of the men who invented new, or improved exisiting, instruments were bandmasters. Civilians in charge of army bands included J. S. Bach's brother J.J., who was a bandmaster in the Swedish army. Handel composed 'Scipio' for the Grenadier Guards *before* it was put into the opera and often borrowed the 'great kettledrums' off the carriage of the Master General of the Ordnance for use at his performances. Jeremiah Clark (alias Purcell !) Arne (of 'Rule Britannia' fame), Mayerbeer, Mozart and Beethoven (whose magnificent 'Yorkscher Marsch' is still in regular use in German band repertoires) are among great composers who were associated with military bands.

Up to the mid-19th century, British bands continued to be the private property of the regiments, with their composition, dress and duties left to the civilian bandmaster, almost always a foreigner, usually German or Italian. The effect of this was that there was no co-operation between bands. In the Crimean War at Varna the massed British bands played the National Anthem in different keys, pitches and arrangements. The resulting cacophony did not go down very well with the Duke of Cambridge, the Royal C-in-C. The military bandsmen were turned into the ranks as stretcher-bearers and the civilians and foreigners sent away. As soon as the war was over the Royal Duke established the Military School of Music at Kneller Hall, Twickenham, near London, to train bandmasters and bandsmen from the ranks of serving soldiers, and regimental bands were brought under War Office control. One of its early professors was a Thomas Sullivan, an ex-army bandmaster and father of Sir Arthur Sullivan.

The new measure was not popular with all colonels. Many were great believers in foreign musicians as directors of their bands, but the days of the foreign bandmasters were numbered. In 1873 an Army Order forbade their further employment and they were gradually replaced by graduates from Kneller Hall. (Ironically enough, the first two directors at Kneller Hall were Germans !) One of the last foreign bandmasters was Ladislao Zavertal, actually appointed after the ban, who presided over the Royal Artillery Band from 1881 to 1907. Under him this band became the largest in the world with 100 players. Italian, a brilliant musician and conductor, he was temperamental and eccentric, sporting a pointed beard 'for health reasons' and poins-nez, he rarely came on parade with the band; when he did he committed all sorts of blunders. He repudiated his rank of bandmaster (Warrant Officer) and, although later given a commission, persisted in styling himself 'Cavaliere' (of a minor Italian order) much to the annoyance of Queen Victoria. Edward VII, however, took a more tolerant view of him and made him an MVO.

This was a period of great international musical activity in which several armies became famous for the virtuosity of their bands. In 1867 the Prussian band of 87 players won top prize in Paris. In 1872, after the Franco-Prussian war, the French Paris Guards and the Mounted Guides became famous, the former distinguishing itself in America. The German Cuirassier Guard Band rose to great heights, and in the Austrian Imperial Army the bandmasters trained at Prague included Franz Lehar. Belgium, Holland and even Norway had army bands famous through Europe for their performances. The British reputation for military music was upheld in this period by the Grenadiers band (under Dan Godfrey), the Household Cavalry, Royal Engineers and Royal Marines (the latter under the leadership of the famous F. J. Ricketts) and the Coldstream under Mackenzie Rogan.

Bands had been an established part of the United States forces since independence. The Marine band dates from 1799 and that of West Point soon afterwards. The size of regimental bands was grudgingly increased from 11 in 1834 to 16 in 1847. The Civil War led to an increase in the numbers of bands on both sides; there are numerous references to the part they took in march and camp and contemporary photographs show their composition. They were the medium by which the lyrics of the rival philosophies were communicated. One of Lincoln's attempts to re-unite the torn country was through a band, when, at a Federal parade at the end of the war, he asked 'Is there a band present?' There was. 'Well then,' he said, 'ask them to play "Dixie".'

By the end of the 19th century American military bands were also internationally known, none better perhaps than the Marine band under John Phillip Sousa, the 'March King', see picture No 25. Forming his own band of 50 players, his world tour of the 1890s brought him lasting fame. All bandmasters are showmen, and Sousa was no exception, one of his innovations being conducting the band with his back to it. Early in the 20th century the United States Army formed its own Music School at Fort Jay, New York, under Arthur Clappe, a Kneller Hall graduate. All the leading US conductors of the period were British-born, with the exception of Sousa, who changed his name from the unpronouncable European to a composition of his own initials and those of the United States of America.

The collapse of so many old regimes following the 1914–18 War led to changes in military musical establishments. Those at Potsdam, Vienna and St Petersburg were given over to the new regime, (and even Fort Jay was closed down 'for reasons of economy'). One outcome of this was the appointment of the Prussian Guards Oberstcapellmeister Fritz von Brasé as Musical Director of the new Irish Free State Army. Whilst it would be an exaggeration to say he became the Sousa of Ireland, he certainly made Irish Army bands widely known by the quality of their performances at the internationally attended Royal Dublin Society Horseshow and other occasions.

Bands had various experiences in the Great War. Some were retained intact to 'bring comfort' to the wounded. My first real memory of military bands is of being taken as a small boy to a concert in the grounds of a militay hospital. In sunshine I sat on the grass amidst invalids in hospital-blue with wheelchairs and crutches and listened to a khaki-clad band play Schubert's Un-

30. *Carts, wagons and limbers; conversions by the author from toys, as detailed in Chapter 10.*

31. *The British Army's first car. Airfix De Dietrich veteran car with converted Britains' metal figures (1:32 scale).*

32. *World War 1 group, showing two types of 1:32 scale lorries converted from Airfix B-type bus.*

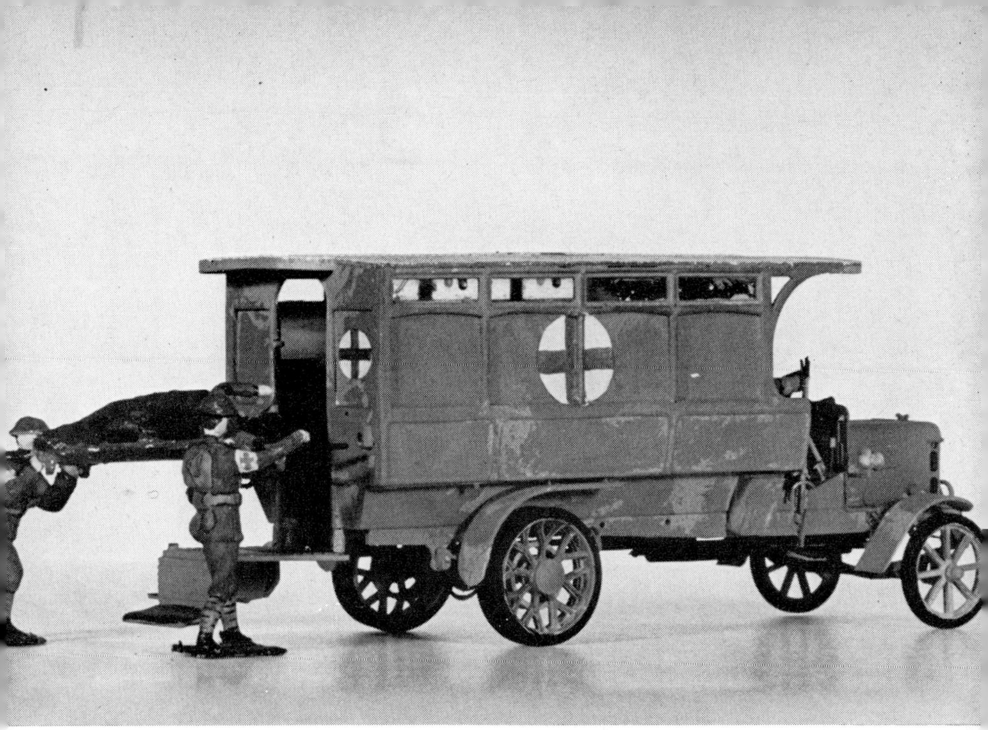

33. *World War 1 motor ambulance converted from Airfix B-type bus, 1:32 scale.*

34. *World War 1 mobile workshap lorry constructed from contemporary pictures on Airfix B-type bus chassis, 1:32 scale.*

35. *Example of horse-drawn 6-inch gun circa 1916. Team of 12 horses (four wheelers) converted from Britains' metal farm horse with postillion legs on bodies of standing gunners.*

36. *Three limbers, scratch-built on Britains' field gun wheels and axles.*

37. *Old sketch from which author built up oven wagon on Britains' metal GS wagon chassis. Note how model measurements were 'scaled' on sketch.*

38. *World War 1 army lorry made from contemporary photographs using Airfix Dennis fire engine chassis. The mechanics are conversions from Airfix motor racing officials and Old Bill bus soldiers.*

39. *World War 1 army light lorry in Mesopotamia, a conversion from Airfix Model T Ford kit.*

40. *Predecessor of the tank; Greek war elephant from Britains' zoo elephant with cardboard 'fighting top'. Warriors are Britains' 'Herald' range.*

41. *World War 2 long-range desert Jeeps; Monogram vehicle kits improved by Roy Dilley. General Montgomery from Airfix motor racing officials; officer on right from Revell polo players legs and Airfix bus passenger body; Gammage heads. Figures in Jeeps are various conversions of Britains' metals.*

42. *Another predecessor of the tank; Queen Boadicea's chariot converted from Timpo Roman chariot with Herald figures.*

finished Symphony. Some bands were dispersed, others given a double rôle of playing on the march up to the line and then performing as stretcher-bearers in action. Many New Army units raised *ad hoc* and unofficial bands, the members of which doubled on more prosaic duties as occasion demanded. The same tended to happen in the Second World War when, in the name of Welfare, bands were given official encouragement. Some enthusiastic officers took this to mean dance bands, and well-known civilian ensembles of this nature joined up en-bloc on the understanding that this was to be their sole contribution to the struggle. This caused resentment by other servicemen and led to a Parliamentary enquiry at which it was said that there were 1,000 full-time dance band musicians in the Royal Air Force alone.

But in both wars the marching bands—and the drums and fifes, bugles or pipes—were the real morale-boosters. An American officer wrote of his unit's arrival, fresh to England, in 1917, on a cold dark rainy night, after an all-day train journey during which his men had had nothing to eat. 'A British Officer asked me to form up the battalion on a road outside the station, which I did. Then occurred one of those demonstrations of the reviving effect of music. Out of the dark marched a splendid British band which played us into camp with all the American marches and airs we know. . . It meant to us that we were welcome. . . I do not think we were ever so uplifted as when we marched along that lonely road that night.'

Twenty-five years later bands, drums and pipes played British troops into the liberated city of Tunis. When the sound of the Irish Guards pipes drifted into the great still Basilica where the white-robed fathers were at Mass, one of them, an Irishman, suddenly sprang from his stall and rushed down the aisle crying 'I must see the boys, I must!' This was the first time he had heard Irish pipes for 30 years.

The British Parliament was once told, in a debate on Defence Costs when cuts in bands were being discussed, that between the wars an officer depressed by the conditions had decided to retire. He had handed in his papers to the Adjutant and was returning to his quarters when he met the band playing the regimental march. The effect was to turn him back to withdraw his resignation. In the war that followed he became a general.

Military bands provide a continuous communications link between the army and the public, ranging from the ceremonial parade, primarily of an internal nature, to the tattoo, which is avowedly intended for public entertainment. At the former the music is mainly martial—salutes, slow and quick marches, and inspection music. The tunes are based on local, national or military traditions, and the public's taste is a secondary consideration. Tattoos are different; here the bands deliberately show off their virtuosity, both by the excellence of their playing, and by the wide repertoire of non-marching music as well as evolutions whilst playing on the move. In Britain, in the inter-war years, tattoos reached their apogee in the Aldershot spectaculars; here often as many as 800 performing musicians would be playing on the move together in full dress. After 1945 the spectacle scene changed; for a number of years the forces' charity organisation SSAFA sponsored splendid shows but at present the outstanding tattoo is that held in Edinburgh during the annual Festival of Music and Drama.

Each evening, as night closes down, the floodlit castle on the hill seems to hang in the sky. Then suddenly a single gun booms out—a rich Scottish voice begins, 'Ladies and Gentlemen . . .' the 7,000 audience in the theatre-like arena cheer, the searchlights point their beams on the gateway and the massed pipes and drums march out. Mini-battles and skill at arms displays are also part but the main events are the performances of the bands, visiting Commonwealth and foreign as well as a mixture of different British types. The music is always a perfect mixture of the old and new, the grave and gay, parade and 'showbiz'. The 'authorities' relax enough to permit the excited teenagers in the audience to come out and caper amid the bandsmen. They always cnd on the same note, a finale like the 'walk down' in classical pantomine, in which all the performers come on in their best uniforms; a lone piper plays 'Light-out'; then comes 'God Save the Queen' from bands and audience; and then—with a great crash of drums and brass—the bands march briskly off to 'Scotland the Brave', 'the Green Hills of Tirol' or some other breath-catching air.

I am often asked about the composition of bands, and my own layouts are sometimes criticised. Like so much else in collecting model soldiers, there are no hard and fast rules on minaturisation of bands. As will be seen from my Order of Battle, in numbers my bands are disproportionate to my cavalry and infantry units. The reason for this is mainly visual, a group of 15 cavalry or 20 infantry look 'right', but if the regimental band was to be in that same ratio, *one* bandsman would have to represent a band, a situation deserving of Euclidian comment.

So a different rule has to be applied for the numbers in model bands; they must be enough to represent all the instruments, which means at least a dozen; in my case I have decided on 14 as the minimum for a normal mounted band, 22 for an infantry band and 16 for drums, as follows:

Mounted Band

Bandmaster/Director of Music
Kettledrummer

1 E Flat Bass	1 Bb Flat Bass
2 Trombones	1 Horn
2 Cornet	1 French Horn
4 Woodwind (2 Clarinets, 2 Flutes)	

Dismounted Band

1 Bandmaster/Director of Music
1 Drum Major

1 E Flat Bass	1 Bb Flat Bass/Sousaphone
2 Trombones	2 Cornets
1 French Horn	1 Euphonium
2 Tenor Horns	1 Cymbals
1 Bass Drum	1 Side drum
1 Saxophone	6 Woodwind (2 Clarinets, 2 Flutes, 2 Piccolos)

Corps of Drums

Drum Major

4 Side drums	2 Tenor drums
1 Bass drum	8 Bugles

Pipe Band

Pipe Major

8 Pipers	2 Tenor drums
4 Side drums	1 Bass drum

If, however, the collection is to consist of bands only, then the full numerical strengths of 25 for cavalry, 40-plus for infantry, 25 for drums, and the groups mentioned earlier above in the chapter could be adopted.

The modeller will see from all this that there should be plenty of colourful subjects to include in his collection. However, to have these he is going to have to make most himself, and from a limited amount of source material. Messrs Britains is the only toy manufacturer in Britain to be still producing bands and these are, of course, in polythene and PVC. The 'Eyes Right' series depict one mounted band, four infantry bands and a few small drum, bugle and pipe sets; their Herald series includes figures for a Scottish kilted pipe band. The metal band instruments are of excellent design and of a high quality plated finish, covering the full range of those in modern use, but are sufficiently few to justify detailing:

Percussion	Brass	Woodwind
Kettle drums	E Flat Bass Tuba	Saxophone
Bass drum	Sousaphone	Oboe
Side drum	Trombone	Bassoon
Cymbals	Tenor Horn	Clarinet/Flute
	Cornet	Piccolo
	French Horn	

There are also Drum Majors' Maces, State Trumpets with banners attached (two positions) and bugles. In all cases except the drums, hands and/or arms are integrated with the instruments. This makes attachment to alternative figures easy, extremely so in the case of straight swopping, and needing only simple paring and sticking in other cases.

The only other source for band instruments in UK is Rose Miniatures (Russell Gammage) who is well disposed towards purchases of accessories. (But would-be buyers should do their best to place an economic order quantity, say £1 to 30s worth of the odds and ends at one time.) He lists (1968 Catalogue) the following in metal:

Egyptian lute	Bugle (with or without tassels)
Egyptian double flute	Bugle horn
Egyptian large harp	Bass Drum for pipe bands
Egyptian small harp	Side Drum
Roman Cornicen	Tenor Drum
Roman Tubicen	Drum Cords
Celtic War Trumpet	Trumpet (hussar)

These range in price from 1s 2*d* to about 5s each.

The French firm Segom produce a range of band instruments and accessories in plastic but have no outlet in the UK at present. These are for the 1st Empire but some or all are suitable for earlier or later periods:

Percussion	Brass	Woodwind	Miscellaneous
Jingling Johnny	Small trumpet	Clarinet	Mace
Side Drum	Large trumpet	Bassoon	Shoulder cords
Tenor Drum	Horn bugle	Serpent	Wing epaulettes
Bass Drum	Horn		
Cymbals	Trombone		
Drum Sticks			

Segom instruments are handless and so a little more skill is required in attaching them to the potential musician's arms. But they are beautifully made and comparatively cheap, ie, from 0·25F to 0·60F each. The firm's price list says 'Minimum to 10 pièces de même sorte', so it seems as if a number of would-be users should club together and elect one of their number to go to Paris to make a bulk purchase!

Grouping of these instruments for playing on the march or in orchestral layouts have a few rules, but in real life a lot depends on the bandmaster and the regiment involved.

Royal Marine Bands always march with side drummers (who are also buglers) in the front, then the rest of the percussion, followed by brass, and then woodwind. (See picture No 24.) British Footguards *always* have the brass in front (generally trombones), followed by percussion and then woodwind. When pipes or drums (ie, fifes) are marching *with* the band they are always at the rear. (The Guards drummers also carry bugles.) Drum and fife, and drum and bugle (known as corps of drums) march with the drums in front; pipe bands march with the pipes in front and light infantry and rifles bands march with the bugles in front. All rather confusing, but the clue to these last layouts lies in the title the leader bears as to which instruments leads, ie, drum major, pipe major, bugle major.

Bandsmen's and drummers' dress, except when on modern active service, is always different from the rest. In the old days they were clothed in the regimental facing colour; ie, if the regiment wore scarlet coat with yellow facings, they wore yellow coats with scarlet facings. This was discontinued at the turn of the nineteenth century and the distinctions marked by variations in head dress and lace and with cross belts and special badges on the sleeves and upper arms.

These distinctions tend to be a little esoteric and the modeller should research carefully on the band dress distinction of the regiments concerned.

Some example of British Army dress distinctions for bandsmen of the 1914 period are as follows:

Regiment	**Normal item**	**Band item**
Household Cavalry	Scarlet or blue tunic. White-metal helmet.	Gold embroidered state frock coats. Velvet 'jockey' cap.
Dragoons and Dragoon Guards (full dress)	Helmet plume.	Plume of colour different from rest of their regiment. Aigulettes on right shoulder.
Royal Artillery	Cloth helmet with ball top.	Busby.
Royal Engineers	Cloth helmet, spike top.	Busby.
Inf of Line	—	'Wings' on shoulders of bandsmen and drummers; 'Cords' (ie, aigulettes) on drummers, who also had lacing along seams of sleeves and backs of tunics.
Footguards	—	An elaborate arrangement of lacing grouped according to set of regimental buttons; 'wings'. Bandsmen or musicians in gold lace (also Drum Majors). Drummers—cloth lace.

Modelling bandsmen, drummers, etc, calls for a little more work than with soldiers of the line:

(a) Most instruments, being double-handed, require the removal of the integral (as well as the usual movable) arm of the basic figure. Dealing as we are nowadays with plastic figures this is easily achieved with a modelling knife.

Where the instruments have integrated hands/arms it then becomes a straightforward fixative operation. The modeller should decide whether the instrument is being played or rested and position it accordingly; the large instruments, E flat and double Bb flat brasses, etc, will exert a drag effect until the fixative takes effect so a wedge should be stuffed temporarily in between them and the model's chest.

(b) All players dressed as bandsmen have the embellishment of 'wings', epaulettes which project from the shoulder seams as the many illustrations available show. They are essential to the models' appearance and can be made from soft thin lead sheet or even paper. The cutting to shape and affixing is somewhat fiddling but well worth the effort.

(c) Shoulder belts and music pouches are also usual for bandsmen, drummers, etc, mounted and dismounted. Like the wings, they do not show up enough by being painted on, but should be cut from the same materials and secured by a good fixative.

(d) All dismounted drummers have aprons in white buff leather, (some old khaki-clad ones had them of brown), or animal skins which, for once, do serve a function. They can be made from similar materials and affixed as for wings and shoulder belts.

(e) Mounted bandsmen control their horses with boot reins (actually adjoined to the stirrups). There are exceptions (I have seen very well schooled band horses without them) but they add to the appearance of the figures and are easily modelled from very thin lead strip, OO gauge fuse wire or nylon cord. These reins are, in fact, included on the recent new Lifeguards mounted band introduced by Britains.

(f) Horse furniture; there are no hard and fast rules about other embellishment, which depends on the regiment and the type of parade. Some kettledrum horses have worn a plume; most kettledrums have drum banners wrapped around them, sometimes in a 'de-colletté' way to show off the ornamentation of the drum shells; some drum-horses have throat plumes, even when these are not worn by Officers' chargers. All have saddlecloths (shabraques) and some (chiefly hussars) a leopard skin (with head) added on top. These again can be added by thin sheeting and the leopard's head done in solder or plastic wood.

(g) Music (band cards) actually on the instruments is not essential for correct portrayal; all good bandsmen are capable of playing some pieces without music, but it certainly enhances the models' appearance. However, band cards are difficult to affix (especially in plastic) and very easily get knocked off.

(h) Band swords, eg, Brass Roman type for Royal Fusiliers and Rifle Regiment bandsmen.

(i) Bandsmen's arm badges—chiefly the lyre, but also the drum, crossed trumpets, and/or bugle, as well as the regimental badge or cipher on the pouches—are quite suitably painted on. My friend Roy Dilley gets a relief effect for these as explained in Chapter 2.

Finally there is another somewhat vicarious pleasure to be derived from collecting model bands and that is the collecting of records or tapes of military music to go with them. There is not the space here to go into what is a wide and very satisfying hobby on its own, but the modeller can combine the pleasures of eye and ear by discriminately acquiring the music related to the bands in his collection. I have done this, perhaps not very efficiently, but my friend John Fowles, who is an expert on collecting military band records, offers some very useful advice to those interested in this side of the hobby which we have put in Appendix 8.

An example of bandsmen derived from extensive conversion work is shown in picture No 26, made from Britains' marching Evzone rifleman. An average of eight cutting and soldering operations was made on each figure to get the desired effect. In contrast to warlike bands, picture No 28 shows a Salvation Army band playing a lively air for, in the words of their founder General Booth, 'it isn't only the Devil who has all the best tunes'.

CHAPTER NINE

'... And Colours Flying'

FLAGS OR TOTEMS have been in use from the earliest wars for two main reasons. Held aloft, they formed a rallying point at the position of the commander, and also they symbolized the deity to whom the fighters worshipped. Surrounded by a specially chosen escort, where the Flag was planted in the ground was where the army or force stood, come what may. If necessary, the last man was expected to give his life to prevent it from falling into enemy hands. One of the most tangible items of evidence of victory was to bring back an enemy standard or emblem, as it was proof positive that the other side had been decisively beaten. To have a standard taken was the greatest military disgrace of all.

In 1778 a writer stated that the use of ensigns in war originated with the ancient Egyptians who, 'being under no regular discipline . . . invented the carrying of some conspicuous sign or token which the soldier might follow and, upon any defeat or dispersion resort to '. Lycurgus took the idea to Sparta from whence it was copied by others, including the Romans. In the latter army they were regarded as sacred emblems (eg, the eagles) and suitably reverenced. This religious homage also derived from the Egyptians, whose chief ensign was of their god Apis, represented as a Bull, the ancient sign of strength and power.

The ancient Jews similarly reverenced battle flags, as is stated in Psalm XX 5, 'In the name of God we will set up our banners' and the Maccabees bore a standard which contained a portion of scripture. According to Tertullian, worship of standards amounted to a form of religion in the Roman Army . . . 'Under the Empire the temples of Rome received some ensigns, but when in camp, following the religious service of the temple, erect the ensign in an inviolate refuge . . .' usually the middle of the general's headquarters, making an altar of turf on which it was placed. According to one authority these ensigns were made of wood, silver and gold, on which were represented the image of warlike deities, such as Minerva or Mars (and later of the emperors). The legionaries swore by their standards and were bound to them by both religion and honour.

When Christianity became the official religion of Rome (due, it is said, to Constantine having a vision of a Crucifix in the sky with the words 'In this sign conquer'), many pagan and superstitious rites were christianised and the veneration of standards was adapted as a means of sustaining *espirit de corps*. From this has come down the consecration of standards and colours in many armies. In his book on this subject, the late Major T. J. Edwards states that the dedication of war flags was so general as to be taken for granted by early writers. Such references as are made confirm the practice, as in 'AD 1060 Pope Alexander II sent the Normans a banner, *which he had blessed*, for them to fight the Arabs under in their conquest of Sicily'.

The British National Flag, with its amalgam of the crosses of the three national saints, reflects the medieval practice of fighting under banners dedicated to particularly appropriate saints (but St George was not an Englishman, and I for one often wonder why our forefathers had not taken King Arthur, that Romanised—and therefore Christian—Briton as their inspiration in battle? The early French adopted St Martin of Tours, a Romanised Gaul, which is what one would expect from the logical race.)

As noted above, banners were originally blessed by the Pope himself, but down the centuries this has steadily been delegated. In the 14th century, Kings and Princes (no doubt as part of their Divine Rights) performed it with a few suitable remarks. In his 'Henry VI' Shakespeare makes Talbot invoke the Almighty to 'bless our colours'. Later in the British forces we find bishops and deans performing the ceremony, but by the end of the 19th century the regulations were providing for the service to be carried out by chaplains. Before leaving this aspect of the subject, in the British Army, which is nominally Church of England, it might be noted that the other religious denominations are covered by providing that 'when the majority of the men' (no mention of officers' persuasions!) 'are Roman Catholic the consecration will be performed by an RC priest'. Provision was also made for Scottish battalions to have this done by a Presbyterian minister on the assumption that *all* ranks were of a dissenting persuasion.

Nowadays the presentation and blessing of new British Colours, Standards or Guidons is done at one formal ceremony, usually of the 'drumhead' nature. The flags are usually, but not always, made by the Royal School of Needlework to specifications laid down by the Ministry of Defence and inspected prior to handing over by two officials—a member of the College of Heralds in the capacity of Inspector of Regimental Colours and, when provided at public expense, a civil servant member of the Inspectorate of Stores and Clothing of the Ordnance Directorate.

The personage presenting the colour depends on the unit concerned. Household Troops and regiments which have Royalty as their Colonels-in-Chief are usually honoured by the presence of the Queen or another member of the Royal Family. Other regiments have it done by a Field Marshal or senior General, who may have served in the regiment or be its Colonel or Colonel-in-Chief. Occasionally, in the case of reserve army units, colours have been presented by Lord Lieutenants of Counties. Presentations must always have official approval and be on the Sovereign's behalf. Readers will be familiar with the form of parade service followed as these always receive good coverage in the press and on television.

As to what types of units carry colours, again taking the British Army as an example (and space precludes the custom in others), there were no hard and fast rules in the early days. The obvious origin was the fighting units, which were of two types—foot and horse. The term standard was, in fact, applied to the flag of those who fought on foot, as it was literally stood in the *ground* (or occasionally set up in a wagon). Cavalry, particularly in the age of chivalry, carried banners or bannerets, but in the course of time the original descriptions have become entangled somewhat, viz:

(a) Colours—which might be thought by the uninitiated to be a generic name for military flags—is the proper noun for *infantry 'flags'*. Nowadays, it usually, but not absolutely, implies a pair—one 'sovereign's' and one 'regimental' colour for each infantry *battalion* (not regiment) *excluding* Rifle battalions. (Also carried by Royal Marines on a group (late divisional) and commando basis; by the Royal Navy on a Command or Station basis—a sovereign's colour only—and by the Royal Air Force as follows:

(i) RAF in the UK
(ii) RAF College Cranwell
(iii) No 1 Technical Training School, Halton
} Each one sovereign's colour the same size as infantry colours)

(b) Standards—Originally the large, rallying battle flag of the King or leader planted in the ground beside him, but now the nomenclature for the flags carried by heavy cavalry, ie, 'horse' *regiments* or *regiments* descended from heavy cavalry. (See chapter 4 above.) In addition to regiments descended from heavy horse, since 1950, RAF Squadrons have been authorised to have standards.

The Royal Artillery had a long tradition that their guns were regarded as their colours, but since 1947 independent sub-units have been authorised to fly a 'standard' (in actual shape it resembles a heraldic standard) at unit HQs on a flagpole. The sizes vary and the unit's crests, formation signs, etc, may be placed on them. (Some artillery units' names embody battle honour titles, eg, Minden, Corunna, Nery.)

Before leaving Standards, those of ex-Servicemen's associations should be mentioned. These only became popular after the First World War and most readers will be familiar with them—those of the British Legion, and the various old comrades' associations at Remembrance Day and other commemorative parade services. These are in the shape of regimental colours and are very numerous, there being one to each branch. In size they closely resemble infantry *colours*, 4 ft 6 in wide by 3 ft deep against the pike.

(c) Guidons—This derives from the old French 'guide-homme', the flag carried by the leader of a troop of horsemen. It has always been swallow-tailed and is regarded as the junior to a standard. In the British Army it is carried by what are regarded as the junior regiments of cavalry, Dragoons, and, more recently, restored to Hussars and Lancers, who were originally Light Dragoons. Modellers will need to be careful about the actual date guidons have been presented to mechanised Hussars and Lancers over the last 10 years or so; as mentioned earlier, for authentic information on individual regiments, it is by far the best to write to the regiments direct, who are always pleased to answer serious enquiries.

(d) Flags—This term is not used in referring to (a), (b) or (c); in military parlance the term flag applies to national colours, flags of truce, and signalling and field distinguishing flags (these latter to indicate Brigade HQ, etc). Most of these are rectangular, but some may be pennants, either pointed or swallow-tailed. These can be, and often are, carried by military personnel to identify national groups at an international gathering, or formations or components of a large parade. Sometimes these have been carried on active service and one of the most dramatic photographs of the last war was that of a group of US Marines struggling to set up a large pole bearing the Stars and Stripes on top of Iwo Jima Island.

In the Middle Ages there were three kinds of flags, the pennant, the banner and the standard. The pennant was a narrow, triangular flag, either pointed or swallow-tailed (not unlike the burgee of a yacht club, but this latter need not detain us). The banner was larger than the pennant and could be square or rectangular in shape. The best-known example of a modern banner in Britain is the Royal Standard. The heraldry boys do not regard it as a standard at all but as the Sovereign's banner, and as such it bears the Royal Arms. According to them a standard is a very long and elaborate affair, with badges superimposed over the bearer's colour. The Royal Artillery standard mentioned above fits into this description, in fact.

The British Infantry pair of colours consist of one Sovereign's and one Regimental colour. In the Foot Guards the Sovereign's or First Colour is Crimson and the Regimental Colour is the Great Union (Union Jack), whilst in the Infantry the Sovereign's Colour is the Great Union and the Regimental Colour is generally the same as the facings of the regiment. In addition, the Grenadier, Coldstream and Scots Guards have 'Royal Standards' of the Regiments (or State Colours). But it should be added that these are not the same as the Royal Standard of the Queen, but more like the Sovereign's Colours, ie, Crimson with the Royal Cypher on them but no battle honours. A further distinction in Foot Guards colours is the practice of bearing company badges on the regimental colours in rotation.

There are many esoteric distinctions about regimental colours which would fill a book, but my advice to modellers, as already said, is this: follow these general rules as far as they go and then move in on the Regiment concerned in depth by reading up their histories and, if necessary, communicating with them.

In the British Army it is the practice for cavalry standards and guidons to be carried (either on horseback or in the open turret of a tank), by a warrant officer. Infantry and Royal Marine colours are borne by junior officers with the Sovereign's colour on the right of the pair. Royal Navy and Royal Air Force colours are also borne by officers. There are occasions, such as guards of honour, when only one colour will be paraded, according to the status of the personage concerned.

A few infantry regiments have traditions of allowing other ranks to briefly hold the colours. During the Foot Guards ceremony of Trooping the Colour (*never* '*the* Trooping of *the* Colour'), a Company Sergeant Major or Sergeant of the battalion performing the duty brings 'the colour' on parade and holds it until the time for it to be trooped. Then the Regimental Sergeant Major marches across, takes it from the Company Sergeant Major or NCO and hands it to the ensign. The South Staffordshire Regiment entrusts its colours to the care of the Warrant Officers and Sergeants for 24 hours once a year to commemorate a battle in India when Sergeants took over the colours after all the officers had fallen.

In foreign armies it is the general rule for officers to carry colours but there are many exceptions which should be enquired into when the moment of modelling draws nigh.

On ceremonial occasions standards and colours are always attended by what is known as a 'close escort'. In the British Forces this is of other ranks; in the cavalry normally two senior NCOs flanking the standard and a trumpeter 'covering' the standard bearer in the rear. In the infantry, one colour is escorted by two senior NCOs and the pair by three (one in between and two covering in the rear). In the Royal Navy the colour escort is of two leading seamen armed with rifles and a Petty Officer 'covering' with a drawn cutlass. A 'full' escort to two colours in the Royal Marines is five senior NCOs. Escorts with rifles always have fixed bayonets and, to eliminate the risk of a colour being caught by the bayonets, these have sheaths or brass-knobbed caps fitted over their points. A small touch when modelling but it indicates you know your subject! An interesting national variation is that of the United States Marine Corps, where the flank escort men carry their rifles on their outside shoulders and also march close together with shoulders touching. This is said to go back to the duty of escorting the colour along the somewhat narrow corridors of the original White House.

Standards and colours proper have not been carried into battle by the British Army since the disasters of the Zulu War, 1879 and Laings Nek, 1881, after which it was decided that 'In consequence of the altered formation of attack and extended range of fire, Regimental Colours shall not in future be taken on active service. . . .' Not all armies fell into line with this new attitude and there are pictures of the French Infantry advancing in August 1914 with Tricolours held high. Unofficial flags and company colours abounded in the Great War, especially in nationalistic-minded units of Wales, Scotland and Ireland. The great painter Matania depicted the Royal Munster Fusiliers being blessed by a chaplain, each company having a flag, which the regimental history tells us were 'green, embroidered with the Irish harp and the word "MUNSTER", a gift from Lady Gordon'. And Edwards records that Princess Patricia's Canadian Light Infantry carried a *Regimental Colour*, presented to them by Princess Patricia of Athlone, on active service in France from 1914–18 and that 'its usual position was at Bn HQ but it flew on the front line trenches on May 8 1915 being hit by shrapnel and bullets, when it gave much inspiration to the regiment, enabling it to hold out against great odds . . .'

An important element of the traditions associated with regimental standards, guidons and colours is the emblazoning on them of battle honours. A single word can mean an heroic attack or loss carried out with great sacrifice; or alternatively months of patient endurance in agonising circumstances, constantly under fire; or perhaps 18 years of incessant warfare under the most cruel conditions, such as is epitomised in 'Tangier 1662–80'. Regiments such as Hussars and Lancers which, up to recently, had no guidons had their honours embroidered on their drum banners. Other regiments without colours ie, rifles, have their battle honours emblazoned on their drums.

The design and emblazoning of standards and colours varies greatly but again, taking the British Army as our example, the general pattern is as follows:

(a) Cavalry Standards and Guidons. Crimson ground with Royal Arms, Cypher, Crest, Motto or other device in the centre in full heraldic colours. Battle honours on scrolls surround this, their exact layout depending on the number granted. Being two-sided, whilst the centre badge is identical on both sides, where the honours are numerous, different ones may be found on each side.

(b) Infantry Colours. Apart from the Foot Guards (see above), the Sovereign's Colour is always the Great Union bearing the Regimental Badge or device in the centre. (This also shows to which battalion, I, II, etc, it belongs). Up to the 1914–18 War no battle honours were embroidered on Sovereign's Colours, but owing to lack of space, up to 10 for that war, and the same maximum number for the 1939–45 War have been authorised. The Second or Regimental Colour is mostly, but not always, the colour of the regiment's facings. Up to the 1880s these had a small Union Jack in the upper canton nearest the pike head and until recently one or two of these were still in service. 'Royal' regiments' second colours are always of blue, whilst regiments with white facings have a St George's Cross on their white colour.

Colours and Standards being made of heavy embroidered silk, it is rare in real life to see all the detailed work on them except in a very strong wind or when lowered in salute. The most normal sight of them is hanging down on the pike or lance and the modeller's aim should be to reproduce this appearance as closely as possible.

I have heard of converters using actual cloth, such as pieces of handkerchief or coloured nylon, but I have found it very difficult to achieve the correct drape effect with these materials. My own experience is that if a hanging colour is required, thin lead sheeting is best, unless a good toy replica is available. Good toy 'colours' are available from Britains' range of US Cavalry and Infantry, US Marines and British Marines, Foot Guards and the Herald range. Painting of colours presents a small problem; if the colour is to hang, most of the details fall out of sight. There is often a temptation to dab a crest on here and a bit of scrolling there, which is called 'suggesting' the paintwork. Colours made of sheet lead which are to be folded in a drooping position do present a slight risk of the paint-work cracking, but I find that if they are folded gently in roll folds cracking rarely takes place.

Another way to obtain an accurate draped standard is for a fair copy of it to be painted first on a spare piece of sheeting and this then pressed into the shape required. Then proceed to paint the actual hanging one, either your own made up one, or a good toy. Painting of the details which show can now be copied exactly on to this.

Our ubiquitous fuze wire will provide the cords that hang from the pike head; the heavy tassels being created by blobs of solder. The table which follows should enable modellers to make up scale size colours for the more popular periods.

As we have seen, the making up of colour parties offers enormous scope. Here in tabular form are some of the possibilities offered by 'toy' figures which are readily available.

Type and period	Size
Colours	*Width and Length (on pike)*
1747 'Windsor' Regulations	6 ft 6 in × 6 ft 2 in
1768 Clothing Warrant	6 ft 6 in × 6 ft
1855 Regulations	4 ft × 3 ft 6 in
1868 Queen's Regulations	3 ft 9 in × 3 ft
1936 and 1953 Clothing Regulations	3 ft 9 in × 3 ft. Length of pike including crest 8 ft 7½ in
1947 RAF	3 ft 9 in × 3 ft 9 in. Also for RN, R Marines
Guidons	
1768 Clothing Regulations	3 ft 5 in to end of point of swallow tails
1936 and 1953 Clothing Regulations	3 ft 5 in to end of point on swallow tail and 2 ft 7 in to beginning of split by 2 ft 3 in on lance*
Standards	
1768 Clothing Warrant	2 ft 5 in × 2 ft 3 in
1873 Queen's Regulations	2 ft 6 in × 2 ft 3 in
1898 Queen's Regulations	2 ft 5½ in × 2 ft 2 in
1936 and 1953 Queen's Regulations	2 ft 5½ in × 2 ft 2 in (Household Cavalry 2 ft 3½ in × 1 ft 10½ in)*
1947 Royal Artillery	3 ft × 1 ft 1½ in on 10-ft pole 4 ft × 1 ft 6 in on 16-ft pole 8 ft × 3 ft on 35-ft pole
1950 RAF (Squadrons)	4 ft × 2 ft 8 in

* Length of Lance is 8 ft 6 in including crest when carried on mounted parades; when carried on mechanised occasions, an infantry-type pike is used but of 7 ft 11 in total length.

Some examples of making up standards and colours

Type of colour	Basic fig available	Alteration required
Household Cavalry Standards (Mounted) 1900–present day.	Standard Bearer from Britains' Set 7835 complete.	Add aigulettes (left shoulder) and repaint to specification.
Same as above, but dismounted.	Britains' 'Herald' range LG/RHG Standard Bearer dismounted.	Attach cords and tassels to pike head. Add aigulettes (left shoulder), repaint to specification.
British horsed cavalry mounted full dress 1914 style uniforms:		
(a) Dragoon Guards.	(a) Britains' No 699 Mounted Police Trooper less head, saddlecloth and right arm with lance. (NB, the cross-belt, pistol holster and pocket need to be erased.)	(a) (i) Rose Model head B129. (ii) Lamb skin saddle cloth from thin felt or plastic wood. (iii) Headrope of fuze wire. (iv) Britains' standard arm from 7835 or Herald standard bearer. (v) Paint up to specification.

Type of colour	Basic fig available	Alteration required
(b) Dragoons (except Scots Greys).	(b) Same Canadian Mounted Police Trooper as above.	(b) (i), (ii), (iii) and (v) above. (iv) Remove standard and trim to swallow-tail guidon or replace by paper one.
(c) Royal Scots Greys.	(c) Same as above.	(c) (i) Rose Model head B138, (ii) to (v) as in (b) above.
British Infantry, full dress, 1914 uniforms:		
(a) Foot Guards, ie, Grenadiers, Coldstreams, Scots, Irish, Welsh, and Honourable Artillery Company Infantry Battalion.	(a) Queens and Regimental Colour Bearers from Britains' No 7226 (Scots Guards).	(a) (i) Alter shape of bearskin caps according to regt by paring and/or adding plastic wood. (ii) Change button sets by paring or adding 'relief'. (iii) Paint up to specification.
(b) Infantry of Line, home service pattern, helmet (ie other than Scots and Fusiliers).	(b) Officers (2) from Britains' Middlesex Regt No 7148, less sword arm.	(b) (i) Colour arms from B7226. (ii) Colour pike shoulder slings from B7226. (iii) Replace empty scabbard with sword in hooked-up position. (iv) Paint up to specification for regiments concerned.
(c) Royal Marines.	(c) Officers (2) from Britains' Marines No 7268 less sword arm.	(c) As for (b) (i) to (iv) above.
(d) Highland Regts.	(d) Officers (2) from Britains' Herald Range Highlanders, less sword arm.	(d) As for (b) (i) to (iv) above. Also sword hilt to be built up into claymore hilt.
(e) Fusilier Regts.	(e) As for (b) above, less head.	(e) As for (b) above, *plus* (vi) Rose Model head B37a.
Canadian		
(a) Governor General's Horse Guards full dress.	(a) As for British Dragoon Guards above.	(a) As for British Dragoon Guards above.
(b) Foot Guards of Canada, full dress.	(b) As for British Foot Guards above.	(b) As for British Foot Guards above.
(c) Princess Patricia's Canadian Light Inf full dress.	(c) As for Royal Marines above.	(c) As for Royal Marines above, *plus* pagris around helmets which can be made by winding narrow strip of thin paper around helmet, as per picture.
Royal Air Force.		
Standard, 1947–50 period dress.	Officer from Britains' US Marines, No 7468 less arm.	As for (b) of British Infantry of Line above.

Messrs Britains' USMC Colour Party—Cat No 7466—is a good example of a high quality toy set designed very accurately from research data supplied by the Marine Corps, Quantico; a group of five figures, with National Standard and Marine Corps flag.

From picture No 27 will be apparent the different types of colours, also their shape according to the material used for the models of them.

Rose Miniatures can supply collectors with the following standards and colours:

Standards—Napoleonic Period—British, French and German.

Colours— 1880–1914—British, German and Russian.

CHAPTER TEN

Transport

LOOKING BACK on his early life, the late Sir Winston Churchill wrote of his own collection of soldiers '. . . all the other services were complete—except one. It is what every army is always short of—transport . . .'

In early times such transport requirements as there were for armies were met by individual arrangements. There were no scales of vehicles and animals to comply with, and the leaders gathered together what they thought they needed or could afford. As plunder was regarded as a legitimate aim of war the animals and vehicles of defeated peoples would be taken over and absorbed into the victor's train. A great variety of vehicles and pack animals followed armies on the march and were regarded as fair game for looting and capture whenever possible. In the English Civil War the reforming instincts of the Parliamentarians disliked such casual arrangements and they laid down rules for regimental baggage trains, including the appointment of wagon-masters. One of these, Shippon, became a general in the Parliamentary Army.

The Parliamentarians quickly saw that any form of organised force was dependent on transport, not only for its men and guns but in order to move its impedimenta and also to keep itself supplied with food, forage and water. The British Restoration and later Parliaments never forgot this and, though the Kings were conceded control over officers and men, the right of 'purveyance'—the authority to requisition transport—was withheld. The Crown was deliberately deprived of the constitutional means to obtain transport to move troops and equipment about. This could only be done at home with the consent of local justices through impressment, and abroad by requisitioning or capture.

What this means for modellers is that, if they are building up collections with transport before the mid-1850s, they will have to rely on contemporary drawings or civilian histories to guide them. There is, it is true, a collection of model vehicles in the Rotunda Museum, Woolwich, said to be of types in use by Marlborough's armies, but I have heard one expert say that the country of origin is uncertain and the various pieces are not all to the same scale. It seems fairly certain that in the British Army before the 19th century GS (General

43. *Leonardo da Vinci with one of his inventions. Café Storme Renaissance-man converted by Alan Cleaver.*

44. *World War 1 armoured car built up from photographs on Airfix 1:32 scale Rolls-Royce veteran car chassis by Roy Dilley.*

45. *World War 1 Mark I tank of cardboard in 1:32 scale, constructed from drawings in RAC Tank Museum booklet.*

46. *World War 1 Mark V tank, made as model above.*

47. *World War 1 Medium A 'Whippet' tank, again made of cardboard in 1:32 scale.*

48. *World War 1 Peerless armoured lorry made of cardboard from illustrations in RAC Tank Museum booklet, based on Airfix B-type bus chassis.*

49. *Scratch-built German Porsche Tiger tank made by Max Hundleby in 1:76 scale. This was one of a large number displayed at Bovington on the 50th anniversary of the Battle of Cambrai.*

50. *Seabrooke armoured lorry operated by RN Brigade in Ypres area 1915. Conversion mainly cardboard on Airfix bus chassis from contemporary photographs.*

Service) Wagon that the 'Flemish' type of wagon was the commonest baggage cart, plus a few special carts connected with artillery. Officers, particularly Generals, took their carriages with them as an alternative to riding and also to sleep in in an emergency. The French model firm of Mignot includes in its products Napoleon's travelling carriage and also his mobile kitchen.

Pack transport has remained a basic form of transport through all ages, remaining in cadre form today in many modern armies to take over in trackless mountain country where even Jeep-type motor vehicles cannot go. Camels, oxen and donkeys have been used according to the country, but mostly the intractable mule and the good-tempered British pony. But those with experience tell us that, despite his vices, the mule has been found to be the toughest for the job. Man himself, of course, is an elementary form of transport. Enlisted as porters thousands of Korean men carried loads for the UN troops on their peculiar 'A' frames, and a little earlier in history white troops used African bearers by the thousands for the movement of equipment and personnel through jungle and bush. (See picture No 29.) Messrs Charbens include African porters with loads on their heads in their No 901 'Safari' set.

Apart from the above there are other reasons why later, even modern, transport is worth the collector's eye. It is always *varied*; obsolescent types remain in service alongside newer models, the former tending to predominate in the reserves of any particular army (or even be the 'latest' in a less sophisticated force). Authorised (and much unauthorised!) alterations to vehicles and mixing of components are carried out by the units holding them; and on mobilisation or other emergency (and here we are back to Churchill), as there is always deficiency, large numbers of civilian vehicles of all shapes and sizes are taken into service off the streets. It is these factors which make collections of vehicles of great variable interest to collectors.

Horsed Transport

Taking the British Army as an example (and, generally speaking, most armies tend to adopt one another's equipment, if with some variations), towards the end of the 19th century military horse-drawn vehicles fell into four groups:

(a) Two-wheeled carts.
(b) Four-wheeled wagons.
(c) Limbered wagon and trailor, each on two wheels, with same amount of carrying space in both.
(d) Pontoon, bridging and other long load vehicles, four-wheeled, basically of the four-wheeled GS type but with longer chassis.

Two-wheeled carts were in great variety at one time. The Maltese cart was the basic vehicle, a simple construction of two shafts, the rear of which formed the frame on which were erected slatted slides and tailboard. This vehicle could be found in most places where the British Army served, drawn, according to the location, by one or a pair of horses, mules or oxen. Britains' farm cart, Cat No 9500, is basically suitable for this vehicle.

The Forage cart was not unlike the farm 'tumbril', with detachable raves at front and rear to help hold the load. Britains' farm tumbril, Cat No 9505, is very similar.

The horse ambulance was a high-sided two-wheeler on a cranked axle. There was a central arch over the inside, from which injured animals could be slung. The tail section, when let down, acted as a ramp. The ambulance could be either a single-horse shafted or two-horse single pole type ridden.

The basic four-wheeled wagon (with the front two of smaller size to allow for turning) was known as the general service or GS type, and as such formed the main element in units' and services' transport. The earlier types had a driving bench flush with the sides, but from about 1900 this was improved and raised above the body on leaf springs. In appearance it resembles a small park bench and this is the item I used from Britains' Zoo and Park series to convert their vehicle into a 1914 model. When the vehicle was drawn by a pair of animals (horses or mules) it was driven from the seat, but when two or more pairs were attached the drivers rode on the near side as with artillery teams.

The chassis of this four-wheeled GS Wagon was used for a number of specialist vehicles, viz:

(a) Early ambulance wagon (until superseded by a specially designed dropped floor type, visible in picture No 22.
(b) Royal Engineers' store wagon.
(c) Royal Artillery store wagon—a feature of which was a spare wheel on the tailboard or behind the driver's bench seat.
(d) Field Forge wagon.
(e) Observation Balloon Winch wagon (see bottom of picture No 55).
(f) Observation Balloon Gas Cylinder wagon (visible on left of pictures 55 and 54).
(g) Telegraph wagon.
(h) Office wagon—as used by Lord Roberts in his field HQ in the South African War.
(i) Mobile pigeon loft.
(j) Field Travelling Oven (see picture No 37).

There is now no toy or model of the GS or any of the above in production. Up to the late 1950s Britains' still produced both a GS Wagon and a limbered trailer, which were very fair reproductions of the real thing. Their Concord Overland Stage Coach in plastic (Cat No 7615) is on a similar chassis, but the body of the wagon would need to be scratch-built from photographs as drawings are very difficult to obtain. I myself have not attempted this as I was able to purchase my requirements of wagons before production ceased. Timpo's Stage Coach and Cowboy Wagon also appear suitable, but their wheels are too thick and would require replacing by lighter types.

The GS limbered wagon and trailer was evolved to meet the need for more flexibility in a vehicle on cross-country journeys as well as ability to turn in smaller space. Very soon the 'specialists' got their hands on the trailer part of this and the following versions were produced:

(a) Field Kitchen; flattish, box-like structure of ovens and boiler, the fire box at the rear dropping below the axle, all topped by a tall, thin chimney.
(b) Cable limber and trailer; the front part was on the design of an artillery limber, but with lowered central seat. The trailer carried four drums

plus racks underslung for poles and ladder. It had three wooden seats on which the signallers perched precariously as the whole team raced across country, paying out line behind. My model of this was copied from one in silver which is at the Royal Signals HQ.

(c) Early mobile searchlights; one or two experimental models were produced on artillery gun carriages attached to artillery limbers. They were drawn by teams of four horses with single pole draft, breast harness, and ridden (see bottom left in photo No 59).

(d) Store trailers of various types for the artillery and veterinary services (see photo No 36).

Apart from the photographs indicated above, most of the vehicles referred to are in photo No 30.

Method of attaching animals to the vehicles (the draft) has changed slowly over the centuries. Despite racing chariots having four horses abreast, wagons and carts had them pulling singly or in tandem, the animal nearest the vehicle (the wheeler) in shafts. Early wagons sometimes had as many as six or eight horses in line, pulling one behind the other. In the 19th century there was a curious arrangement of pairs, one inside a pair of shafts and the other (that ridden) on the outside. Then in the 1890s pole draft for the wheelers was introduced, and this was soon followed by a changeover from collar harness to breast, this becoming universal until mobilisation in 1914, where reserve and impressed harness included the old collar type, especially for the heavier loads.

The number of animals attached depended on circumstances. The normal one, two or four would be augmented by extra animals to pull uphill or across marshy ground. In the devastated areas of the Western Front, 1914–1918, especially in wet weather, it was often necessary to employ two or three times the normal teams to get vehicles through (see picture No 35).

Both Britains' and Timpo's artillery limbers can be cut down and altered to a GS Limbered Wagon, but it would be an expensive item as it would mean purchasing two complete outfits to obtain one limbered wagon. Picturesque as these vehicles are, I foresee a lot of difficulty in making them and advise collectors to keep their eyes open for the secondhand ones which are offered for sale from time to time.

Mechanical Transport

Prior to the development of the internal combustion engine, attempts to supersede the horse (or mule or camel) had been confined to steam tractors, known to the troops as 'Steam Sappers', unwieldy substitutes with a low speed and limited scope.

But the IC engine revolutionised road transport. The lorry (or truck), which could carry three to four times the load of the horse-drawn wagon, only took up the same amount of road space and could travel six times as fast. Hitherto the capacity of railways had been limited by the amount of horse-drawn vehicles which could distribute their freight, but now, with the motor vehicle, supplies (and troops) could be brought quickly from railheads to the front line and the movement of much larger armies became possible.

By now readers will not be surprised to learn that, at first, British military authorities took little official notice of the horseless carriage, although one or two were acquired for the use of senior officers at HQs (see picture No 31).

Then, in 1908, as a result of local initiative, troops were moved from London to Shoeburyness in 94 London omnibuses. The following year, more as a publicity stunt, the Automobile Association organised the movement of a battalion of Guards with full equipment from London to Hastings and back in one day, including a stop for dinner.

The British War Office's reaction to these demonstrations was to convert some of the horse-drawn transport companies of the ASC (Army Service Corps) to mechanical transport (MT). These carried stores between units and railheads as well as providing staff cars for HQs and motor ambulances for the Medical Services. But the cavalry and infantry regimental transport remained horsed all through the 1914–18 War, and was not finally changed until the mid-1930s when the official mechanisation of the whole British Army was put in hand. Up to then the RASC remained the sole user of MT vehicles, relying on a committee to influence the motor trade to produce vehicles more or less suitable for military use. This was the period when Churchill, speaking critically of the paucity of British rearmament, said 'It is true that the British Army is being mechanised in the sense that all its horses have been taken away and nothing given it in exchange!'

So collectors will find both horsed and mechanical transport serving side by side in this period, which makes a collection of transport doubly interesting. Generals rode in sedate staff cars escorted by horsed lancers, despatch riders rode on both horses and motorcycles, MT and horse ambulances operated together and stores lorries and GS wagons loaded up at the same railhead. It was no uncommon sight to see one or other form of transport come to the aid of the other, according to the nature of the mishap.

Field artillery remained horse-drawn all through the Great War but the new range of medium and heavy guns sometimes employed teams of 12 shire horses (picture No 35), sometimes making use of steam traction engines or IC powered tractors, such as the Holt caterpillar. When field artillery began to be mechanised in the between-war period the first means of traction was a curious little tracked vehicle called a 'dragon'. Then in 1939 came the distinctive 'Quad' tower, made mainly by the two firms of Guy and Morris.

Apart from the Airfix 'Old Bill' bus with soldier passengers, which is really a modification of their Type B, LGOC vehicle of about 1912, there are no model kits made of the period in 1 : 32 scale. But the situation is not as gloomy as with horse-drawn vehicles; there are a large number of civilian kits of the period which can be converted. A helpful factor in this is that the great majority of MT employed by armies in the 1914–18 War were civilian types impressed into service and variously modified. This could not be better for the collector/converter who, once he has read himself into the period and studied the mass of photographs available, can produce almost every type of military vehicle of the period. Government parsimony extended the life of some of these well into the post-war period. I have produced the following military variations from the excellent Airfix 1 : 32 vehicles:

Basic Vehicle	**Conversion**
'B' type bus	Single decker hard-top ambulance (picture No 33) RFC general-purpose lorry

	Troop carrying lorry (picture No 32) Stores lorry with hood and tilt (picture No 32) Mobile workshop lorry (picture No 34) Peerless armoured lorry (picture No 48) Seabrook RNAS lorry (picture No 50) Austin armoured lorry
Dennis Fire Engine	Army lorry under repair (picture No 38) Searchlight lorry
Rolls-Royce 1906	Staff car Machine gun carrier Tender for repair crews
Rolls-Royce 1911	Staff car Armoured car (picture No 44) Light ambulance
Lanchester	Armoured car Light ambulance
De Dietrich	Field Marshal French's first staff car (picture No 31)
Ford Model T	US Army staff car Light lorry (picture No 39)
Mercedes-Benz	German Army staff car

My friends Roy Dilley and Alan Cleaver also have made up many military vehicles using these and other kits in 1:32 scale. Those who feel it is vital to work to fully detailed assembly instructions and drawings may not approve of our methods, ie, proceeding solely with the basic kit, some plastic card (available from model shops), a range of photographs and a great deal of confidence. I can assure them, however, that the results are satisfactory, as the pictures show.

In the late 1930s, the British Government took the conscious decision to mechanise the army with vehicles specially designed for service use. This was barely begun when the 1939 War started and, to meet the requirements of the vastly expanded forces, impressment of all sorts of makes and types was resorted to. No collector would be wrong if he included a coach, a furniture van, a bread van, plus all sorts of civilian cars in his Order of Battle for 1939–42. By 1942 war production was giving the troops AEC Matadors, Scammels, Austins and Morrises of all shapes and sizes. US Lease Lend provided them with Chrysler, Dodge, Ford and GM products. Of all the vehicles of that war, two are probably the most representative and at opposite ends of the size chart; the tank transporter and the Jeep.

The latter vehicle, of American origin, and first known to them as the 'peep' (the Jeep was a larger-size personnel car), was quickly seized on by armies and became the workhorse of all units. It was subject to a wide variety of uses and changes to body and was, above all, very rugged and robust. Jeeps could be turned over, buried under debris, flung about by explosion and then be righted, started up and would go. Fortunately for collectors at least two US makers of kits which are available in UK include this great little vehicle in their lists (see picture No 41).

Some idea of the growth of use of MT in the British Army can be gauged from the number issued by the British Ordnance Corps; in 1936 the vehicle population was 4,000; in 1944 it was over one million. In the post-1945 cold war period MT has come to mean the life of an army. Every unit now depends on MT to move, to eat, to fight and to live. Without motor vehicles armies of today would be useless. Despite strenuous efforts to standardise, the multiplicity of makes and types still runs into several hundred divided into combat, CT, GS, etc, of which Britains' No 9760 Champ is one. So model collectors of armies of today have as a prime activity the gathering together of a large quantity of vehicles.

As indicated above, drawings or plans of many of the more intriguing vehicles no longer exist, or can only be obtained by much wearisome research. Museum specimens may be available from which one can sketch the necessary detail. There are, however, photographs and these should not be despised for vehicle modellers; after all, we are all happy to accept them as data material for dress if a regulation is not available and it is probably a photograph of an unusual vehicle which has triggered off the desire to make it.

This is how Roy Dilley, Alan Cleaver and myself go about it. We try and get as many different views as possible (a minimum of two) and make a rough drawing using any men in the picture as a scale line. If the man standing by the rear wheel is 5 ft 9 in high and the wheel comes up to his shoulder the latter is 4 ft 6 in. We then extend this yardstick to the rest of the vehicle, length, height, width, distance between axles, the different angled views acting as a check on these measurements, plus our common sense which tells us the vehicle is unlikely to exceed or be less than certain dimensions. We then do a mock-up and get it right by trial and error. In our view, as we are usually doing a 'one-off', a lot of well executed drawings are not necessary and this is the reason I have none to reproduce in this book!

CHAPTER ELEVEN

Armoured Fighting Vehicles

THE ANCIENT WAR CHARIOTS and war elephants (pictures 40 and 42) can be regarded as ancestors of the tank, as can some of the early engines of war, ie, movable towers and battering rams. The Romans perfected these, though an old Irish saga tells of such machines being used by the men of Ulster in one of their legendary wars with Connaught. Renaissance thinking produces 'battle carts', one version of which was employed in Scotland. Leonardo da Vinci (see picture No 43) designed an armoured vehicle driven by a system of crank handles and, in 1599, an inventor produced a landship on four very large wheels and propelled by sail. A Dutch version driven by a windmill is said to have covered 40 miles in two hours on the shore of the Zuider Zee. Voltaire was a firm advocate of the use of battle carts propelled by horses inside them. The Frenchman Cugnot produced the first steam-driven vehicle but unfortunately on its initial outing it collided with a wall. For this he was thrown into prison and the experiments perforce abandoned.

Despite the rapid development of steam-driven machinery in the Industrial Revolution there were few applications of it to land vehicles. 'A philanthropist' produced a self-propelled battery of scythes to mow down the Russians in 1855, but Lord Palmerston rejected it as too brutal for civilised warfare. In 1902 a Mr Simms exhibited a war car with an IC engine at the Crystal Palace and he offered the patented design to the British War Office but they declined. In 1904 Gottlieb Daimler (the motor inventor's son) built an armoured car with four-wheel drive and a revolving machine gun turret, but neither the German nor Austrian military authorities to whom it was offered took it up.

Ability to move across country was restricted until the caterpillar track was perfected by Diplock and Holt in America for agricultural purposes at the turn of the century. H. G. Wells wrote a prophetic thriller in the 'Strand Magazine', which must have given an intellectual stimulus to many. The official history of the Tank Corps records that a Mr de Mole submitted in 1912 a design for a fighting vehicle which forecast many features of the tank;

unfortunately it was pigeon-holed in the War Office and not found until after the war.

No one concerned can be called the 'inventor' of the tank, although many combined in the imaginative and technical efforts to produce it. Sir Winston Churchill was quick to see the potential of an armoured vehicle, but his share was to give aid and encouragement to others, first through the Naval Armoured Car Division and then the Landships Committee at the Admiralty. It was an RE Officer, Lieut-Colonel Swinton, who first thought of the idea of an armoured vehicle capable of destroying machine gun posts and crossing trenches on caterpillar tracks. Various types were then experimented with, including one with 15 feet wheels resembling a monstrous daddy-longlegs and which existed only as a 'mock-up'. When Churchill left the Admiralty the encouragement changed to hostility, but fortunately Mr Lloyd George, then at the new Ministry of Munitions, took an interest, and Swinton also got British GHQ in France to back the idea for a 'machine gun destroyer'.

When the first prototypes were built, in order to keep them secret a less informative description than 'landships' was required. In a conversation Swinton had with a Lieut-Colonel Dally-Jones the latter suggested 'tank' which was short, gave nothing away and would be plausible to anyone who saw strange shapes in transit under tarpaulins. After more trials and demonstrations, the War Office ordered 100 of what became known as the Mark I Heavy—25 ft 6 in long by 13 ft 9 in wide by 8 ft 2 in high, driven by Daimler 6 cylinder 105/1,000 bhp/rpm engines. The tracks, which were 20 inches wide, went all round the body. Half the number were armed with two 6-pdr guns in side sponsons and were known as 'males'; the others had four machine guns in lieu and were known as 'females'. The tactical concept was that the 'male' tanks' guns would drive the enemy out of his emplacements or pillboxes whilst the 'female' stood by to kill the occupants as they fled. These tanks had a 'tail' assembly of two wheels which was intended to improve the obstacle-crossing power and also to aid the steering. Steering was very cumbersome, involving four out of the crew of eight to make a change of direction.

Readers may be interested to know that the information in the above paragraph, plus a few photographs, was all I had to make my first model of a 1916 tank. The result can be seen in picture No 45.

Owing to training handicaps and mechanical troubles, only 36 tanks took part in the first battle in which tanks were used—Flers-Courcelette on the Somme, September 15 1916. The action began with the advance of one tank followed by two companies of 6th Bn KOYLI who thus had the distinction of being the first infantry to go into action with tanks. But the results of the battle were disappointing, mainly due to the way the tanks were employed, in ones and twos in support of the infantry and not massed together. However, the moral effect was great; the awesome appearance of these monsters out of the mist was a great shock to the Germans, some of whom bolted as the tanks crawled towards them, whilst the British troops were greatly boosted by the modest success they achieved. Field Marshal Haig sent back a request for 1,000 more, including heavier types with improved armour.

A year later at Cambrai, nearly 400 British tanks, led in person by General Elles with the Tank Corps pennant flying from his own, smashed through a defence zone of the Hindenburg Line, capturing 9,000 prisoners and 100 guns.

This time the mass tank attack was so rapid that the following infantry were unable to keep pace with them and so a great opportunity was lost. But in August 1918 the co-ordination was better and the British attack with tanks and supporting troops scattered the Germans on what Ludendorff called 'the Black Day of the German Army'. This attack made them realise further resistance would be useless. These tanks included the second major design of the period, the Medium A or 'Whippet' tank, with a much greater speed to take advantage of the opening made by the heavier types and to keep up with the cavalry. Whippets were 20 ft long by 8 ft 7 in wide by 9 ft high, driven by two 45 hp Tyler engines. Their tracks were on a lower loop than the heavies and the turret protruded well above. To reduce weight they were only armed with three machine guns and carried a crew of three (see picture No 47).

Gun and supply carrying 'tanks' were also produced but not in any great numbers. The Germans also produced some tanks but not enough to make any difference to British usage. The French specialised in light tanks and used them with success in their 1918 battles. US tank production did not get going in time to supply their own armies, which were equipped with French and British types.

Armoured cars were introduced by the Royal Navy in Belgium in 1914 by affixing steel plate protection to ordinary Rolls-Royce and Lanchester civilian cars. This was copied and improved by the army in other theatres, practically every make of vehicle being adapted to suit the terrain, ie, Western Desert, East Africa, Palestine, Mesopotamia, South Russia, India and lastly Ireland. The makes and types, in addition to the two already mentioned, included Delaunay-Belleville, Wolseley, Mercedes, Minerva, Seabrooke, Fiat, Standard, Leyland, Jeffrey-Quad, Austin and Peerless. Tactical use of these included their towing by heavy tanks across broken ground, so that they could be unleashed on the good roads of enemy-occupied country beyond (see pictures 44, 48 and 50).

As Sir Basil Liddel-Hart has said, the post-1918 history of armoured forces—not only in the land of their birth—is a record of checks imposed and confusion caused, by the way higher authorities continually refused to consider them a fully-fledged arm of their own. This was done in many ways; one was to scale the tank force down so as to make it only capable of supporting infantry, and another was to repeatedly appoint to key posts officers without tank experience.

In France, Britain and the US, inter-war tank development was practically nil, although a few dedicated soldiers in each strove to keep ideas alive and carry out experiments. Among these latter was an amphibious tank at the Tank Corps Centre at Bovington. In 1928 the first two horsed cavalry regiments were converted to armoured car units; the 11th Hussars at Aldershot and 12th Lancers in Egypt, each with 34 Rolls-Royce armoured cars (these vehicles were still in use by these regiments in Egypt and Palestine in 1940) and 15 supporting vehicles. The mechanisation of cavalry, especially in Britain, was a delicate matter as many of these regiments had 250 years of proud tradition as horsemen. For many years a tank-versus-horse controversy raged in most armies and a large part of military opinion felt that the claims of the 'tank school' had by no means been proved. Consequently Britain, the birthplace of the tank, fell behind continental armies, such as the French, Russian and Czecho-Slovak, in armoured units (not to mention the Germans, whose leaders made a deep study of armoured warfare and conceived the blitzkrieg panzer forces which swept Europe for four years).

When the Second World War began, the British 1st Armoured Division had been formed only a few weeks before. The Germans then had ten. It was composed of a mixture of tank battalions and recently mechanised cavalry of what was now the Royal Armoured Corps. The equipment was a mixture of light and 'infantry' tanks, the heaviest armament being the 2-pounder guns in the latter. When the Germans attacked in May 1940 it was rushed over to France, committed to battle piecemeal and its striking power frittered away. Mostly out-ranged and under-armoured, on the few occasions they were able to close in, the British tanks fought well. So did the French in the few instances where they were used in bulk, such as the action where they were led by General de Gaulle.

Following Dunkirk (at which all the armoured vehicles of the BEF were left behind) there was a great shake-up in the British Army and armour-minded officers, such as General Martel, emerged who built the British tanks up into a powerful, balanced hard-hitting force. Max Hundleby, President of the Miniature Armoured Fighting Vehicles Collectors Association, describes the general situation as follows:

'In the Second World War, AFVs rapidly became the decisive element and their employment and technical improvement can be studied in three phases.

'The first phase saw the well-balanced German armoured divisions advance through equal or greater forces which were less well organised. The British and French tanks of 1940 were still mainly employed as infantry support, while Guderian had organised the German armour so that the other forces supported the tanks. To do this everything was mechanised to match the speed of the tank and nearly half the infantry was carried in armoured halftrack vehicles. In attack, the armoured or panzer divisions were grouped together as a mass and this technique succeeded against even the superior numbers of Russian tanks, which at the beginning of 1941 numbered about 20,000, some seven times more than the German.

'The second phase saw the development of the British and Russian armoured forces along the lines of the panzer divisions, though the Russians were handicapped by their continued loss of territory and material, while the British economy was severely strained by the requirements of the Bomber offensive and the Navy.

'By the end of 1942, the effects of time and American aid were being felt and the Germans suffered the reverses at Stalingrad and Alamein. In the former, Russian armoured armies were using tanks in mass and, as there were no armoured infantry carriers, each tank carried a specific number of infantrymen on its upper deck. The fighting that followed, as the Russians advanced towards Poland and the Allies cleared North Africa, saw the armoured divisions settle into their final form except for minor variations due to the type of country.

'The final phase of 1944–1945 saw the Allied armour increase in size and power while the major change again took place in the German forces. The requirements of defence produced the heavily armed and armoured, less mobile tanks, such as King Tiger, and the cheaper turretless mobile anti-tank guns. The final months saw a change in German employment forced by events. The more mobile armoured divisions, particularly the well-equipped ones of the SS, were used as a 'fire brigade' and rushed from one trouble spot to another.'

The British 7th Armoured Division in North Africa became probably the most famous armoured formation of the war. The open wastes of the desert were ideal 'tank country' and the elite corps the Germans sent there under Rommel proved and disproved many theories. Painfully, the British and Americans learned the meaning of blitzkrieg and tank-versus-tank battles: In these to-and-fro fights across hundreds of miles, tanks were tried out, discarded or confirmed. Amongst the types the British tank formation used were:

- Light tank Mk IV
- Infantry tank Mk II ('Matilda')
- Covenanter cruiser tank
- Tetarch light tank
- Crusader cruiser tank
- Valentine infantry tank
- Stuart light tank (US)
- Churchill infantry tank
- Lee medium (US)
- Grant medium (US)
- Sherman medium (US)
- Ram (Canadian)

There was also the Chaffee light tank (US) and the British Cromwells and Comets used in North West Europe later in the war. Between them the model kit makers supply most of these and I need not give much details on how to make them up if readers have Chris Ellis' excellent book 'How To Go Plastic Modelling'. But collectors often want the only one which is *not* produced in kit form, and for these Max Hundleby offers the following advice:

'The scratch building of tanks is not a difficult operation so long as care is taken and the model made in separate sections. The best method is to make the major portions from wood as this ensures resistance to distortion and gives the model a feeling of weight (see picture No 49).

'The Panzer 2 drawn on page 136 is a good example of a normal tank and the body and the turret should be carved from wood. It is best to make the parts undersize so that they can be covered with plastic sheet. This material produces hard sharp corners characteristic of metal. If rivet detail is to be incorporated, it can be simulated by pin pricking from the rear face of each plate before sticking to the wooden block. The wheels can either be taken from another kit or built up from dowel or plastic. The Panzer 2 is particularly simple since the bogies are almost plain and can be sliced from a suitable rod.

'Trackwork can either be cut from a kit or fabricated from plastic sheet. The latter method is tedious but well worth the effort as the characteristic sag can be made in the top run between the return rollers. Details can be added to any desired extent though all turrets should be made to rotate. This is easily done by means of a pin in either turret or body. The large side springs can be made from separate leaves and a pliable bristle is most durable as an aerial. In scales such as 1:32 the gun should be bored out and this can be suggested even in the smaller sizes.

'Many German vehicles were covered with an antimagnetic plastic material called zimmeritt and this can be suggested in several ways. In the larger scales it is possible to cover the relevant areas of the model with one of the putty-type compounds now available and then pattern it with a steak fork. In the smaller sizes it is better to draw the pattern directly on to the plastic with the tip of a small soldering iron.'

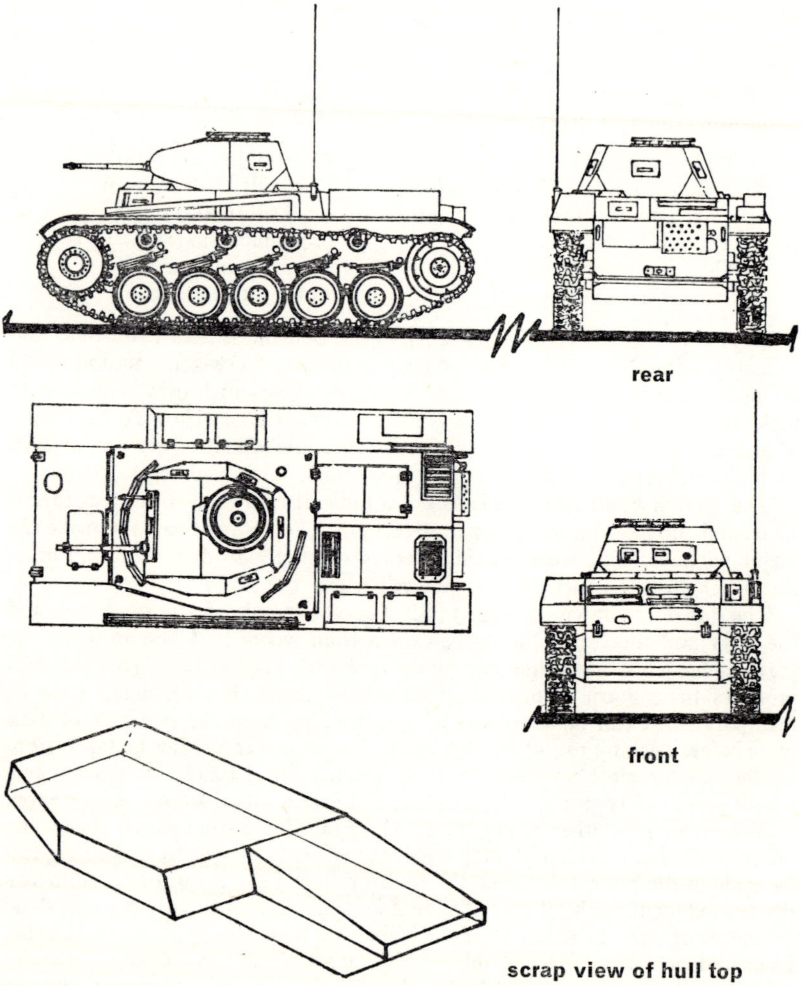

Drawing of Pz II tank 1:76 scale by Max Hundleby.

On post-1945 tanks he also writes: 'With the ending of hostilities in 1945, the armoured forces of the Allies were vastly reduced and the only improvements in the tanks themselves were of a minor technical nature. Thus the Centurion, the main British tank until recently, was only a marginal improvement on the German Panther. With the reduction of quantity there was, at least, an improvement in quality, not only technical, but also in the organisation and equipment of divisions. Thus the opportunity was taken to make the Armoured Personnel Carrier fully tracked and to bring the formation up to full complement; an ideal not attainable in wartime.

'The Russian forces were reduced little and this continuing powerful force, mainly armoured, led to the formation of NATO, their forces being increased and forged into a single command of 15 nations.

'The most important weapon to influence military thinking since the war has been the nuclear device. Due to thick armour, which acts as a shield, the tank is relatively unaffected and can operate over nuclear battlefields with the least inconvenience. The development of tanks was influenced by two ideas, contrasting experiences, the major war and the Korean type sideshow.

'In the first, the powerful battle tank has a place, together with the balanced armoured division. Modern tanks have the necessary technical improvements to fit them for such conditions; for example, multifuel engines, wading capability and air filtering. All mechanised infantry is now carried in armoured carriers though not all are fully tracked and not all allow fighting from inside.

'In the smaller conflict there is a need for a smaller mobile AFV but the duties are almost as well carried out by the efficient APC and this vehicle has been increasingly used for these duties. The tank and APC together will be in demand for a long time to come.'

Tank personnel dress falls into two types; the combat or working dress and the parade or walking out uniforms.

The 1916–18 period personnel wore the ubiquitous service dress of the period, including the peaked cap. This latter was very unsuitable for wear inside tanks. It did not fit close enough to the head and the wearer could not apply his eye to the visor slots or gun sights unless he wore it back to front. Also, continual handling with oily hands stained it. A close-fitting leather crash helmet was in use by 1918, but tank officers were more impressed with the beret-type headdress worn by the French Chasseurs Alpin attached to them that same year. After the war they recommended the adoption of a black beret, not as large as the French, and more like a tam-o'-shanter.

For security reasons up to 1917 the new arm had been known as 'Heavy Section, Machine Gun Corps' and tank personnel wore the MGC badges or that of the regiment from which seconded. Early in that year approval was given for a badge of a Mark I tank without its rear wheels in worsted embroidery to be worn on the upper right arm, and this was adopted in metal as the cap badge of the Tank Corps when it was formed in July 1917, after being inspected in France by King George V.

A distinctive feature of Tank Corps Officers which should be included in any models made was the ash walking stick used by them, when reconnoitring routes or leading tanks up to the start line in mud and darkness, to probe ground that seemed hard on the surface but might be soft underneath.

In 1931 a full dress for officers was approved. The tunic was of blue cloth with black velvet collar and cuffs edged with gold lace, twisted gold shoulder straps and waist sash of black and gold. The trousers were overall type of the same cloth and colour as the tunic with black lace stripe. The black beret was worn in full dress with the addition of a cloth patch brown/red/green behind the badge. The sword carried was infantry pattern with gold/black sword knot and slings. Field officers wore spurs in full dress. In this period the other ranks' equivalent to full dress was the blue patrol jacket and trousers in dark blue with corps embellishments.

For work with tanks black combination overalls came into use; at the Silver Jubilee Royal Review at Aldershot all ranks wore them in a drive past.

The fusion of the cavalry regiments into the Royal Armoured Corps has provided modellers with a number of colourful accessories. These famous old regiments retain a small portion of their last full dress which is worn by the band, parade markers and quarter guards for ceremonial occasions. (It has been alleged that some of the converted lancer regiments affixed lances on the outside of their vehicles; I have never seen this but sub-unit pennants are flown from radio aerials for identification purposes.) All ranks of these regiments now embody in their No 1 Dress shoulder chains of burnished steel and various facings according to their old full-dress colours. In addition, the 5th Royal Inniskilling Dragoon Guards and the 11th Hussars wear trousers and overalls of green and crimson, respectively.

To bring out this type of colour, ceremonial groups make the best models, for example the following ensemble of, say, an armoured regiment in BAOR marching past.

Tanks

3 Tamiya 1 : 35 scale Chieftains
3 Nichimo 1 : 35 scale Centurions
3 Tamiya 1 : 35 scale Saladins (armoured cars)

In the open turrets the figures should be trimmed up to be at 'attention' position; they can have either beret or tank helmet heads. One in each group of three vehicles can be saluting to the right. Making-up of these vehicles is advised in accordance with Chapters 3 and 6 in 'How To Go Plastic Modelling'.

Personnel

(a) **Standard party in old pattern full dress—say Dragoon Guards (Queens, 3rd, 4/7th, or 5th Inniskilling).**

Take six Britains' 'Herald' dismounted Household Cavalry trumpeter figures (these do not have cuirasses). Replace five trumpet arms by four sword arms and one standard arm from other figures. Carefully pare down the jacked-boots tops, etc, with your favourite cutting tool to give overalled leg effect. Add spurs by embedding short pieces of thin pins into heels. Attach shoulder cords and strings to trumpeter figures made of plaited fuze wire. Add standard sling to bearer, made as detailed in Chapter 9. Paint up in accordance with details for regiment of choice.

(b) **Detachment in No 1 Dress**

Take 24 of Britains' US Marines marching (Cat No 7468). Trim down rifles to represent FN type *or* replace with FNs from stretcher bearers (No 4336) for

22 only. For other two, replace arms with sword arm at 'carry' and affix 'empty' scabbards from Civil War figures. Paint up in accordance with details of regiment chosen.

The above will give a good layout of a British Armoured Regiment on a ceremonial parade. The Standard Party in Full Dress can be at the saluting base (with a visiting VIP to take the Salute in Britains' Land-Rover or Champ), and the Detachment in No 1 Dress can be passing the saluting base with the three sections of armoured vehicles in 'one-up' formation following behind.

Picture No 51, a composition of a photograph of a parade of French armour in Paris in 1968, with two of Roy Dilley's models in the foreground, conveys the impression such a grouping can make.

CHAPTER TWELVE

Sea, Air and Civilians

THE INCLUSION of Marines, Sailors and Airmen (as well as of civilian figures associated with the military scene) is a legitimate extension of model soldier collecting. This will be apparent from their inclusion in the producton of toys and models by the manufacturers, as well as the collector's own historical knowledge. What is perhaps more questionable is how far should the model soldier collector go into the realms of collecting ships and boats, balloons, airships and aircraft, as well as civilian impedimenta such as street furniture, buildings, rail layouts and the like?

The answer is, of course, as far as he likes. There are no hard and fast rules determining the collection of models of any sort. It's up to you, the collector, to include them in or, as the late Sam Goldwyn is reputed to have said, 'include them out'. Most collectors of model soldiers find sooner or later that they want to have sailors and airmen because in real life there are few military situations in which they do not figure. To my mind the only aspect to be thought about is how far into other spheres of collecting can you afford (in terms of space and time, as well as money) to go? By this I mean the extensive collecting of ships and aircraft to the same standard, and more or less in the same scale, as the figures themselves.

I do not think we need labour the point. Very few readers of this book are likely to be able to afford fleets of scale ships and aircraft or have the space in which to deploy them. What is worth mentioning, however, is that this should be thought out at the planning stage—when drawing up the Order of Battle. This is what I did, and in my case I saw sailors, marines and airmen appearing mostly in parade groups with soldiers. They had to have a certain amount of their own background as well, and my way of providing this was by a naval dockyard gate, with one or two boats and small ships, putting them in the garb of landing parties or, in the case of air, confining my collection to the period of the Royal Flying Corps. The following historical review of the part played by sailors and airmen may assist the reader in making his own choice.

51. *Armour today: AFVs from Roy Dilley's collection cleverly simulating a typical ceremonial parade in Paris.*

52. *'Colours.' Exhibition model showing Navy and Marine personnel on mock-up cruiser stern. Conversions are from F. Winkler's figures, but modern Britains' Marines and Zoo Keepers could be used instead.*

53. *Group of Marine historical figures made by Rear Admiral C.M. Blackman and presented to RM Museum, Eastney Barracks, Portsmouth. 1:32 scale.*

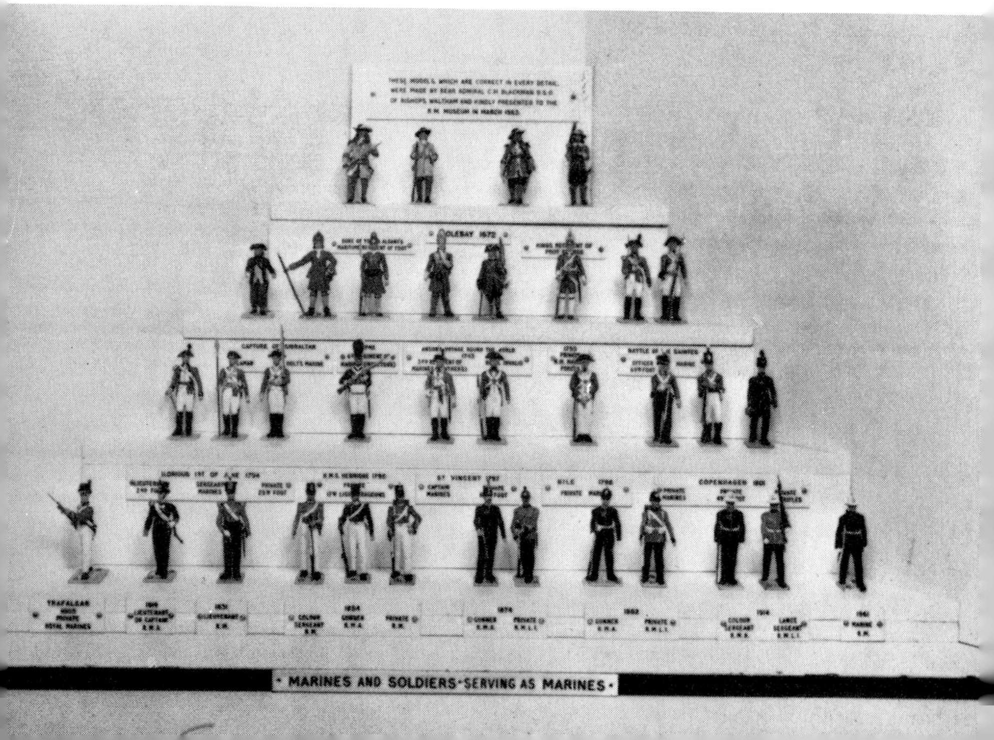

54. *Part of the author's exhibition at the Aldershot Tattoo, 1960, showing models of S.F. Cody and an early aeroplane being moved on a horse-drawn tender.*

55. *RE balloon with winch wagon and crew. Scratch-built by the author, based on contemporary photographs.*

56. *'Horse Marines.' Detail from a group made by Mr and Mrs W.G. Harle of America and presented by them to US Marine Corps exhibit in the Smithsonian Institute (Nat Mus), Washington. (Figures in metal, 55 mm, of Marine mounted detachment in winter dress, Peking pre-1939.)*

Sailors

The first sea fight between collections of ships is lost in the mists of antiquity. One of the earliest recorded is the great fights of Salamis and Artemisiam in 480 BC between the Greeks and the Persians. From this it appears there must have been more on which these and other earlier warriors based their tactics and knowledge.

British tradition is that King Alfred was the founder of the Royal Navy; earlier records indicate that the Romans had fast scouting vessels in British waters, the crews of which wore a garb of blue. (Would this have been of woad?). Alfred's 'navy', however, was not a properly organised permanent force in its own ships, but simply the 'Fyrd' or call-up of able-bodied peasants embarked on a collection of odd ships and boats, impressed for the occasion. Harold had a similar force cruising in the Channel up to September 1066 when he had to let them go to return to their lands. (Poor Harold, probably the unluckiest king in British History; the Normans were, in fact, ready and waiting to put to sea but contrary winds held them back for three weeks, by which time the demands of the thegns to return to get the harvest in compelled Harold to disperse his ships.)

After the Conquest, as part of the Feudal System, the Cinque Ports were ordered to hold a certain number of vessels in readiness, and we know from accounts of the Edwards' and Henry's expeditions to the continent that ships were used for the passage of the soldiers. If cannon were at Sluys in 1346 they would have certainly been manned and fired by the personnel accompanying them, the sailors being there to work the ships. For, throughout the ages up to well after the invention of cannon, sea fights consisted mainly, apart from ramming or setting fire, of getting ships alongside each other, holding on by grappling irons and throwing boarding ladders over, across which soldiers swarmed to do battle with other soldiers as if assaulting a castle or fortified position ashore. The soldiers did the fighting, either because they met other ships sent to stop them coming or because the commander wished to have a go at an opposing fleet. Carthage was one of the ancient powers to employ soldiers regularly at sea; their prowess was so great that at one time they threatened Rome itself. But the Romans quickly copied the Carthaginians' skills and in a sea fight off Sicily defeated the Carthaginian fleet. So Roman legionaries became soldiers at sea, assaulting opposing galleys held alongside their own or jumping ashore from them when they were run up on shallow beaches.

This is not to disparage the part played by the sailors; masters, mates, boatswain, fore-top-men, even the man who beat the big drum to keep the slaves' oars in unison were as important as the soldiers. They sailed or guided the ships towards the enemy, but they didn't do the fighting.

As well as the cannon there was one other development which made the sailor into a fighting man. The opening-up of the New World meant long voyages by ships heavily laden with stores, as well as being fitted out with guns. One of the first ships built primarily for fighting purposes was the 'Great Harry'; so, too, were the 'privateers' (the polite name for nautical highwaymen). In these the place of the soldier had to change from a passenger into a participator. Drake said, 'I will have the gentlemen' (ie the soldier adventurers) 'to hale and draw with the mariners'. But soldiers were still embarked for shorter voyages. The Spanish Armada (which meant army) contained a large number for landing in England, as did the fleet the British sent out to harry them and drive them around the North coasts.

In the 17th and 18th centuries the Dutch and the French Navies were more professional than the British, who still employed as Lord High Admiral, leaders such as Prince Rupert and James, Duke of York, who had, 'one foot in sea and one foot on shore', so to speak. Cromwell's Dutch war produced a great soldier-admiral of this breed, Blake, who was also an exponent of combined operations.

The slow evolution of the gun and the emergence of naval gunnery, in which ships fought each other instead of being mere vehicles to bring fighting men together, then began to impinge on navigation, so a new art came about, naval tactics. The men who sailed the ships now had to know something of ballistics and such fighting formations as line ahead, line abreast, 'crossing the T' and so on down to the famous German naval manoeuvre performed at Jutland 'Gefechtshehrtwendung', or 'all turn away together'.

It is at this time, ie mid 18th century, that British naval officers first had a distinctive uniform. (Readers who can acquire a delightfully illustrated booklet from Moss Brothers will see the whole story of naval dress told lightheartedly but accurately by a Royal Marine officer.) Before that, uniformity was the exception rather than the rule, and this was to continue to be so for men, the ratings, for another hundred years. Paintings and drawings show Naval Officers standing proudly in the ensembles of blue coat, white breeches and hose. The cocked hat was worn variously; for some it was the tricorne, for others it was the bicorne which was worn by some fore-and-aft and others 'athwart ship'. When there were midshipmen, their rank was denoted by brass buttons on the cuff. Another old legend is that this was to deter them from wiping their noses on their sleeves, hence the nickname 'Snottie' by which they were long known. Up to 1795 the officers' ranks were denoted by the amount of gold lace on cuff, breast, and collar. Then the epaulette came in, for lieutenant one on the left shoulder, on next promotion to the right until it eventually became a pair.

The age of steam and technical gunnery brought in first the engineer officer and later other specialist classes, and by late Victorian times the system of rank lace was much the same as we know it today, with distinctive colours between the rows to distinguish the wearer's qualification, ie, purple for engineering, red for surgeons, white for supply branch, etc. Until after the end of the 1939–45 War there was a further distinction in rank lace between the regulars and the RNR* (interwoven lace stripes) and the RNVR* (the 'wavy navy stripe'). Instead of resenting what some might feel was a type of discrimination these reserve officers were intensely proud of the differences and many mourned its replacement by a small 'R' inside the curl on the topmost row. The curl also has a story attached to it. In the Crimean War there was an officer named Elliot who had his hand shot off. He looped a piece of torn lace from his damaged sleeve around one of the buttons of his coat so he might continue in action.

Although at first sight naval dress may appear to be a much simpler matter

* RNR: Royal Naval Reserve; RNVR: Royal Naval Volunteer Reserve.

for modellers there are, in fact, many pitfalls for the unwary. The 1948 Naval Dress Regulations, for example, listed 14 orders of dress together with the occasions on which they were to be worn. The 1957 Defence changes by the British brought about a radical difference in the naval officer structure. The rank lace remains the same, the branch distinctions of colour between has changed. Modellers of the navy today should study these before perpetuating what may be a tragic *faux pas*.

For long, too, there was happily a general resemblance in dress matters between most navies of the world, which the British flattered themselves by assuming was due to their superiority in nautical matters. There is, of course, something in this where the Royal Navy has frequently acted as foster parent, such as to the Japanese in the 19th century and to most of the Commonwealth navies. But new operational conditions in the Pacific in the 1939–45 War caused the US Navy for one to break with traditional dress and adopt a greenish colour tropical uniform, topped by what Britishers think of as a baseball cap. A further blow at the universality of naval dress has been the decision of Canada in 1968 to merge all three services into one with army type dress and rank titles predominating. So, modellers of Canadian naval officers from 1969 onwards, beware!

Up to Tudor times the dress of the seaman was similar to that of the fisherman, but with a belt in which was held privately acquired sword or pistol for defence whenever he might be caught in the general mêlée of soldier-versus-soldier on board his ship. In 1513 crews of the Cinque Port ships are said to have worn 'jacks' (jackets) of white, with St George's crosses thereon. As there was a great deal of tar about on a sailing ship in those days, seamen wore a short canvas apron or skirt to protect their trousers or pantaloons. This garment is a noticeable item in drawings of the period. It is said that the combination of these two articles led to the nickname of 'Jack Tars'.

From Stuart times there was the ship's 'slop chest' whereby certain articles of clothing and materials for making-up laid down by the Navy Board were sold. This gave some measure of uniformity but their wearing was optional. The Dutch and French wars led the British to copy some of the uniformity found in their adversaries' clothing. The 18th century authorised clothing for ratings included a grey jacket, red waistcoat and striped breeches with some extraordinarily fancy hats and stockings.

A curious and colourful feature of the Royal Navy during the Napoleonic period was the liveries worn by the crews of captains' boats and gigs. Rivalry between them for the most smartly dressed (as well as best at rowing) reached great heights of their captain's fancy on colour and style. HMS *Tiger*'s boat's crew wore black and yellow striped jerseys; more than one Scottish flag officer dressed his boat's crew in tartan and HMS *Blazer*'s boat's crew had blue jackets trimmed with white and with brass buttons which may be the origin of the semi-sporty article of attire we call the blazer today. All of these were worn with high top hats. Some crews' outfits were eccentric, such as that of the *Harlequin*, which had to wear a clownish outfit. What they themselves thought and what their messmates and men of other ships said of them is not recorded!

The brutal methods of 'recruiting' seamen, such as the press gang ashore, and by culling a proportion from merchant ships met at sea, retarded the development of the Royal Navy which, from the model collector's viewpoint, is a factor affecting the late evolution of naval dress. But by the early 19th century the 'customary' dress of the sailor was white trousers, blue jacket, and tarpaulin or straw hat plus pigtail. The men themselves made decorative additions to these, including piping and ribbons with or without the ship's name on for the hat.

Uniform dress for ratings was not officially introduced until after the Crimean War, and then it endorsed what was in general wear. Due to the Nelson cult in the Navy certain of the items are said (erroneously) to be in his memory. One such is the three white tapes on the collar to commemorate Copenhagen, the Nile and Trafalgar. The collar itself goes back to 1660, but the regulations specified two stripes. This was during the time the sailor made up his own clothes and it seemes he just liked three stripes instead of two. So after ineffectual attempts to dissuade him the Authorities altered the rule to meet the situation. The black scarf is also said to be a Nelson memento, but was originally a practical item introduced to protect the jacket from the grease of the pigtail, and also for wearing around the forehead in action to protect the eardrums from the noise of the guns and to stop the sweat running into the eyes. Up to the 1939 War there were still recognised breaks in the sailor's routine for him to attend to his clothes—'make and mend' spells—and Rope-Yarn Sunday was the Thursday afternoon set aside for major sewing jobs. Many sailors had sewing machines and also were experts at knitting, crochet, and embroidery. (Perhaps these were some of the things that made 'all the nice girls love a sailor'?)

Part of the 1857 dress regulations was the special dress of petty officers and chief petty officers—dark blue serge jacket with buttons, narrow trousers, white shirt and collar and a peaked cap (known as the 'fore and aft' rig). Certain other junior ratings, such as stewards and writers, also wore a form of fore-and-aft until the 1957 regulations, which laid down that all ratings below petty officers should be 'dressed as seamen'. Up to then also there had been one minor seasonable change in naval dress at home or in temperate waters—the donning of white caps or cap covers on May 1 to denote 'Sumer is encoming inn', and their prompt removal on September 30 to indicate its passing and the onset of wintry weather. British weather had a perverse habit of not complying with the Admiralty and Fleet Orders on this, but it did give a noticeable variety to the dress and made landlubbers aware of the seasons. However, the postwar dress regulations put RN personnel permanently into white plastic cap covers at, it is said, the suggestion of Admiral Mountbatten. At the same time, the jumper and bell-bottomed trousers were given zip fasteners.

Sailors serving ashore have a special attraction for modellers, as they can be integrated with soldiers in a collection, not just in parade groups but as part of contingents where sailors took part in land battles. Ceremonial parade groups of sailors give you the opportunity of including mounted naval officers, which always seems to attract attention, as well as bands and colour parties. The 19th and 20th century wars provide much historical evidence of the part played by sailors, sometimes in places far away from the sea, for example, during the Indian Mutiny of 1857.

The author (a friend of mine) of a book about this wrote, 'As a small boy I was fascinated by the swords, muskets and pistols which I was told had come from Lucknow as part of my great-uncle Edmund Verney's adventures as a young man . . . This seems very odd for I knew Uncle Edmund had been a sailor and I could not understand how he had come to fight on land, such a long way from the sea. . . .' Victorian elders did not encourage questions from small boys so Gerald Verney never found out until he was a grown man and a Major General in the army. When he did, he put it all into a book, an exciting story of the ship his great-uncle served in, HMS *Shannon* and the naval brigade it supplied, one of several to serve ashore during the tragic Indian Army Mutiny of 1857–58. The *Shannon*, a screw frigate of 2,667 tons, had a crew of 510 and 51 guns, mainly 32-pounder and 8-inch. Her Captain, Peel, had won the VC fighting ashore in the Crimea. After going some way up the Ganges as far as they could in boats they landed 24 of their 32-pounder guns for a siege train drawn by oxen and made their way at some two miles per hour to Cawnpore, Lucknow and Futtenshur. They found the bullocks very temperamental: 'sometimes they would take it into their heads to lie down and nothing would induce them to get up until they felt like it. Again they might be frightened (or pretend to be) and rush away down the road to the peril of the wagons and their passengers.'

The sailors wore their normal clothes but were issued with army boots for the long marches and also haversacks and water bottles. They collected many pets, monkeys, parrots, pigs, dogs, cats, mongooses . . . 'Some of the monkeys became very tame and affectionate and would follow their masters like dogs.' When they all got back aboard, Peel complained that the *Shannon* looked more like a menagerie than a ship!

In the 1884 Nile Expedition there was a naval brigade doing what one would expect sailors to be doing—manning the boats of the Nile flotilla—but, in addition, there was a machine gun detachment complete with round straw hats, mounted on camels, for guard and escort work. In the early days of the South African War the Boers had superiority over the British Army in heavy guns, so heavy guns were landed from warships at Cape Town for conversion into siege artillery. Captain Scott, of HMS *Terrible*, devised carriages and wheels from timber baulks and boiler plating and, thus fitted, 20 4·7 inch and 32-pounder guns of that ship set out for the front. (It is this that the 4·7 gun, Cat No 9730 of Britains' is based on and it must now be the oldest item in their catalogue.) Naval Brigades fought at the Modder River and Colenso and the British reverses might have been greater without them. At Graspan they suffered very heavy casualties.

In the 1914–18 War sailors surplus to the fleet were formed into a Naval Brigade which fought in Flanders and also a Division which fought at the Dardanelles. Although untrained in infantry tactics, and without artillery, they scored one of the few successes on the Peninsula. An interesting mixture of dress was worn by naval officers in the Division; Khaki army-type tunics, pantaloons and puttees, Sam Browne belts, naval peaked caps with khaki covers over the crown and gold lace rank insignia on the cuffs of the khaki tunics.

The Naval Division fought on the Somme (dressed as soldiers), where it suffered terrible casualties, but it remained as a formation until the end of the war, taking part in the Final Advance of 1918.

'Lone Star' are the only British firm to make toy sailors at present. Their Naval Officer in Duffel Coat with marine glasses has conversion potential.

The pirate set of Charbens is ideal for portraying 17th–19th century sailors (one figure has a wooden leg, not an uncommon sight in those days; and also a pet monkey). Messrs Britains' 1969 list has a naval cannon with two seamen of the Nelson period (No 9736). The Zoo Keeper—Britains' No 1391—is basically suitable for conversion into a Naval Officer in reefer jacket rig of approximately the 1914–57 period.

Marines

In Britain the first force to be raised as Marines was the 'Lord Admiral of England, HRH Duke of York and Albany's Maritime Regiment of Foot' in October 1664, consisting of 1,200 men taken from the trained bands of London for sea service. This, of course, was not the first regiment to be used on board ship but was the first to be specially so raised. They had uniforms of tawny yellow, carried no pikes and were armed with flintlocks rather than matchlocks in view of the fire risk on board from the latter.

In the next 80 years there were many maritime operations, in the course of which more marines were raised, some of which were transferred to the line as infantry; also some existing infantry served afloat. Most noteworthy in this period was the capture and then successful defence of Gibraltar in 1704—the only battle honour of many to be borne on the Royal Marines' colours. In 1740 a newly raised marine force included companies of 'invalids'—the official designation of men below normal medical category or over age. Many died on a voyage round the world, four obtaining unending fame when, as crew members of HMS *Wager*, they volunteered to be left to certain death on the coast of Patagonia there not being enough room in the boats for them all. They were soldiers, they said, who knew how to die and they shouted 'God Save the King' as the boat left them.

Marines were stationed in Scotland in the '45' rebellion and were at Culloden, but apart from Gibraltar the many other amphibious operations in this period had been mainly failures and showed the need for special forces raised and equipped for sea service. Warships were now making very long voyages and when they stopped to re-provision or repair, often in unfriendly parts, they required a tactical screen of troops ashore to protect them as the crews worked. So, all old marine corps were disbanded and on April 5 1755 a regular body of 50 companies of marines was authorised to be under Admiralty control.

The new Corps served at Majorca, at Quiberon Bay under Admiral Hawke, and were with Wolfe at the capture of Quebec, and most other sea battles of the Seven Years War.

The laurel wreath which encircles the globe in the badge is said to have been won by their action at Belle Isle.

Marines fired some of the opening shots of the War of Independence at Boston, and so impressed was the Congress by them that one of its first actions was to form a Marine Corps which came into existence in November 1775. The British Marines served afloat throughout the French War, and in the naval mutinies at Spithead and the Nore in 1797 Marines were conspicuous by their loyalty.

In 1802, as a result of the representations of Admiral St Vincent, they became the Royal Marines, and their facing colours changed from white to blue. At this time Colonelcies in the Marines were given to naval officers as sinecures. Nelson held one and the Royal Marines' history records that when he was hit at Trafalgar he fell into the arms of a Marine Sergeant-Major. Royal Marines' losses at Trafalgar were heavy due to the exposed positions they had to occupy as marskmen on the top decks and foretops.

In 1804 an artillery company had been added to each division of marines to improve their striking power in combined operations. In 1827 the Corps was granted the badge of the globe instead of further battle honours, King George IV saying 'it was the most proper and distinctive badge for a Corps whose duties had carried them to all parts of the globe in every quarter of which they had earned laurels by their valour and good conduct'. At the same time their motto, 'Per Mare, Per Terram', was approved.

During the Crimean War the marines manned bomb vessels as well as serving ashore as infantry and artillery. Three of the first batch of Victoria Crosses were awarded to Marines—one officer and two men. In 1855 the Marine Corps was designated a light corps, a highly prized distinction in the army, but also in recognition of the type of service they had to perform ashore.

In this period the dress of the two bodies followed generally on that of the army. The Royal Marines Light Infantry wore scarlet tunics edged with white and had blue facings; the Royal Marines Artillery dark blue tunics with facings and piping of red. Both wore a distinctive white helmet surmounted by a brass ball, with a star badge on the helmet front. For drill, training and landing parties both corps wore 'frock' tunics of blue serge without facings, distinguishable only by a difference in buttons. With this, in the early 20th century, they wore a Broderick Cap—named after the politician in whose time it was introduced. This was a peakless type of the modern forage cap (resembling the contemporary German and Russian fatigue cap) and was as much disliked as the loathsome shapeless berets of the 1940s.

Royal Marines were in the international force sent to Peking in 1900 to protect the legations there, and formed a joint unit with the US Marine Corps. Both Corps have the highest regard for each other and share a number of traditions. (See pictures No 52 and 53.)

The United States Marine Corps have also had world-wide service expressed in the lyric 'From the Halls of Montezua to the shores of Tripoli'. They provide special guards for US Presidents and at most embassies; Messrs Britains have in their current catalogue an excellent set of a USMC Colour Party on White House duty. I had the pleasure of researching on this for the firm and found the US authorities most helpful. We discovered that, as a result of the narrow corridors of the White House, the colour party had to march rubbing shoulders. As a precaution against tearing the colour the two flanking men always held their rifles on the outside shoulder. For many years the USMC detachment at Peking included a mounted escort—Horse Marines come true! which US modellers Mr and Mrs W. G. Harle and Mr J. C. Wirth have immortalised in models now in the US Marine Corps Museum. (See picture No 56).

In 1914 a British Royal Marines Brigade was hurried over to try and save Antwerp from the advancing Germans but had to be withdrawn when the Belgians fell back. Photographs of the period show them in marching order with London 'Old Bill' type buses behind them which were part of their transport. In 1915, when the Navy made its first attack on the Dardanelles, parties of marines went ashore with demolition equipment and blew up some Turkish fortifications, and the story is they had a picnic meal before re-embarking. A Marine Brigade formed part of the Naval Division which fought ashore in Gallipoli, and later in France and Flanders. There were nearly 6,000 marines in the 250 British ships at Jutland, manning a quarter of the guns. A marine officer won the VC in HMS *Lion* by, though mortally wounded, giving orders to flood the magazines and so saved the ship from destruction. Total marine losses in the battle were 589. A composite Marine force—'4th Bn'—took part in the St George's Day landing at Zeebrugge, the raid which tried to block the German submarine base. Two VCs were won and the Admiralty decided, as a mark of honour, that no other unit would be given the number '4th'. A Royal Marine battalion was in the British final advance in November 1918, as one Divisional Commander put it—'On starboard bow of the army'.

US Marines were among the first American forces to land in France in 1917 in 1 and 2 Divisions, but did not go into action until the following year. They also manned railway-mounted heavy guns. In 1923, as part of the British post-war economies, the RMLI and the RMA were amalgamated. The common uniform adopted was that of the 'Blue Marines' (Royal Marine Artillery) with minor variations.

In the 1939–45 War Commandos are popularly associated with the Marines, but in point of fact the first commandos were army special volunteers. As the nature of their activities was amphibious it was only natural that Marines should also take part and at the end it was logically decided that this rôle should be given exclusively to the Royal Marines. Apart from Commando work, Marine units and brigades, dressed and equipped as soldiers, were in action in Norway, Holland and at Calais and Boulogne in 1940. They fought in the last rearguard action in Crete and in the Dieppe raid the following year, incurring heavy casualties at both.

In the siege of Singapore, Marine survivors of HM ships *Prince of Wales* and *Repulse* were formed into a composite unit with survivors of 2 Bn Argyll and Sutherland Highlanders, which was appropriately known at the 'Plymouth Argylls.' The Royal Marine Division was the main formation in the capture of Madagascar, Marine Commandos were among the first troops ashore at Sicily and in the fiercely contested Salerno landings. A large force of Marines were in the NW Europe invasion forces, manning guns on ships, and in Commando and armoured support groups ashore. They were also in the crossing of the Rhine operation and in the last amphibious operations at the Scheldt Estuary and Walcheren. In the Far East Royal Marines assisted in the take-over of the forts in Tokio Bay.

The US Marine Corps also played a major part in this war, the US Pacific strategy of capturing islands making their rôle in this almost indispensable. The hoisting of the US Flag on the top of Iwo Jima in 1945 was done by Marines, although it has since been stated it was a posed photograph and not that of a cameraman taken spontaneously. In the Korean and Vietnam operations the USMC has emerged as a self-contained 'pocket' army with its own integrated armour, air, artillery and supporting services. Two years ago this force was larger than the whole British Army. It is the elite force of America, in some ways analogous to Napoleon's Imperial Guard.

Other nations with naval traditions also maintain Marine Corps. Brazil, for example, has had Marines since 1808, when a Portuguese Naval Brigade brought the Portuguese Royal Family into temporary exile from Napoleon. Today, they are 10,000 strong, distributed round the long Brazilian coastline. They also recently took part in the Inter-American Peace Force which guaranteed order and tranquillity in the disturbed Dominican Republic.

Good quality plastic Royal Marines in blue with white helmets are available ex-Messrs Britains' Eyes Right series. They require little more than careful painting to turn into presentable models. A simple but effective change can be made by painting some as Royal Marine Light Infantry, ie, with Scarlet Tunics. If this is done, however, it will be necessary to change their rifles to the Lee-Enfield type of the early 1900s. Marines of today in combat dress are easily portrayed by taking any of the toy action fighters and re-painting as Commandos, ie, green beret (if appropriate), with blue shoulder 'flashes' indicating the Marines' special arm sign. (Royal Marine recruiting literature gives examples of this.)

Airmen

The first record of anyone attempting flight is the Greek Legend of Icarus who flew with his father from Crete but, going too near the sun, the wax with which his wings were fastened melted and he fell into the Aegean Sea. Leonardo da Vinci visualised a flying machine—an airship with flapping wings—but his design lay hidden until Victorian times.

In the late 17th century there was much experimenting with balloons using hot air. The discovery of hydrogen gas by Cavendish in 1760 gave this work an impetus and there were many ascents. In 1784 and '85 ascents were made in Dublin, one of which, coming down in the sea, had to be rescued by a boat. The first-ever air-sea rescue, surely! In 1794, at the Battle of Fleurus, the French general Jourdan used a balloon to survey the Austrian lines. This must be the first recorded aerial reconnaissance. In 1785 two men drifted in an airship across the English Channel, but this does not appear to have caused much concern, and in 1852 a man called Giffard made a powered flight in an elongated balloon drawn by a steam-driven propeller. Balloons were used for scouting in the American Civil War and in some of their little wars against the Indians afterwards. In 1867 both sides in the Brazilian–Paraguayan War used them but the British Government, to whom the use was pointed out, was not impressed. Balloons were used by the French during the siege of Paris to operate a postal service.

Ballooning in the British Army began in 1878 when two officer enthusiasts were allotted £150 for experimental work. Some of their early problems were the leakage of hydrogen from the balloon fabric and the cumbersome equipment required to store the gas. The first was solved by discovering a material known as goldbeaters skin, the making of which was a closely guarded secret of a family in the East End of London. They refused to divulge it, but eventually were persuaded to do so by the whole family being taken into Government employ. Their secret processes were preserved until 1912.

Thanks to the enthusiasm of a few officers, military ballooning made progress. An RE officer took some very successful photographs of the Halifax, Nova Scotia, fort from a balloon in 1883 and balloons were on active service in Bechuanaland and the Sudan in the following year. These operations were very hampered by difficulties in transporting gas, but a report said that 'the presence of the balloons gave the troops confidence'. Ascents were made in 'marching order' of scarlet tunics, riding breeches, knee boots, spurs, helmet, belts, swords and sabretaches. The slightly unconventional RE Officer who discarded some of these items received a reprimand from watching staff officers! A balloon detachment went with the British Contingent to Peking, where ascents were made and equipments compared with other balloonists there. Balloons acquitted themselves well in the South African War, where they were used widely in reconnoitring, sketching and gun spotting. The Boers, who had no balloons, disliked the British balloon activities and made great efforts to bring them down. Balloons were most vulnerable near the ground and the ground crews became highly skilled in rapid hauling down and letting up (see picture No 55).

In 1906 balloons were supplemented by Cody's man-lifting kite. Cody was a picturesque personality of genius who, in his early days, had been a stunt cowboy and he brought his long hair, large cowboy hat and enormous spurs with him to Farnborough. During the early army trials of his kites he used to provide light relief for the troops by lasso displays and shooting down glass balls and coins thrown up in the air at full gallop. He was also associated with early fixed-wing aircraft experiments. He made the first officially observed flight at Farnborough on October 5 1908—a distance of 500 yards. He contributed greatly to British military aviation—both airships and aeroplanes—until he was killed in August 1913 testing a machine for landing on both ground and water (see picture No 54).

Count Zeppelin's success with dirigibles in 1900 led to experiments in Britain with airships, some of which were humorous as well as thrilling. In 1907 one flew to London and encircled St Paul's Cathedral; strong head winds prevented the return journey by air so it was brought down in Crystal Palace and, part-dismantled, came back to Farnborough by road. In 1910 HMA *Beta* achieved a speed of 32 mph driven by a radial air-cooled REP engine with two propellers abreast of the chassis. At first there were only rudimentary navigational instruments and airships frequently got lost in cloud or fog. *Beta* once just missed colliding with the spire of Salisbury Cathedral; and on another occasion, returning to Farnborough, short of lift and ballast, petrol cans had to be hastily jettisoned over St Michael's Abbey, narrowly missing the monks strolling in the grounds absorbed in their breviaries. Another airship returning collapsed in the garden of an officer's quarter, coming to rest outside the window of a room in which his wife was dressing for dinner. (A part of my model of *Beta* can be seen in the background of picture No 57.)

Fixed-wing aircraft development had an equally exciting beginning. Proceeding from gliding experiments in Britain in 1906, the early efforts were disappointing and the War Office banned further expenditure. The enthusiasts, however, carried on their work at private expense in Scotland. The Marquis of Tullibardine gave loan of his estates and keepers, and ghillies of the Duke of Atholl's private army kept intruders away. Then in 1909 Louis Bleriot flew the Channel and a new era was ushered in. (The French, as a result of Government encouragement, were well in advance in aircraft construction at this time.) Re-appraisal of the military aspects of aviation led to the purchase and building of various aircraft, some of which were of novel design, such as the 'tailfirst' type. Names which are part of British aviation history now appear—Hon C. S. Rolls and his tailfirst SEI, Mr G. De Havilland with his specially designed Farman-type bi-plane, and the Duke of Westminster and his 60 hp Wolseley propelled Voison pusher bi-plane.

All these efforts gradually overcame official reluctance and in April 1911 the developing arm was officially formed as the Air Battalion, Royal Engineers. A few months later it formed the nucleus of a separate air arm; the Royal Flying Corps was formed in May 1912 with a Naval and a Military Wing and a central flying school on Salisbury Plain.

The khaki uniform for the corps was completely different from the rest of the army, the most distinctive feature being the plastron fronted tunic. This was primarily to protect the wearer against the wind whilst flying, but it was issued to all RFC personnel. Bit by bit necessary items of flying kit were added, helmets, motoring goggles, thick gloves and lined boots, but many pictures of RFC men taken outside messes, or gathered around aircraft show them in the service dress of various other arms and corps. A full dress uniform was designed but never taken into general use. A specimen is held in the Imperial War Museum (see picture No 57).

The Royal Air Force uniforms have a lot of interest for model soldier collectors. A full dress for officers of blue-grey, following the cut of that for infantry, was introduced; with it was worn a waist sash and a sword with white metal scabbard. The most distinctive feature was the head-dress—a small round-topped busby-type cap with a large plume in front. The ordinary service uniform was of the same colour—a tunic modelled on the army item, worn with pantaloons and puttees of the same colour and with a peaked forage cap. The rank lace worn on the cuff will be so well known that I need not detail it here. The RAF Band's dress uniform is of a special material with gold braiding on collars, shoulders and cuffs, not unlike the officer's full dress for which it has sometimes been mistaken.

Uniforms of the RAF in the Second World War differed but slightly. The pantaloons and puttees were replaced by trousers and, like the soldiers', all ranks adopted battledress and collars and ties. Press photographs abound of RAF types wearing all sorts of combinations of non-regulation dress and undress, a favourite mixture being uniform trousers, woollen slipover and a gay cravat or scarf. Pilot Officer Prune and Squadron Leader Prang will be found in many magazines and journals.

Out of the last war emerged a special RAF unit which is, so to speak, right up the modeller's street. This is the Royal Air Force Regiment. Formed to provide protection for airfields and for general security, this unit has rapidly built up a well-deserved reputation for smartness in dress and drill. It includes a Queen's Squad of specially picked men, which is to be seen often at Tournaments and Tattoos.

Civilians

Many collectors tend to look at toy civilians with the eye of a recruiting sergeant—what military types can they be turned into? And there is no doubt that a modeller with imagination can get the most surprising results from a clever, but often simple, conversion.

In the good old days of lead toys there was a great variety of both country and town figures; farmers with their wives, milkmaids milking and carrying pails on a yoke, carters, ploughmen, shepherds and drovers. Then there was a whole range of railway people, too, engine drivers, firemen, guards, porters and also passengers—men with overcoats slung over one arm, men with bowler hats, men with straw boaters, women in various styles and also children. There were as well clergymen (two types—high and low church), boy scouts, blacksmiths, navvies, coalmen, costermongers, footballers (but never cricketers) and policemen. For two or three years after the end of the last war, as well as the production by the larger firms (Britains, Hills and Crescent), there were innumerable small firms producing pirated versions as well as original lines of their own. There was also a wide range of horse-drawn vehicles, farm carts, wagons, milk floats and traps. Collectors who could look in on the toy and model shops in the big towns almost always found something new.

My friend Roy Dilley was a great snapper-up of such items, which he usually saw through the eyes of a recruiter. One of his most brilliant coups was the acquisitioning of a lot of Britains' AA Road Scouts. Whenever I look at his collection I see an additional officer who unmistakably has the slim legginged leg of an AA man, and it makes me very envious!

But nowadays the range is much smaller, so there is little point in describing the wonderful changes we did in the past. In the here and now there are very few. Britains' still produce a farmer and a farmer's daughter (but no farmer's wife!), a trousered land girl, a driver, a shepherd and two labourers. They also make two Zoo Keepers (one of whom also doubles as the human in their Chimpanzee's Tea Party). Among the four horsedrawn vehicles there is one solitary figure—a plastic milkman with the milk float. There is, too, a family in the Floral Garden range of five adults, two teenagers, two children and a dog which can be adapted to a number of other rôles. Crescent and Cherilea also produce a few farm workers, and Airfix have a set of spectators and track officials for model motor racing. Apart from Cowboys and Indians made by the above and a few other small firms that's the lot.

Cowboy and Indian toys have possibilities; their horses can be used to vary action groups, but the legs of the riders need a lot of cutting down to obtain the neat-booted effect of regular cavalry. It is better to use only the horses, but the collector must remember to give them a full set of head harness and saddlery.

Some collectors try and build up all the trappings of a community around their military figures, creating a garrison town, complete with outlying farm, a railway and civilian road traffic. I am content with introducing the fringe of these to my military scene; a bus or tram by the barrack gate, a nursemaid pushing a pram, a newspaper boy and, of course, children and dogs. Wherever soldiers march by there are always children, and whoever saw a parade in real life on to which a dog has not strayed at some part of the proceedings?

CHAPTER THIRTEEN

Displays and Exhibitions

A VERY IMPORTANT PART of collecting model soldiers is where to keep them. The simplest solution is to wrap them up and put them in boxes in a cupboard, under the stairs or under the bed. This may be necessary at times, but no collector will accept this as the final solution of his collection's storage. Collectors are always proud of their pieces, whether made by themselves or acquired from an expert of the art, and part of the pleasure of collecting is to regard the items from time to time and have them admired. It can, in fact, be an excellent form of relaxation to go and sit in front of a case of your models and let your eyes travel over them, recalling their acquisition, when, where and why you obtained them. A further pleasure is, of course, to display your treasures to others, whether it be at your home or in an exhibition. It is very hard at times to convince non-collectors of the value of a model. To such a person there is often nothing discernible between the good toy and the item you have perhaps spent a hundred hours on, from researching, through visualising, converting or casting, to painting. Meaning well, and to be polite, such a person will grab the model and distort some protruding detail or perhaps drop it! Models have to be protected from their admirers, but they have to be seen as well.

In Chapter 8 of *How To Go Plastic Modelling** the author gives much excellent advice on displaying, which I feel is worth summarising again here. (I also especially endorse his Laws of Domestic opposition!)

(1) Do not leave delicate or intricate models on sideboards, window ledges or mantelpieces, etc.

(2) Dust is one of the greatest enemies of all models.

(3) Protection from dust is often protection from clumsy handling (and misappropriation!).

(4) Polythene display cartons or units are good *temporary* display protection.

(5) Simple showcases in the whitewood kitchen cabinet series are good *permanent* display units. They can be painted to choice and their sliding front

* Published by Patrick Stephens Ltd at 25s.

panels can be replaced by similar pieces of clear glass. They should be hung *firmly* before heavy models are in.

(6) In addition to hanging units, such 'do-it-yourself' furniture as three-shelf bookcases with sliding glass fronts are comparatively inexpensive storage/display cases. Usually 36 inches wide by 10 inches deep, the three levels give you 1,000 square inches—enough for 200–300 mixed mounted and dismounted figures. Such a unit can be purchased for £5–£6.

(7) Secondhand furniture—here one just has to keep looking out for 'something'. If you've decided on an old china cabinet it will be the last thing you'll see! Keep an open mind on the style, shape and size and weigh up critically all the potential items in the dealers' shops as you come upon them. I have an excellent storage cabinet for 300–400 figures arranged in seven pull-out drawers (four with trays), which began life as a birds' egg collector's cabinet. All I did was to baize line the drawers and put in sheets of thin clear glass as lids to them.

In addition to the above 'Ellis Rules' I would add the following:

The majority of toy and model soldiers available at present are in 54/55 mm scale, so collectors of these have to 'think bigger' than those who go in for 1:72 and HO/OO sizes.

Collectors do tend to allow their enthusiasm to overcome their normal good sense, which can be embarrassing at one's home. I remember once calling on a friend who was going through a phase of making large flat plywood soldiers 9 inches high or so (he is very expert at the flat type of figure). He and his wife were at tea so I excused myself and, to make light conversation, looked quickly around their sitting room for anything to discuss. Along the wall next to the communicating doors with his 'den' was a large shelf full of plywood grenadiers marching briskly towards the next wall. It seemed new to me so I blurted out—'Oh, I see you are beginning to display your models in here now'. There was a silence, then my friend's wife said coldly, '*That* wasn't there when I went out this afternoon.' He said nothing and I got away as soon as I decently could afterwards.

The moral of this, of course, is to have, if possible from the beginning, an 'understanding' about where and when you can display models in your home. To those who have a den, study, or bed-sitter this is fairly easy to arrange—but, if you have such a place and leave fragile pieces about, you should also assume responsibility for the tidiness (if not the cleanliness) of this room. You should very strictly confine your models to it to keep your side of the bargain. The day will come when you need more 'lebensraum' and it is then good 'public relations' to win over interest by inviting attention to your latest additions, either by making a good display in an attractive case, which would harmonise with another room, or by putting them out in the garage, shed, or even WC. If they are colourful, sooner or later, *someone* will say 'That's a nice case (or picture frame, etc) you have. Why don't you bring it in here and put it in that corner near the window?'

The 'picture frame' idea mentioned above is not a new one; I have seen it in many versions, from the ornate gilt to the severe trendy style. One acquires the frame and then replaces the picture by a shallow box—not more than 2–3 inches deep, otherwise it will project too far out on the wall and spoil the effect. A back, painted in some light contrasting colour, the area divided by glass shelves, and you have a most attractive display unit. Don't forget to make the box part reasonably easy for access for when you want to change the exhibits!

Damp is another but more insidious enemy of models. Some collectors may have no option but to hang thin-sided cases on outside walls or in outhouses. These should have some form of damp insulation between the surfaces and, where space permits, small quantities of silica gel should be put unobtrusively inside the cases and changed at intervals.

There are two other display-storage items which I have evolved and which deserve mention. Starting with a small section of model wall with an archway gate in it I have gradually progressed to a series of three-dimensional buildings in what I call 'telescoped' 1:32 scale. By this I mean that heights of doors, windows, entrances, etc, are suitable but length and depth have been reduced for space reasons. Some of these are, if not exact replicas, 'after' actual buildings, eg, my Horse Guards Parade (see picture No 60), Grand Entrance to Woolwich Arsenal and Prince Consort's Library, Aldershot; others are what film scenario writers say, 'based upon an idea', to give the most appropriate background to the figures to be displayed. A feature of all these I would like to mention is that I made use of their '3-D properties' by having them hollow as far as possible, with roofs as lids, and use them for storing the figures for which they act as a background.

Sooner or later, whilst building up your collection, you will be asked to put on a display somewhere as part of your Society's Exhibition, or in support of a charity or as a promotional item in connection with a film or trade show. You will naturally be delighted and do all you can to 'air' that portion of the collection packed away; this spurs you on to finish off those long outstanding items you've been talking about and also stimulates new ideas as a result of the show itself. But there are a number of snags in such a display, some of which one has to accept, and others which a little tact and experience will eliminate.

The display will almost always be on a 'stand'. I put it thus as some 'stands' turn out to be a couple of trestle tables. The troubles with this are:

(1) It will not be firm enough. Visitors will push and jostle and bump against it and knock the figures over.

(2) It will almost certainly not be big enough for the display you have been visualising, so rearrangement becomes necessary.

(3) It will have absolutely no form of protection against prying or acquisitive fingers.

(4) To protect it you will have to supervise it personally all the time the display is on.

(5) If in a marquee or in a hall for several days or more the amount of dust from normal walking in and out of visitors, plus the activities of cleaners, will take the bloom off your treasures.

The way to avoid the above and other difficulties is to know of the exhibition as soon as possible. A model soldier society knows of all this and their approach is basically to eliminate the problems, *if* they themselves have control of the hall, stands, etc. But even the most experienced advertising and display firms may not have put on model soldiers before and will not be aware of these headaches. Get to see the exhibition organisers as soon as you can give them *your* idea of what *you* want in the way of a stand; provide a sketch showing:

(1) Overall dimensions, with key to layout of model groups, etc.

(2) How stand is to be made bump-proof—affixed to floor, ground or wall by brackets; if in sections, trussed firmly together.

(3) Pilfer-proofing. Either by roping off at least three feet away from nearest models or by a screen of glass or Perspex about two feet high erected all around the edge. If it is up against a wall, incidentally, or one side is to have a backcloth, these will serve in part substitute.

(4) Lighting required. You may want to animate your scene by having parts of it unlit at times—for instance, to convey searchlight tattoo effect. This must be mentioned as soon as possible to make sure it fits in with the organiser's overall lighting plan.

You may find, of course, that it is impossible to obtain the size of stand you hoped for, and in such a case there is nothing you can do about it except to adjust your layout accordingly. But you should try and be as tactfully firm as you can over the other matters; after all, it is as much in the organiser's interest as yours that your exhibit should look smart all the time the show is on. As part of this smartness, try and ensure that your stand's title and any captions about the models are up to professional standards. If you can't do these yourself you will probably find that the organisers will supply them as part of their overall style for the show if you let them have the necessary copy. Another item which adds to overall smartness is to have the legs or supports of the stand concealed. Here again the organisers may have made something for all stands. But if your display is a 'one-off' they may not have thought of it so mention it at an early stage. They may only provide coloured draping paper, but whatever it is it will enhance the appearance of the display and also provide a screen under which you can stow all the cases and cartons in which you brought the models.

The only satisfactory way of laying out such a display of loose figures is to do it yourself. You know the groupings, having visualised them previously, and probably you even had a dress rehearsal at home. So you must fit in with the organiser's timetable for this, even if it means being there late the night before or, more likely than not, having to do it at the last moment because of some hold-up, and be putting the last few out as the VIP who is opening the show approaches! (See picture No 58 for an example of this!) But this is inevitable with exhibitions and it is no good going in for them unless you accept this sort of thing. Organisers do not leave everything until the last moment from choice, but there is so much dove-tailing-in to be done that one snag can throw their timetable out of gear. I always vow at the time, especially during the aftermath when I am packing up, surveying my 'damages' or hunting for missing figures, stiff and tired with leaning over the layout that I'll never do another! But I always do and I always learn a little more each time about how to put on such a display.

The above remarks refer to the (more or less) temporary display, ranging from the one-day village fête to a local trade fair of a few days or in support of a military tattoo or a 'good cause' exhibition of a week or so. In these, in my experience anyway, it has always been a matter of a large layout, specially set up for the occasion. But there are others. A lively model soldiers' society like, say, Harry Middleton's in the Manchester area, can participate in most

57. *Types of Royal Flying Corps 1914. Britains' and Hills' 54 mm metal figures converted by the author.*

58. *The author's centenary display at Prince Consort's Library, Aldershot, just before the opening ceremony.*

59. *An example of a home display hanging wall case (glass door open), 28 inches wide × 32 inches long × 4 inches deep, holding approximately 200 assorted figures.*

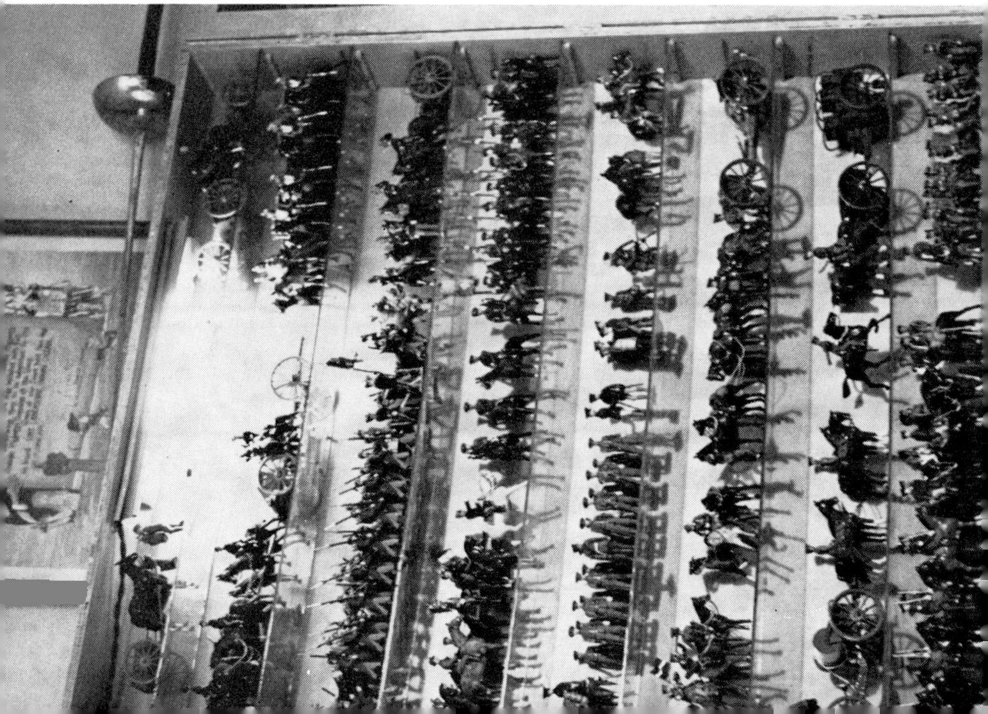

60. *Example of 'telescoped' 1:32 scale buildings. The author's Horse Guards Parade units, which are hollow and permit storage and transit of associated model soldiers.*

61. *An example of a diorama (case removed for photograph), at the Northern Model Soldier Group exhibition at Oldham Museum, 1968. Left to right: Messrs H. Middleton, J.W. Carter (Director of Museum), J. Fielding, D. Goodman and Max Hundleby.*

62. *'Les Adieux de Fontainbleau', diorama by M M. Meitschel in 55 mm metal French figures at 1960 Paris Exhibition.*

63. *An example of the author's portable exhibition units—small dioramas in old TV cabinets.*

64. *Wellington and his Staff. Conversions by W.Y. Carman, the historical modeller, from Britains' metal castings. These pieces are at least 30 years old.*

65. *'Blinded by gas'—diorama in TV cabinet—after painting by Sergant.*

66. *'Let battle begin!'—Donald Featherstone (right) explaining the wargame to actress Anette Whiteley and Major York of the Middlesex Yeomanry. (Note this officer's uniform as described in Chapter 11—page 138.)*

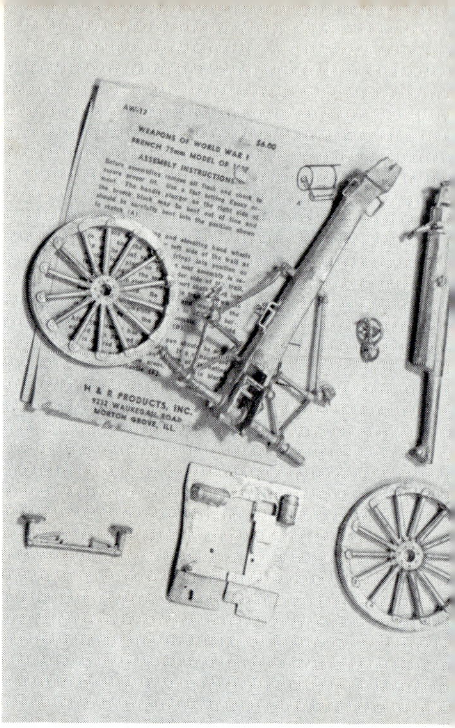

67. *Scratch-built waterline model of British 1914 submarine in 1:32 scale; a vessel which does not involve problems of size.*

68. *An example of a kit of a metal gun—1914–18 type 75 mm field gun in 1:32 scale, supplied with full assembly instructions. An H-R Product, USA.*

69. *Metal mould. Casting achieved by pouring lead through hole at figure's feet whilst held by clamps. E. Walker, Liverpool.*

social, cultural and trade shows if they become known and form an active and continuing part of local life. Harry Middleton and his lads (if I may call them that) have, by lots of hard work and great enthusiasm, put model soldiers on the map in that part of England. Some of the exhibitions they take part in last for months and call for considerable planning. Such as these lend themselves to another form of display layout—the diorama.

Dioramas are defined as 'pictorial representations, partly lit up by strong reflected light hidden from spectators, partly by transmitted light and seen through an opening in a partition—a dissolving view . . .' With some variation as to subject and layout this covers most dioramas. They are seen at their best in museums, especially in the US, in France (at Normandy and Strasburg) and at Kulmbach Castle in South Germany.

Essential elements of dioramas are that the figures in them are fixed for permanent or semi-permanent display and also that they contain scenery. The scenic factor enters into this form of model soldier display very much, and my view is that, despite the above definition, without well contrived scenery model layouts fail to achieve their objectives as dioramas.

Up to quite recently the classical flat figure, as evolved in Germany, was the ideal model, but diorama makers are now resorting to the 1:72 and HO/OO sizes more and more, and the Airfix range in this scale is wide enough to meet most requirements. As with 'free' displays, some thought must be given to the quantity of figures to be deployed and once the size of case or cases is decided upon the next most important aspect is the internal terrain. Free standing displays limit the use of 'terrain' severely, but when the figures are to be fixed the subject can be given full scope.

To those entirely without ideas on miniature landscaping I would suggest one of several books on railway model layout, and I also endorse John Ahern's 'Landscape Modelling'. But most readers will have a few ideas of their own to which I would offer the following for inclusion:

(a) Large areas of undulation can be made by an underlay of wire netting. Lightweight wood blocks, rolls of old cloth pieces, etc, underneath will provide basic foundation for the features. This can be covered by material of the hessian type, which can be pressed and folded into the desired hollows and areas of dead ground. Papier-maché-type egg containers can be easily reshaped by soaking in water and then squeezing about as required; these are particularly good for gun emplacements, trenches and torn-up battle areas.

(b) Soil, grass, etc, can be depicted in a number of ways. The railway versions will probably suit many people; others may prefer a layer of wet sand which can be painted over (but remember, for lifting purposes, that sand is very heavy). A mixture of sawdust with thin paint of the desired colour is also effective. That wonderful 'do-it-yourself' material, Polyfill, also has a hundred and one uses in the diorama, either as a base or as a medium.

(c) Trees can be a mixture of the many realistic models available, with a judicious mixture of actual twigs. For shelled or devastated areas of the 1918 Western Front type, twigs on their own give a most realistic effect.

(d) Ponds, pools, shell holes, etc, are best simulated by pieces of glass painted to give the desired reflection of surroundings and sky (just in case anyone should not know—you paint the *under* side of the piece of glass, thus leaving the upper part to catch the light as well as simulate reflection).

(e) Buildings are at present in good supply for most scales. Messrs Britains and Timpo have a good series of buildings in 54 mm, basically of the Farm and Ranch type but which will lend themselves to almost anything. Bombed or shelled houses can be quickly built up from balsa wood, the ubiquitous Polyfilla and sheets of brickwork from the railway hobby shops.

(f) Lighting of the diorama is all important, just as it is in stage production. A modeller who builds up some expertise in the use of lighting can dispense with a lot of scenery, and a lot of models. This is an aspect well worth going into with some personal experiments and the results will always be exciting. A different aspect of lighting dioramas is the deliberate one of providing switches in front for viewers to press on. This is important but is more an aid to animation than to scenic effect.

Making a diorama on the above lines for exhibition for some months, or even years, at a museum, is not to be entered into lightly, and it is not for the beginner to rush into as it calls for skills over and above those found in the usual collector. Dioramas also tie up quantities of your collection; you can't do anything else with these models whilst they are embedded in the terrain of a large dust-proof and pilfer-proof case. If you have made the figures for that purpose only that does not worry you; but if you would like some out for something else it can be awkward.

I am not a diorama man myself—few collectors of 54/55 mm figures are, for obvious reasons. But I have made up small groups of figures for specific purposes and for these I have evolved a sort of mini-rama using as the basic case old television cabinets of the deep variety. They are still very easy to acquire, providing you are prepared to take them 'as is', ie, complete with their useless worn-out innards which you have to take out and dispose of. But when this is done you are left with a trimmed polished cabinet in which to erect a platform and layout of your group of figures plus scenery. A small strip-light fitted inside, and suitably screened, provides all the lighting and a round backcloth gives a good perspective effect. If the cabinet is one of those that had its controls in front, a title or long caption can be placed over the apertures. I have six such mini-ramas for groups which do not form part of any order of battle, and with these can provide a display of models at literally a moment's notice.

CHAPTER FOURTEEN

Wargames

By Donald F. Featherstone

THE DUKE OF WELLINGTON compressed his lips and dug tightly clenched fingers into sweat-damp palms. He was fast losing his composure. The tight-packed squares of red-coated British infantry were being torn and shattered by showers of grape-shot from French guns. He wondered whether they would be strong enough to beat off the fierce attack about to come from the cavalry massed colourfully at the foot of the Mont St Jean. On the far side of the battlefield, Napoleon loosed up the gentle slope his Cuirassiers, his Dragoons, his Hussars and his Lancers. At full gallop, the cavalry crashed into the British squares to send them reeling in disorder. Napoleon ordered forward the Imperial Guard—he knew he had the battle in his pocket now. The Duke of Wellington made a gesture of despair, his voice was choked with emotion:

'All right! I'll concede!'

Britain had lost the battle of Waterloo—but there was always another day! The lights were switched off and the miniature combatants, so recently locked in fierce combat, were frozen in attitudes of belligerence. Wellington and the Emperor Napoleon reverted to their substantive ranks of physiotherapist and accountant—another Thursday evening wargame had ended.

This puzzling reversal of history will not affect the destiny of Europe one little bit because it is not war but a wargame, the soldiers are only one inch in height, the ridge at Waterloo and the undulating ground around it are moulded in sand, realistically coloured with distemper, the farms of Hougomont and La Haye Sainte are made to scale in wood and plastic and laid out on a large table 12 feet long by 6 feet wide. The battle might be part of a campaign that has been going on for months, and it may proceed for another year before Wellington asks for an armistice after failing to throw back a French invasion on the South coast of England.

Wargames with model soldiers are no new craze, they have been fought both as a pastime and as military training since the 17th century, when the Princes of France were taught, with model soldiers, how to command the fine French Armies, the best troops in Europe. The idea took a real hold in the second half of the last century when the manufacture of lead soldiers became almost an art. The military minds of the major European nations used wargames to work out tactics for their future wars—the Schlieffen Plan for the invasion of France and Belgium in 1914 was worked out on the wargames table, but they must have done something wrong because it did not work out in real life! The German defeat of the Russians at Tannenberg in 1914 had been practised for years as a sand table exercise—but the Czar was not to know this! Today, practically every army in the world uses sand tables and models to train their soldiers and the writer recalls with nostalgia a model landscape in the Tank Regiment Depot in Dorset, where model tanks were made to manoeuvre by means of magnets under the table!

Model soldier collecting became really popular during the second half of the last century, when makers in Germany, France and Great Britain began to turn out the large and relatively cheap 54 mm (2⅛ inch) figures so well known during our boyhood days. Now, human nature being what it is, no boy will be content with amassing large and gleaming armies to merely be stood upon shelves and looked at with covetous pleasure. He soon wants to *do* something with them, so he lines them up and fires wooden shells at them from a toy cannon. But this soon palls and he seeks something less childish, a pastime that requires skill and which provides some sort of situation in which he can pit his brains and cunning aganist an opponent. Most of us are frustrated generals at heart and field-marshal's batons imaginatively exist at the bottom of every boy's (and man's) wardrobe!

Most boys collect model soldiers at some time in their lives, but only a few of the more enlightened carry the fascinating hobby into later life. This is a pity, because there is considerable skill and research required to turn out accurate figures of Napoleonic troops in all their colourful glory, or even the less ornamental modern infantryman with his great variety of weapons and equipment. It is a hobby that puts one in good company because many famous men have found enjoyment and relaxation in fighting battles with model soldiers. Tin soldiers were the chief amusement of the boyhood days of Sir Winston Churchill, who commanded one army and his brother Jack the other. They had 1,500 men each, organised as an infantry division with a cavalry brigade—typically, Winston's army could muster 18 guns whilst his brother Jack was allowed no artillery and only coloured troops! Today, model soldiers are collected by many well-known people—Charlton Heston, hero of many a screen battle, has a fine collection; so have actors Peter Cushing and Douglas Fairbanks. Television actor Deryck Guyler not only has probably the finest model Roman Army in this country but is also an authority on the period. The Swedish Ambassador in London and at least two famous dress designers are avid collectors, as are men of all ages and from all walks of life.

Two famous writers had much to do with the birth of wargaming—Robert Louis Stevenson and H. G. Wells. In the 1880s, Stevenson was convalescing in Switzerland when he devised and played a fascinating and most intricate wargame on an attic floor, with hills, roads, rivers and villages erected on the bare boards. The fullest details of this game can be found in Lloyd Osborne's *Stevenson at Play*. Wells' rules form the basis for practically every set of conditions under which people fight with model soldiers. In 1912, Wells was famous as the author of what would today be called space fiction; he prophesied space flight in his books and his ideas in the field of aviation were years in advance of their time. He wrote two articles for a magazine, describing a game which he called *Little Wars*—'. . . a game that may be played by two, four or six amateurish persons in an afternoon and evening with toy soldiers'. On its title-page, the book says:

'LITTLE WARS—A game for Boys from Twelve Years of Age to One Hundred and Fifty and for that more Intelligent Sort of Girl who likes Boy's Games and Books'.

Today, there are hundreds of wargamers in all corners of the world. They have their own monthly magazine, *Wargamer's Newsletter*, which goes out to nearly 1,000 subscribers in 24 countries. Regular conventions, tournaments and National Wargames Club Championships are held regularly. In celebration of the 150th anniversary of that conflict a military festival in London featured a re-fought Battle of Waterloo—more than 3,000 model soldiers were used and nearly 1,200 enthusiasts turned up to give their support. The aspiring wargamer need not flounder around in the dark—there are text books covering wargames on land, on the sea, and in the air.

Wargamers use small soldiers about an inch in height because a very spacious table would be required to fight battles with the once-popular large figures. Although soldiers are not difficult to obtain, many wargamers find great pleasure in making moulds and casting their own figures. Cleaned up, the figures are given their accurately painted uniforms, finally to parade in all their pristine glory in battle where they never disobey an order!

Wargaming can be as simple or as involved as one requires; it can be dabbled with and enjoyable, elementary games fought out using small numbers of unpainted plastic figures amid hills made of books and houses of matchboxes. Or it can assume vast proportions so that it almost becomes a way of life—recently, a wargamer coming home from Kuwait (in the Persian Gulf) drove a car right across Europe so that he could visit wargamers and other places of interest in Italy, France and Germany! Instead of the excellent and cheap OO gauge plastic figures, the more affluent wargamer can use expensive and exquisitely formed metal figures that are painted with the aid of magnifying lenses to incredible degrees of perfection. He will recognise the various makers' soldiers, and become familiar with the individual characteristics that distinguished those figures made by the master-makers from their less expensive counterparts.

There is more to wargaming than amassing two armies and then manipulating them according to some pre-ordained rules; in fact, the actual battles themselves can become the climax of many fascinating hours spent making and/or painting the soldiers, carrying out research into their uniforms, weapons and tactics, reading up specific periods, planning and making a wargames table and the innumerable variations of scenic terrain to be laid out upon it. Then, most important, rules have to be formulated so that they give a realistic representation of the specific period and manner of battle of the troops involved (one doesn't give battle with Marlburian armies using the same rules as those for Napoleonic wars, nor do Lee's American Civil War soldiers fight as did their great-great grandsons in World War II). The preliminary skirmishes will probably take place under the most elementary rules—a good battle can be fought with a set of rules filling up only the back of a postcard.

With experience will come the desire to accomplish the more involved and difficult manoeuvres of real-life warfare, thus rules have to be formulated that allow this to be done.

Experience indicates that the wargamer devises his rules to suit his temperament and character. The brisk, impatient man has rules that give a fast, hell-for-leather and devil-take-the-hindmost sort of game; the steady plodder finds that his rules give him a satisfying defensive sort of game. The ideal combination might be to have a pair of opponents of each type! Rules can be very simple or so complicated as to allow for such problems as supply; fatigue; morale; natives against disciplined troops; wounded men; prisoners; sieges; mining and, probably most difficult of all, the myriad calibres and types of weapons for modern warfare. One enthusiast of the latter school has a rule that permits a nuclear weapon to clear, in one go, an area of 8 ft × 6 ft from his 9 ft × 7 ft wargames table! Truly, wargaming can be called Chess with a thousand pieces'!

To avoid discouraging potential generals, let us hark back to the statement that a workable set of rules need only fill the back of a postcard. With such a set of simple rules, the writer was fighting most enjoyable wargames within two weeks of commencing to collect model soldiers. Briefly, all that is required are rulings to cover the movement of troops, the firing of their weapons and hand-to-hand fighting when they come into close contact.

Movement: Infantry can move 6 inches per move. Cavalry can move 12 inches per move.

Firing: Guns will fire one shot per move at a maximum range of 3 ft, when one dice is thrown and the dice-score is the number of men hit. At 2 ft range, throw two dice and at 1 ft range throw three dice—casualties equal numbers thrown on dice (or half scores if this is considered too severe).

Infantry will fire in volleys of five men, one dice being thrown for every group of five men. At 18 inches range deduct THREE from each dice at 12 inches range deduct TWO from each dice and at 6 inches range deduct ONE from each dice—the total remaining is the number of enemy casualties.

Hand-to-hand: When two opposing groups meet—count infantry as one point each and cavalry as two points each. Then throw ONE dice for each lot of five points (thus, a force totalling 20 points would throw four dice). The enemy casualties are HALF the total dice score. At the end of the mêlée (when both sides have decided their casualties), count the number of survivors and throw a dice for each side, multiplying the number of survivors by the dice score. The lowest score retreats one move distance (6 inches for infantry, 12 inches for cavalry). Thus, side A has ten men remaining at the end of the mêlée and throws a two, giving a total of 20. Side B has eight men remaining and throws a three, giving a total of 24, so that Side A, although strongest, has to retreat. Simple, isn't it?

There are innumerable variations that add interest and make for greater realism. For instance, in the very beginning of the battle each side lines up its troops on its own base-line at the rear of the wargames table—if a curtain or some other form of concealment is erected, so that neither commander can see his enemy, then there are often horrible surprises when the curtain is lifted! Another idea is for both sides to throw a dice to determine who moves first, the throwing being done before each move. In real-life, opposing bodies of troops do not fire at each other at exactly the same time, one force may be better trained or more alert than the other and get in their volleys before the enemy have loaded. To represent this, a dice is thrown for each formed regiment within range of the enemy—the dice is either left lying by the side of the formation or else the score is noted. When firing begins, all units who have thrown sixes fire first, then the fives, then fours and so on. When the turn comes to fire for an unfortunate unit who threw a one then they may not have many left to fire! When a body of troops is hit by a fast-charging unit of cavalry there must be a certain 'shock value' about the impact—to represent this the cavalry unit making the charge is given a 'shock-bonus' for the resulting mêlée by adding one to each of their dice scores. Other ideas and variations will come naturally to the wargamer as he progresses with the hobby.

The model soldiers that form the table-top armies are the basic element of wargaming and the collector has many fascinating choices to make as to their scale, numbers, period, painting, whether to buy ready-made or to make (or convert) his own with his own moulds of synthetic rubber or plaster of Paris. Conversion is an intriguing business and is a means of turning plastic or metal figures ito completely different troops of another period or country.

Earlier collectors of the period of H. G. Wells were stuck with either the large 54 mm soldiers made by William Britains of London, or with the wafer-thin two-dimensional metal flat figures usually made in Germany. In Wells' immortal book *Little Wars*, the now legendary battle of Hooks Farm is described with the aid of illustrations showing various stages of the conflict with posed 54 mm soldiers. To fight a battle with these large soldiers obviously requires a large table, a garden (and the warm, dry weather to go with it), or the wargamer can acquire an acute case of Housemaid's Knee by crawling over the floor as he moves his men. As time passed, smaller soldiers were produced —first the Britains' 'W' range (about 40 mm) then 30 mm figures made specifically for wargaming, and now the fashion has turned round to the small but perfectly formed and inexpensive 20 mm figures in metal and plastic.

Using these smaller figures, the wargamer finds that he can get so much more into a small layout, so that it is possible on an average-sized table of about 6 ft × 6 ft to have an excellent and most realistic battle with flanking movements and with reasonably large numbers of troops involved. The ever-increasing availability of these small warriors means that the wargamer need not be tied to any one specific period but can amass armies of perhaps 350 men each side for many different periods. In this manner, the writer has gathered together nicely balanced forces for the American Civil War; the Franco-Prussian War; Victorian Colonial Campagns; 18th century wars from Marlborough to the French-and-Indian Wars; armies of Henry V, complete with plenty of archers to fight the mounted knights of the King of France; an Austrian Army of the 1880s; a Russian force with large numbers of Cossacks, all bent on flowing down into India aided by the Afghans and hillmen of the Khyber Pass; an early World War I set-up and some primitive tanks and armoured cars for a 1917 Colonial affair; a World War II set-up in which two scaled-down infantry battalions, each about 250 men strong, plus suitable attached armour, fight each other; Romans take on Ancient Britons and, last but by no means least, that most popular of all periods, the Napoleonic Wars.

From this list it can be seen that limitation lies solely in the mind of the individual wargamer, who can have whatever types of troops or period of warfare he covets. In so acquiring them, he will find that he is opening the doors to hours of stimulating reading and research, coupled with the making of new friendships and incentives gained from mingling with fellow enthusiasts in wargames groups and clubs,

The terrains upon which wargames are fought range from a card-table to huge affairs of hardboard and trestles that cover perhaps 100 square feet. The table should not be wider than 6 ft because that is about the maximum distance that can be comfortably reached when moving soldiers in the middle of the table. It can be as long as desired so as to give vast ranging battles with exciting flanking movements. The permanent table can have a landscape built up in damp sand, moulded into the hills and valleys with coloured-in roads and rivers. Portable tables of hardboard can be erected and dismantled in a few minutes; terrain can be set up on them that is made of shaped pieces of wood piled on each other and perhaps covered by a suitably coloured cloth; Plasticine can be moulded over wooden shapes into hills; rivers and roads can be marked in chalk or laid in strips of cloth or card; villages can be made from plastic kits or constructed from card and balsa wood; fences and walls made from wood or plastic and trees from lichen moss stuck on to twigs.

Land battles rarely become a bore but wargamers sometimes feel the urge to become a Nelson, a Hornblower or a Beatty and re-fight Trafalgar or Jutland, using exquisitely scaled model ships made up from kits. Such games have a true fascination because they can be fought with exactly the same numbers of vessels that took part in the original battle. Sea activities can be combined with land wargaming and the resulting grand strategy can almost completely take over a wargamer's leisure hours! It is also possible to fight wargames using model aircraft, the inevitable difficulties of space and speed surmounted by intricate rules and devices. Both of these exciting facets of wargaming are completely described and explained in their own text books. No war was ever fought in a civilised country without railways playing a sometimes vital part—this means that the model railway enthusiast can easily combine the two hobbies to the advantage of both.

Wargaming is not a bloodthirsty pastime followed by frustrated lance-corporals and ex-lieutenants (one of the best known wargamers in this country is a retired Brigadier with strings of medals on his chest). It is a skilful relaxation, made as involved as one wishes or simple enough to permit the children to take a hand. There is a big kick to be obtained from manoeuvring obedient armies in the comforting knowledge that there is no one braver than a lead soldier with no metal wife or plastic children to mourn his passing!

CHAPTER FIFTEEN

Hints and Tips on Making-up Models

I AM INCLINED TO THINK that anyone who has a genuine interest in the miniature soldier hobby will want to work out his own way of making-up his models and that, in any case, the way I have gone about making mine will not be of much help to him. However, 'practical hints' are a fundamental part of a book of this sort, so I offer the following as a basic guide.

Place of Work

I think it is manifest that anyone setting out to build up a planned collection cannot do it on the corner of the kitchen table. He must have a *permanent* work place where work-in-progress, materials, tools, pictures and drawings can be left. *If* the home allows it, the spare room, attic, study, shed or garage can provide this (although the latter can be jolly cold at 2–3 am on a winter's morning!). But many readers may not have these; at best a young enthusiast may have his bedroom (shared with a totally unsympathetic brother), or be a family man living in a crowded house or flat.

For these, and for other situations too, the ideal work 'place' is an old roll-top desk. With the desk top as a working surface, the little drawers and recesses to hold the tools and pieces, the deep side drawers for materials, books and papers and a roll-top to pull over it all without disturbing the work in hand, these desks could have been specially designed for us! They even have pull-out flaps at the side for extra working space for one's apprentice or young willing helper. This capacity to hold-all and cover-all is a great boon to the modeller. As we all know one of the most tiresome parts of 'do-it-yourself' modelling is the setting-up and clearing away. It takes so long that the time available for work after allowing for it is often so little that one decides it's not worth it. But with a roll-top desk a push of the lid and Voilà!—it's all there just as you left it last time. And when the time comes to stop, the top is closed down and it's locked out of sight until we return. My friend Roy Dilley and I produced well over 1,000 figures in under two years with the help of a roll-top desk, despite the constant presence of four young children, two dogs, three cats, and the undoubted distraction of his very attractive wife.

At the time I speak of, roll-top desks, whilst not exactly a drug on the market, were plentiful and inexpensive. They are not seen so much now but are about and I only hope these remarks of mine won't send their values up unduly. They are in several sizes and colourings but, having been well made originally, most have survived in good shape. The modeller should not acquire one that is too battered, otherwise the lady of the house may object to it coming into the home. A further sociological point in favour of the roll-top desk is that it enables the modeller to remain with his family whilst he is working and not shut himself away from them for hours on end. With the desk installed in one corner, the children playing in another and his wife sitting in an armchair knitting and/or watching television one can see a picture of family life of an ideal sort.

If a roll-top desk is unattainable, a tool chest-cum-work-in-hand box, which can be quickly opened and put away, would be an austere substitute. Readers will be familiar with the type of box I mean as they are regularly publicised in handyman periodicals. With this one needs a piece of flat hardwood suitable as a working surface. Its underside should be smooth so as not to cause scratches to other surfaces.

Lighting

This, too, is somewhat obvious. Modelling requires good, strong, shaded light. The adjustable 'Anglepoise' type of electric lamp with a conical shade, as used by draughtsmen, is ideal. This should, of course, be safely connected to a proper point and the cable stowed neatly. If metal figures are to be worked on with an electric soldering iron, an adaptor should be included in the wiring arrangments and all the usual safety precautions taken.

Tools

These are very much a personal matter. Some modellers go in for complete sets of the various types, others seem to get along with just a broken saw, a razor blade and half a file. The old 'saw' that cheap tools are false economy is not true with our hobby; it does, of course, depend on the usage, but I have converted some 5,000 models over 23 years with tools bought originally for 6*d* each in a well-known chain store. The tools need to be looked after, and replacements—especially of things like hack-saw blades—is necessary, but the work is light in nature and almost invariably carried out in warm, dry conditions indoors. So 'care of tools' is not something likely to be a problem. (Yet I have read of one converter who burnished all his tools and, after every session cleaned and polished them before putting them away in old cutlery canteen boxes. There's perfection for you !)

Some or all of the following will be required, according to the reader's fancy or dexterity. (Remember to think of the *small* sizes in each case; we are not building a house.)

Putting a price on a minimum set of modelling tools is difficult; most people will have household and/or other tools already in their possession. Allowing for these, the 'special' items required to get one going should not cost more than £2. I also recommend a 'pinny' to wear; it is useful to keep filings and scrapings off one's clothes and obviates the need to go and change into old trousers. It also serves to catch the odd piece that breaks or flies into the air during working.

A small vice—the flat type, which can be stood on its side for preference (or alternatively a D Clamp).

Small saws, fretsaw type, and if obtainable the jeweller or mechanic's type. Also a 'razor saw' which the reader will probably evolve himself.

Lightweight electric soldering iron, as used by radio mechanics.

Pliers, various, square-jawed, pointed ends, side-cutting.

Very small screwdriver; will be found useful as a scraper and spatula.

Scissors, and possibly a small pair of snips.

Small drill. Small awl. Small gimlet.

Knives, various; the plastic modelling 'Craft' type is an obvious one, plus old discarded ones with blades honed down to one's own requirements.

Files (probably more of these than any other tool), course and fine in flat, round, triangular, needle, etc; and I suppose handles for same though I gave up using these years ago.

Pin drill and chuck, say 1/32 to ⅛ inch sizes.

Ruler, (metric and inches). Set square. Magnifying glass.

Small tweezers, possibly old ones from the wife's eyebrow kit.

Small brush of brass bristle (ie, suede cleaning type).

Paper clips, various, to act as extra hands or finger holds.

Paint brushes, various, preferably of sable in the small 'O' and 'OO' sizes.

Expendable Items

Emery and glass paper. Solder (the multi-core electrician's type). Plastic wood. Candle (for warming plastics). Putty. Epoxy fixatives (various to suit the materials to be joined). Fuse wire—various sizes. 'Polyfilla' or similar. Thin lead sheeting, plastic card sheeting or similar. Old pipe cleaners (for plumes, etc.). Bottle corks (for shakos, etc.). Paints, in tubes or tins and, of course, the reserves of old heads, limbs, bodies, weapons, etc.

Appendix One

SOME ABBREVIATIONS AND MILITARY TERMS (BRITISH) REFERRED TO IN THIS BOOK

'A' Branch or Adjutant-General's Branch of the Staff: Responsible for all personnel matters, such as recruiting, education, pay, discipline, welfare, allocation of medals, arranging of burials, ceremonial matters.

AA: Anti-aircraft.

ADC: Aide-de-camp (Fr). A military personal attendant of Officer rank for a sovereign or General. Wears a special uniform or insignia or armband.

Adjutant: (from the Latin—assistant). The Staff Officer of a regiment or battalion. Not a rank but an appointment; usually held by an up-and-coming Captain. (In the French Army an 'Adjutant-Chef' is an 'Other Rank' approximately equal to a British Regimental Sergeant Major (RSM). Abbreviated as Adjt.

Army: A generic term for a large number of organised soldiers.

Armies: The largest normal operational organisation, although in the Second World War there was the British 21st Army Group in NW Europe of two armies. In the 1914–18 War, although there were five armies in the British Expeditionary Force ultimately, they all came directly under GHQ, BEF (FM Haig).

Artillery Brigade: Used in British Army up to late 1930s for a unit of two or more batteries. Usually commanded by a Lieutenant-Colonel, RA. As a mark of differentiation their numerical titles were always given in Roman *not* Arabic figures. Now known as Artillery Regiments.

AFV: Armoured fighting vehicle, ie, tank, armoured car.

AQMG: Assistant Quarter Master General. A Staff Officer usually of Colonel's rank on the 'Q' Branch Staff of an HQ.

Battalion: From the Latin battuere—to strike. The usual division of infantry; consisting of a number of companies. Commanded by a Lieutenant-Colonel. Correct abbreviation is Bn, eg, 1st Bn Irish Guards.

Battery: A unit of artillery, usually with guns of one size or type. In case of field artillery the number of guns varied from 4 to 6 to at present 8. Abbreviated as Bty.

Brigade: Two or more regiments of same arm, ie, cavalry, infantry, tanks, with a small HQ, but usually without any supporting arms or services, commanded by

—up to 1914—a Major-General or Brigadier-General; 1914–1921—a Brigadier-General; 1922–28—a Colonel-Commandant; 1929 to date—a Brigadier. Correct abbreviation is Bde.

Brigade Group: A brigade as above with augmented staff and elements of other arms and services permanently integrated under command. Abbreviated as Bde Gp.

Brigadier: A senior officer rank above Colonel and below Major-General. (In some continental armies it used to denote an NCO rank equal to Corporal.) Abbreviated as Brig.

Brigadier A/Q: A Brigadier in charge of the 'A' and 'Q' branches of a headquarters. Abbreviated as Brig AQ.

Cadre: The basic structure of a regiment or unit.

Captain: From French 'capitaine'—the head of a company or small unit. Abbreviated to Capt.

Chief of Staff: The executive head of an Army in peacetime. (Prior to establishment of Ministry of Defence in 1964 the British title was Chief of the *Imperial* General Staff—a vestige of a pre-1914 plan never fully implemented.) The post is usually held by a selected senior General or Field Marshal. But in the field in large armies the Chief-of-Staff is subordinate to the Commander-in-Chief. Abbreviated to C of S.

Colonel: From the Italian 'colonello'—a little column. So called because he led the small group at the head of a regiment. Called by the French the clique; the present RHQ or BnHQ. Abbreviation is Col. Without wishing to confuse, it should be mentioned that Colonels do not command the basic fighting units, ie, regiments of cavalry and artillery and battalions of infantry. This is done by Lieutenant-Colonels. There are Colonels of regiments who are almost always Generals, these Colonelcies being honour titles. In the footguards, whilst the battalions are commanded by Lieutenant-Colonels, on the RHQs of the five regiments there are Regimental Lieutenant-Colonels who are Colonels in rank. The Colonels of the Regiments are, as stated above, Generals. Their Colonels-in-Chief are always the sovereign or a royal duke. Some corps, eg, RA, RE, RAOC, etc, have Colonels Commandant—titular appointments with nominal duties, held by Generals. A further point in the case of royalty is that the Colonel of a regiment may hold a junior rank in the Army List, viz the Queen, when Princess Elizabeth, on becoming Colonel of the Grenadier Guards was a junior officer in the then Army Territorial Service (ATS). A point to note regarding dress is that when Colonels, Colonels-Commandant and Colonels-in-Chief visit or represent their regiment they wear the regimental style of uniform with appropriate facings, stripes, braid, etc, but with badges of rank of a Colonel.

Company: Evolved in Middle Ages and applied to groups of soldiers of fortune who banded together and agreed to serve for pay, booty and ransom. Had a commercial meaning not dissimilar to that of today. Abbreviated as Coy.

Corporal: A non-commissioned officer. From the Italian 'capodi' or head of section. Abbreviated as Cpl. (Known in the Royal Artillery as Bombardier—Bdr.)

Corps: (1) An operational or army corps is composed of two or more divisions plus corps troops, supporting artillery, engineers, medical and supply services. Corps HQ commanded by a Lieutenant-General with 'Chief' Officers for the principal supporting services. (2) Is also used to denote titles of other groups of units not organised on a regimental basis, eg, Corps of Royal Engineers, Royal Army Ordnance Corps, Women's Royal Army Corps. (3) Is further used as a group description of all units of a particular type for indirect administration, eg, Royal Armoured Corps (cavalry and tanks) and as a quasi-military-legal term for the whole of the Royal Artillery.

'D'-Day: The first day of an operational programme as visualised by the planning staffs; D+1, D+2, etc, second and third days by which objectives are calculated and the build-up of troops is phased.

DAAG: Deputy Assistant Adjutant General. A staff officer of rank of Major dealing with 'A' matters in an HQ.

Division: Until the nuclear age this was the internationally accepted smallest self-contained fighting formation, capable of maintaining itself for a limited period; the recognised yardstick by which fighting potential of armies was measured. It had a small HQ Staff, commanded by a Major-General, consisted of three brigades plus divisional artillery, engineers, signals and administrative services. Normally the brigades were of infantry unless the title indicated otherwise, eg, Cavalry, Armoured. The British Army had 90 divisions in the field in the First World War and 60 (including 12 armoured and 2 airborne) in the Second. Abbreviated as Div. With the heavy cuts in the British infantry (from 152 to 46 battalions), a system of grouping the single battalion regiments for recruiting and cross-posting, etc, led to the use of the term 'division' being applied to these groups, eg, King's Division, Prince of Wales' Division, etc, which is likely to cause confusion in the use of this term in future.

Field Marshal (or Marshal, foreign): An international military rank (except in America), derived from the old German words for a person in charge of horses, it is the highest in the military world. It owes its rise to the part played by mounted troops in the Middle Ages. In England it then became one of the great offices of state. As a military rank it was only introduced in 1736. Promotion to Field Marshal does not depend on seniority as a General; royal princes and foreign royalty have had the Baton conferred on them and there is at least one instance of a retired General being made a Field Marshal. Unlike other general officers, there is no age limit for Field Marshals; they remain on the active list until they die. This means they qualify for the highest grade of military funeral. (NB: The Royal Air Force embodies the title of Marshal in four of its senior officer ranks—see Appendix 9—but only one—Marshal of the Royal Air Force—equates to Field Marshal.)

General Officers: The seniority of the three grades of Generals derives from the 17th century. An army in the field was under the overall command of the General; its cavalry, which was more mobile, was commanded by the next senior officer, the Lieutenant-General, and the assistant to the Commander was called the Sergeant-Major General. In the course of time this became shortened to Major-General. (A similar complimentary shortening of a rank is done in some infantry regiments where, in the sergeants' mess, the Regimental Sergeant Major is addressed as 'Major'.) There is also the little-used title of Captain-General, which is an appointment and not a rank. Its usage preceded the introduction of Field Marshal. Captains-General titles are only held by the royal personage at the head of the Royal Artillery, the Royal Armoured Corps, the Royal Marines and the Honourable Artillery Company. The use of the term arose to indicate an Officer in general or overall command of a body of mixed troops.

'G' Branch: The General Staff Branch, the senior of the three departments of military staff work. Sub-divided, depending on size of HQ, into Operations (Ops), Intelligence (I or Int), Staff Duties (SD), and Training (Trg). On a Brigade HQ the General Staff Officer is known as the Brigade Major (Abbreviated to BM).

GSO1 (2), etc: General Staff Officer, Grade One (Lieutenant-Colonel; General Staff Officer, Grade Two (Major); General Staff Officer, Grade Three (Captain) These are appointments in a Headquarter's 'G' Branch.

HQ, etc: Headquarters—of a military formation, either static or mobile. Usually prefixed by a letter or abbreviation indicative of which. Examples: BnHQ= Battalion Headquarters; GHQ=General Headquarters (only used for the highest HQ in that theatre of operations, etc); RHQ=Regimental Headquarters. (NB: Abbreviations 'DHQ' and CHQ' for Divisional and Corps Headquarters are never used, but are indicated as 'HQ5Div' or 'HQIICorps'.)

Lieutenant: From French 'one who stands in for', or in lieu of; a Captain, Colonel or General. Abbreviated to Lt.

Major: The 'greater' or more important Officer, originally, than the other company Officers. Abbreviated to Maj.

MP (CMP): Military Police—the 'Red Caps'. The Corps of Military Police, responsible for traffic control, provost and some disciplinary duties in the army. (NB: Police duties *inside* a unit are done by men assigned to the work and known as Regimental Police; they do *not* wear red caps, only armbands as a distinctive insignia.)

MT: Motor transport or mechanical transport.

Order of Battle: The manner in which military forces are organised and disposed. Can also mean a tabulation of organised units and formations for an action or campaign. Abbreviated to Orbat.

Private: Originally meant a fighting man who was only responsible for himself. Is of honourable origin but there has been a flight from it in the British Army by substituting regimental names, such as Trooper, Guardsman, Sapper, etc. Abbreviated to Pte.

'Q' Branch: The Quartermaster General Branch of the Staff. At one time regarded as the least important of the Staff but not now, as a result of the recognition of logistics. Responsible for organisation of supplies, equipment and materials, accommodation, transportation and movement control. Supervises the various Corps and Services of specialists who perform these functions.

Sergeant: From Latin—possibly the oldest rank of all—meaning one who serves. In use in Norman times. Abbreviated to Sgt.

Soldier: A generic term for organised fighting men on land. In its widest sense includes *all* ranks, ie, 'the Soldiery'. From Latin and old French—the 'soldati'—those who gave military service for pay.

Regiment: From Latin—'regimen'—rule or system of order. Came into use at the end of 16th century to describe a body of troops of more than one company. At present generally means a named unit of one or more battalions (or equivalent), each consisting of a number of companies (or squadrons or batteries). Also used in another sense in the formal title of the British Artillery, ie, the 'Royal Regiment of Artillery', which consists of a large number of artillery regiments, each consisting of two or more batteries. (NB: The Royal Horse Artillery is not part of the Royal Regiment of Artillery for purposes of precedence.) Abbreviated to Regt.

SP: Self-propelled—appertaining to artillery.

Appendix Two

ORDER OF BATTLE—HARRIS MODEL ARMY
TABLE 1—SUMMARY OF SUMMARIES

Serial No	Formation or Establishment	Ladies	Gentlemen	Mounted Officers	Mounted Men	Dis-mounted Officers	Dis-mounted Men	Draught horses	HD vehicles	M' cycles	MT vehicles A	MT vehicles B	Guns	Misc Eqpt	Vessels	Aircraft
1	The Court, General-Headquarters and Base Units	8	59	34	60	250	579	43	24	—	—	2	7	—	—	—

Serial No	Formation or Establishment	Ladies	Gentlemen	Mounted Officers	Mounted Men	Dis-mounted Officers	Dis-mounted Men	Draught horses	HD vehicles	M'cycles	MT vehicles A	MT vehicles B	Guns	Misc Eqpt	Vessels	Aircraft
2	1st Full Dress Corps	—	—	129	304	58	654	96	74	—	—	—	20	2	—	—
3	2nd Expeditionary Corps	—	—	72	93	78	390	140	34	14	17	26	8	1	—	—
4	The Naval Division	—	—	7	—	59	366	6	4	2	5	3	6	—	7	1
5	The Air Corps	—	—	2	—	29	133	—	—	3	—	8	1	—	—	11
6	Miscellaneous Formations	10	20	146	217	97	995	87	45	—	—	5	10	4	—	—
	TOTAL	18	79	390	674	571	3,117	372	181	19	22	44	52	7	7	12

As will be seen from these figures, my overall planned collection consists of just over 5,000 figures and some 530 guns, vehicles, small boats and aircraft.

It surprised me, when I did a physical stock-check of the present collection for this book, to find how close I had followed my original plan, laid down well over 12 years ago. Inevitably, some models which were specified then have not yet been made. This is due to three main reasons: I have not got the basic materials, the research has not yet been completed, or (and I must confess this is the main reason), I have just not felt like making them! But I find that I have at least 90 per cent of the total completed, plus quite a few which I had not programmed but which I was excited into making by something I saw or heard, since compiling the original Order of Battle.

TABLE 2—SUMMARY OF 1st FULL DRESS CORPS

Serial number	Formation	Mounted Officers	Mounted Men	Dis-mounted Officers	Dis-mounted Men	Draught horses	Vehs & limbers	Guns	Misc	Remarks
2a	Corps headquarters and Corps Troops	18	40	7	30	24	17	2	2	C in C, Staff Officers, orderlies, Mounted Escort, Signal Section and Mounted Police. Also Artillery, Engineers and Supply Services.
2b	HQ 1st Cavalry Division and Divisional troops	10	20	1	22	15	7	3	—	Div Comd and Staff; Sigs, Escort, Transport and Div artillery.
2c	1st Cavalry Brigade	13	58	—	4	3	4	1	—	Each comprises Bde Cmd and 2 SOs, M/C gun section, transport section, one band, one standard party and 3 regimental groups each of 15.
2d	2nd Cavalry Brigade	13	58	—	4	3	4	1	—	
2e	3rd Cavalry Brigade	13	58	—	4	3	4	1	—	

Serial number	Formation	Mounted Officers	Mounted Men	Dismounted Officers	Dismounted Men	Draught horses	Vehs & limbers	Guns	Misc	Remarks
2f	HQ 2nd Infantry Division and Divisional troops	10	20	1	22	15	7	3	—	As for 2b (above).
2g	4th Guards Brigade	7	5	8	91	3	4	1	—	As for 2c–e (above). Regimental groups of 21 each are either all marching or standing in each brigade to give uniformity when massed.
2h	5th Infantry Brigade	7	5	8	91	3	4	1	—	
2j	6th Infantry Brigade	7	5	8	91	3	4	1	—	
2k	HQ 3rd Infantry Division and Divisional troops	10	20	1	22	15	7	3	—	As for 2b above.
2l	7th Infantry Brigade	7	5	8	91	3	4	1	—	As for 2g–k (above).
2m	8th Infantry Brigade	7	5	8	91	3	4	1	—	
2n	9th Infantry Brigade	7	5	8	91	3	4	1	—	
	Grand Total	129	304	58	654	96	74	20	2	

Total personnel = 1145

LIST OF REGIMENTS FORMING BRIGADES (circa 1900–1914 dress)

Notes: 1. **(M)** indicates all group is at a moving position. **(S)** indicates all group is at a standing position.
2. Facing colours of Infantry are denoted as follows:
(B): Blue, (W): White, (Y): Yellow, (G): Green, (Bu): Buff, (Sc): Scarlet, (Bl): Black.

1 CAVALRY BRIGADE (M)

King's Dragoon Guards
5 (PCW) Dragoon Guards
Royal Scots Greys

2 CAVALRY BRIGADE (S)

8 KR Irish Hussars
13 Hussars
14 (King's) Hussars

3 CAVALRY BRIGADE (M)

5 Royal Irish Lancers
12 PWR Lancers
17 DCO Lancers

4 GUARDS BRIGADE (S)

1 Grenadier Guards
1 Scots Guards
1 Irish Guards

5 INFANTRY BRIGADE (M)

1 R Welch Fusiliers (B)
2 Worcestershire Regt (W)
1 Middlesex Regt (Y)

6 INFANTRY BRIGADE (S)

1 Royal Irish Regt (B)
1 Connaught Rangers (G)
1 R Dublin Fusiliers (B)

7 INFANTRY BRIGADE (M)

1 Royal Scots (B)
2 Black Watch (B)
1 Highland Light Infantry (Bu)

8 INFANTRY BRIGADE (S)

1 R Warwicks Regt (B)
1 Somerset Light Infantry (B)
1 W Yorks Regt (Bu)

9 INFANTRY BRIGADE (M)

1 Scottish Rifles (G)
2 KR Rifle Corps (Sc)
1 R Irish Rifles (G)

Appendix Three

SELECTED LIST OF BOOKS, ETC

THIS LIST is very much a personal choice, and many readers may have or know of different books on the same subject. I have not put in details of prices, as these vary with editions and some of them may be out of print and rare. But modellers should have little trouble in obtaining most of them, either from fellow modellers' private libraries, from the bodies mentioned in Appendix 5, or from any good public library.

Title/Author	**Publisher**
Frossiarts Chronicle	History Book Club Joliffe edition
Military Antiquities (Grose)	Egerton & Kearsley
History of British Army (Fortescue)	Macmillan
History of Uniforms of British Army – 4 volumes (Lawson)	Peter Davis & Norman Military Publications
History of the Regiments and Uniforms of the British Army (M. Barnes)	Seeley Service
Armies of India (Lovatt and McMunn)	A & C Black
India's Army (Donovan Jackson)	Sampson Low & Marston
British Military Uniforms from Henry VII to present day (W.Y. Carman)	Leonard Hill
Dress Regulations (Officers) of British Army (NB: These are official publications and very difficult to acquire. The 1911 edition is the last fully illustrated one; the last edition was issued in 1934.)	—
Rules relating to Dress 1953 onwards – various pamphlets. (This also is an official publication and to some extent supersedes Dress Regulations.)	—
Clothing Regulations, various parts & dates (British official publication)	
Intelligible Heraldry (Lynch-Robinson)	—
'Observer' series book of Heraldry	Warne
Heraldry in War (for formation signs on vehicles (Howard Cole)	—
Military Music and other books on military bands (H.J. Farmer)	Max Parrish
Standards, Guidons and Colours of British Forces (T.J. Edwards)	Gale & Polden
Early English Artillery (O.F.G. Hogg)	Royal Artillery Institution
International Military Uniforms – Kannik (English translation by W.Y. Carman)	Blandford Press
Dress of British Sailor (Dickens)	HMSO
Navy List (Official) – various editions. Appendix of dress regulations for Officers and ratings and men, Royal Navy and Marines	—
Regimental Histories of regiments – as required	—
Blandford's Military Uniforms of the World in Colour. (Written and illustrated by Prebeu Kannik. English edition by W.Y. Carman)	Blandford Press

Books on Model Soldiers

Collectors Guide (J.C. Garratt)	Seeley Service
Tackle Model Soldiers This Way (D. Featherstone)	Stanley Paul
*The Wonderful World of Toy Soldiers (In French) (Paul Martin)	Charles Massin
*Steadfast Model Soldiers (In German) (Paul Martin)	Frankh'sche V'-lung Stuttgart
†Little Wars (H.G. Wells)	—
*Figures and Soldiers (In French) (Marcel Baldet)	Edition d'art Gonthier
*Military Models (US and French editions) (Peter Blum)	Odipsley Press
Making and Collecting Military Miniatures (US) (Bob Bard)	Robert McBride
Model Soldiers' Guide (US) (C. Risley and W. Imrie)	S.S. Publishing Co (NY)
*Model Soldiers (English, US, French, German and Italian editions) (H. Harris)	Weidenfeld & Nicolson

Books on Wargames

War Games (D. Featherstone)	Stanley Paul
*Charge! (P. Young and J. P. Lawford)	Morgan Grampian

* These are profusely illustrated.
† Now out of print and rare.

Magazines, periodicals, booklets, etc. (see also Appendix 7)

Airfix Magazine (monthly – very useful for conversions, hints and tips, etc).

Soldier Magazine (monthly – British Army).

Soldier – New US publication for collectors. Obtainable in UK from Box OO5, 61 Benares Rd, London SE18.

Miniature Warfare – monthly – from same address as 'Soldier'.

Tradition – monthly for collectors, wargamers and antique buyers – 44 Dover St, London W1.

Exchange and Mart – weekly classified sections on models and toys for sale and wanted. (Readers must be very strong-willed as regular reading of this turns one into a compulsive buyer!)

Publicity and Recruiting Literature. All services, regiments and corps, as well as central recruiting authorities, produce very good material in this field. Often profusely illustrated and almost always free.

Regimental magazines and journals. Published variously by the regiments and corps, a few monthly, most quarterly or annually. A 'must' to keep collectors of regiments up to date.

Appendix Four

SOME CENTRES FOR INFORMATION AND REFERENCE

Notes

1. Personal visits to the museums are recommended.
2. In some cases books may be borrowed but precise advice cannot be given as some Institutes restrict this to members only.
3. All will do their best to answer serious questions from bona fide researchers. To assist I recommend asking for information in the form of a questionnaire, providing space for answers to precise questions; this saves time in processing answers in the establishment concerned. Stamped addressed envelopes for replies also seem to speed things up.

Ministry of Defence Libraries:
(a) Main and Army: Old War Office Building, Whitehall, London SW1.
(b) Naval (including Royal Marines): Old Admiralty Building, Whitehall, London SW1.
(c) Air: Air Department, Kingsway, London WC2

Royal United Services Institution, Whitehall, London SW1. Now Library only; museum dispersed. (See also Societies, Appendix 7.)

Imperial War Museum, Lambeth, London SE1. For general matters on all sections of HM Forces in battle from 1914 onwards. Includes book, portrait and photographic libraries. Photographic prints can be obtained at very reasonable cost.

National Army Museum, Camberley, Surrey. (Due to begin transfer to new buildings in Royal Hospital, Chelsea, in 1970.) Includes Indian Army and Disbanded Irish Regiments' sections.

National Maritime Museum, Greenwich, London SE16.

Royal Air Force Museum, Henlow, Beds.

HMS *Victory* and Royal Dockyard Museum. Portsmouth, Hants.

Royal Marines Museum and Reference Library, Eastney Barracks, Portsmouth, Hants.

Scottish National War Memorial and Museum, The Castle, Edinburgh.

Royal Armoured Corps Tank Museum, Bovington, Dorset.

Royal Artillery Institution Museum and Library; also Rotunda Museum, Woolwich, London SE18.

Corps of Royal Engineers Library and Museum, Brompton Barracks, Chatham, Kent.

Royal Corps of Signals Museum, Catterick Camp, Yorks.

Royal Corps of Transport (late Royal Army Service Corps) Museum, Buller Barracks, Aldershot, Hants.

Royal Army Medical Corps Museum, Mytchett, Aldershot, Hants.

Royal Army Ordnance Corps Museum, Deepcut, Camberley, Surrey.

Corps of Royal Electrical and Mechanical Engineers Museum, Aborfield, Berks.

Prince Consort's Library, Aldershot, Hants.

Brigade of Guards, Cavalry, Infantry and other Corps' Museums; these are too numerous to list here and *all* are unlikely to be of interest to every reader. Addresses of these can be obtained from a useful book called *Military Museums* by T. Wise (Bellona, 5s).

Public Relations Officers at all main Navy, Army and Air Command Headquarters can assist with information on current affairs but should *not* be asked for historical details.

Foreign Forces: provision of general information by Military Attachés at Foreign Embassies is usually provided as part of their PR services. Addresses of those will be found in the London telephone directory. If the information required is at all detailed or obscure they will probably provide you with an address in their homeland with which you can communicate direct.

Museum of Childhood (toys and games of the past), High Street, Edinburgh.

The Toy Museum, Bethnal Green, London E1.

Appendix Five

MUSEUMS, ETC, WITH COLLECTIONS OF MODEL SOLDIERS

THIS LIST is not exhaustive, and also museums are continually re-arranging their displays, so although model soldiers may be in their collection they may not always be on display.

UNITED KINGDOM & IRELAND

London Area

Tower of London, London EC1.
Imperial War Museum, London SE1.
The London Museum, London W8.
Royal Artillery Institution, Old Academy, London SE18.
Duke of York's HQ, Chelsea, London SW3.

Camberley, Surrey

National Army Museum (moving to Royal Hospital, Chelsea in 1971).

Pirbright, Surrey

Household Brigade Depot Museum.

Woodstock, Oxon

Blenheim Palace.

Bedfordshire

Woburn Abbey.

Lichfield, Staffs

Staffordshire Regimental Museum.

Beverley, Yorks

E Yorkshire Regt Museum.

York

Castle Museum (Military Section).

Nottingham

Castle Museum (Military Section).

Deal, Kent

Walmer Castle.

Edinburgh

Castle.
Museum of Childhood.

Co Cork, Ireland

Kinsale Folk Museum

ABROAD

Belgium
Royal Museum of Military History, Brussels.

Czechoslovakia
Hradrany Castle Museum (The Graffifti House).

Denmark
Danskfolk Museum, Copenhagen.

Egypt
Cairo Museum.

France
Arromanches, Normandy (Inter-Allied Museum).
Compiegne.
Arc de Triomphe, Paris.
Musée de l'Armée, Invalides (Salon Ney), Paris.
Musée de la Mer, Palais de Chaillot, Paris.
Strasbourg.

Germany
Kulmbach-Schloss Plassenburg (Bavaria).
Leipzig.
Bayerisches National Museum, Munich.
Hersbruck Museum, Nuremberg.
Potsdam Museum.

Italy
Museo del Commune, Milan.
Museo Civico, Naples.
Museo Civico, Rome.
Museo Civico, Turin.

Netherlands
Leiden Dutch Museum.

Spain
Museum of Industry and Arts, Barcelona.
Artillery Museum, Madrid.
Museo del Ejercito, Madrid.
Military and Naval School, Madrid.
Naval Museum, Madrid.

Sweden
Gottingen Museum.
Uppsala University Museum.

Switzerland
Zurich Landesmuseum

United States of America
Annapolis Naval Academy Museum.
New York Metropolitan Museum.
Gettysburg Memorial.
Marine Corps Museum, Quantico (Va).
Smithsonian Institute, Washington.
US Military Academy Museum, West Point.

Union of Soviet Socialist Republics
Artillery Museum, Leningrad.
Hermitage Museum, Leningrad.

Appendix Six

SOME MANUFACTURERS, SUPPLIERS AND STOCKISTS OF MODEL SOLDIERS

THIS INFORMATION is based on replies to a questionnaire sent out by the author in July 1968. It is confined to those who have toy or model soldiers and military accessories, eg, firms that make car and aircraft kits as well as soldiers are *included;* those that do *not* make soldiers, or essentially military items, despite their other items, are not. The symbol (T) means that the items are produced primarily as toys, (M) produced as models. For kits, etc, see Appendix Three of *How to Go Plastic Modelling.*

UNITED KINGDOM

ACTION MAN

Messrs BXL Toy Division, Owen Street, Coalville, Leicester.

A basic male figure in plastic 11½ inches high for which is provided a large range of uniforms in fabrics (cotton, canvas, nylon, etc). Also weapons and personal equipment. Action Man is very well jointed and can be arranged in a large number of positions. Uniforms range from British soldier and sailor, through German, French and Russian. The firm are adding vehicles and 'scenery' in same scale. (T)

AIRFIX

Airfix Products Ltd, Haldane Place, Garrett Lane, London SW18.

Within their large range of other items this firm produces a good selection of plastic soldiers in OO/HO scale which are particularly attractive for wargames. There are also kits of OO scale guided missiles and armoured vehicles. Military figures in 54 mm appeared with their 1:32 scale Bus and in 1968 some 1:32 scale British paratroopers were also released, but the quality of these is not as high as their other products. In 1969 two more sets of 1:32 scale figures were introduced, German and US infantry of World War Two. The Germans are particularly fine figures. Of interest to keen converters are also the motor racing officials and spectators, which have many possibilities for the experienced modeller who has worked his way through all the military figures. (T)

AURORA PLASTICS

See Hales

BRITAINS

Messrs Britains Ltd, Blackhorse Lane, London E17.

Still the largest manufacturer of 54 mm scale high-quality toy soldiers (plastic), and guns and vehicles (die-cast metal) in the UK. Production now limited to selected British and American Armies type plus a few ancient Greeks and Medieval figures. Many of their Cowboy, Indian and civilian figures are useful for swopping parts and conversion. Introduced a range of figures in 40 mm in 1968. (T)

CHARBENS

Charbens and Co Ltd, 219 Hornsey Rd, London N7.

Makers of metal and plastic toys to approximately 54 mm scale. Moderately priced toy-standard Guardsmen, American GIs, Afrika Corps; also American Civil War and British Guardsmen with removable and interchangeable bodies, legs etc. (T)

CRESCENT

The Crescent Toy Co Ltd, Cwmcarn, Monmouthshire

Die-cast metal artillery and 'Saladin' type armoured car not all to constant scale, some approximately 54 mm. Also polythene commandos, medievals, American Civil War and British Guards of toy quality, reasonably priced. (T)

GAMMAGE R.

See Rose Miniatures

GAMMAGE A.W.

Gammage A. W. & Co Ltd, Holborn, London EC1.

Departmental store with toy and model departments which usually stock a variety of items of interest to model soldier collectors.

GARRISON, THE

W & P (Militaria) Ltd, Knaresborough, Yorks.

Stockists of 20 mm wargame and 54 mm models of most known manufacturers. Also tank and vehicle kits.

HALES

Hales A.A., Ltd, PO Box 33, Hinkley, Leics.

Distributors in UK of Monogram kits, including Jeeps and tanks, also of recently introduced high-quality Merité model 55 mm soldiers in metal by Monogram. (See under USA). (M)

HAMLEYS

Hamleys, Regent Street, London W1.

One of the best-known toy shops in the world. Usually carries stocks of model soldiers, painted and unpainted, as well as toys and kits.

HERALD

See Britains (above)

Range of ancient Greeks, Knights, British Guards, and Highlanders toy soldiers produced by Messrs Britains. Regarded as less well made than 'Swoppet' range but contains some interesting items. (T)

HINTON HUNT

Hinton Hunt Figures, Rowsley, River Road, Taplow, Bucks. (Also at 9-10 Camden Passage Boutique, Islington, London N1.

Designer and maker of 20 mm and 54 mm collector quality figures in metal. The range is largely the Napoleonic period. Figures supplied either painted or unpainted. (M)

HUMBROL

Humbrol Ltd, Marfleet, Hull.

Major manufacturer of paints and fixatives, such as Britfix, (cement and PVC repair outfit), plastic wood and a wide range of paints specially prepared for painting models.

HUNT

Hunt R.J., 36 North Rd, Brighton, Sussex.

Dealer in militaria, including secondhand toy and model soldiers, Britains, etc.

KOHNSTAM

Kohnstam, Richard, Ltd, 13/15a High Street, Hemel Hempstead, Herts.

UK distributors of Japanese Tamiya Mokei models which include 1:35 and 1:21 scale AFVs of 1939-45 War and later. (M)

LUCK

Luck E.J., Ltd, 34 High Street, Southgate, London N14.

Dealer in Britains' toy soldiers. Mailing lists of items available.

LONE STAR

Lone Star Products, 168 Great North Rd, Hatfield, Hertfordshire.

Manufacturers of toy plastic figures, including some suitable for conversion, eg, interchangeable part Indians and Medieval figures. Not to any constant scale but reasonably priced. (T)

MINIMODELS

Minimodels Ltd, Havant, Hants.

Introduced in 1969 three sets of soldiers of approximately 50 mm size, Japanese, German and US of World War Two. Each set of 12 to 15 different types. (T)

MODEL TOYS

Model Toys Ltd, Torbothie Rd, Shotts, Lanarkshire, Scotland. (Also known as Timpo Toys.)

Manufacturers of toy plastic soldiers, ancient and modern, in polythene and polystyrene, to approximately 54 mm size. Also a range of cowboys and farm people with some conversion potential. A feature of the processing is that, instead of painting, hands, gun belts, etc, can be given their exact position and actual colour. They recently introduced a 'historical' gun carriage and limber with various teams and also some sets of Waterloo (British, French and Prussians). Proposing to introduce a brand-new set of Guards, including mounted officer and also French Foreign Legion. The design of their later figures, particularly the Romans and Waterloo items, is particularly good. (T)

MONOGRAM

See A.A. Hales (above).

REVELL

Revell (GB) Ltd, Cranborne Rd, Potters Bar, Hertfordshire.

This firm makes a wide range of military aircraft and some tanks but an irritating feature is the multiplicity of scales used with no apparent reason, eg, Sherman tank is 1:40 but helicopters are 1:32 scale. (M)

ROSE MINIATURES

Russell Gammage, 45 Sundorne Road, London SE7.

This little firm produces a wide range of very high quality model soldiers and associated figures and accessories in tin alloy, 56 mm and also wargame size. Some are in one piece and others multi-piece, supplied painted or unpainted. Because of their quality the price of painted complete figures is rather high, but the proprietor is prepared to sell direct to modellers such parts as heads, weapons, musical instruments, etc, providing an economic order quantity is asked for at one time. (M)

SURÉN

Edward Surén, 60 Lower Sloane Street, London SW1.

Manufacturers of 30 mm high-quality model figures. (M)

HISTOREX

Historex Agents (UK), 3 Castle Street, Dover, Kent.

For fuller details of these see under foreign section. Mr Sangster, the proprietor, is a model enthusiast himself and will be helpful to collectors requiring spare parts, such as heads, harness, weapons, etc. (M)

TRI-ANG

Tri-ang Toys Ltd, Liverpool.

Have introduced (1969) a number of military vehicles into their non-mechanical series, such as Land-Rover, troop- and load-carrying trucks. Whilst the vehicles are toys, the seated figures, British officers and men in fighting dress, with detachable weapons, are almost of model quality. (T)

OVERSEAS

BELGIUM

Cafés Storme (Messrs Storme Coffee), Grand Place, Mouscron (near Ypres).

This firm is giving away with its coffee plastic figurines of the history of Belgium (from Roman to modern times). The figures include many of international fame and are of high quality. Almost all so far produced are in 55 mm (1:32 scale). Whilst limiting distribution with its product the firm has set up centres, where duplicates, etc, may be exchanged for others, and publishes newsheets of the figures available and projected. It has also fostered clubs in various parts of Belgium for displays, conventions and historical meetings. (M)

GERMANY

Ochel A, Feldstrasse 24b, Kiel.

Maker of high-quality flat figures. Until recently, as a result of world opinion, these were restricted to cultural and pastoral items, but more martial figures are beginning to appear. (M)

FRANCE

Baldet M.P., 109 rue de Rome, Paris 17eme,

Maker and painter of high-quality full figures in metal, 54 mm, of all countries and all periods. (M)

Baptiste, E., 19 rue Poncelet, Paris 17eme.

Producer of various models, also painter and illustrator. (M)

Bardou, R., 31 rue Raynal, Rodez, Aveyon 12.

Maker of high-grade models of celebrities of French history. (M)

Bieville, Pierre de, 50 boulevard Malesherbe, Paris 8eme.

Proprietor of the SEGOM firm which produces an excellent range of plastic 45 mm figures and accessories, supplied complete and painted or in kit form. At present the range is mainly First Empire but many of the accessories are suitable for use with other periods. (M)

Boverat, Madame R., 'La Montjoye', rue des Graviers, Mareil-Marly, Yvelines 78.

Maker of very fine flat models of all periods. (M)

Bretegnier, P., 'Le Gravelot', par la Chaussee d'Ivry, Eure-et-Loir 28.

Maker of flat figures of all countries and all periods. (M)

Daniel, R., 2 avenue Jan Boin, Choisy-le-Roi, Val de Marne 94.

Maker of toys and very good small-scale model soldiers in plastic. (T)

Dejean, S., 298 rue Henri Deshals, Toulouse 03.

Maker of models of 18th and 19th century French history. (M)

Duretz, R., 15 place Phillippe le Bon, Lille, Nord.
Part-time maker of plastic figures of First Empire. (T)

Historex Société, 23 rue Petion, Paris 19eme.
Makers of military figures in kit form (plastic), at present of French First Empire only but it is planned to cover all periods of all armies. Items cast in white shock-proof polystyrene; a mounted figure is composed of some 40 parts, which enables the modeller to make various changes. For UK supplier see Historex Agents (above). (M)

Metayer, Madame F., 18 rue Nelaton, Paris 15eme.
Maker of model figures, chiefly of Louis XV and XVI and French Revolutionary periods. (M)

Mignot, Maison, 1 rue de Vieux Columbia, Paris 6eme.
Probably the oldest toy soldier firm in the world, having incorporated Lucotte, the first makes of round or solid figures. Although specialising in French types, the production of other national figures is also included but they are now being rivalled by the new plastic model makers. (T)

Mokerex Coffee Co, 101–107 avenue Jean-Jaures, Epinary-Sur-Seine.
Another coffee manufacturer which has made its give-aways in the form of national military and costume figures in plastic. Always very faithfully reproduced in detail, they resort to at least three different scales, but employ leading experts to advise on designs. They also run an exchange centre in Paris for swapping of duplicates, etc, by individuals. As with Cafés Storme there seems no other way of acquiring these excellent figures than by buying their coffee, but I suppose enterprising British people could ask their French friends to switch to this brand of coffee and save the figures for them ! (T)

SPAIN

Almirall Fuste, Jose, Rosallon 285 bis pral 2, Barcelona.
Spain has been lacking a good figure maker until now, but Almirall, who concentrates on Spanish figures, at present is becoming increasingly known and admired outside Spain. (T)

SWEDEN

Eriksson, Holzer, Sommarrovagen 8, Karlstad.
More a designer and sculptor of military miniatures, Eriksson is sought by many firms to design master figures for them. He has an international reputation for this work but does not produce in volume. Specialises in cavalry and artillery of late. (M)

UNITED STATES

Bussler high-quality figures. Obtainable from most stockists below.

Eagle Hobby Center, 2004 Colorado Blvd, Los Angeles, Calif, retails all the best American and foreign figurines; also paints and brushes.

H-R Products, 9232 Wauhegan Road, Morton Grove, Ill.
Specialists in miniature weapons, eg 54 mm scale model of famous French 75 mm field gun. Also architectural items, trees, cars, people, etc, in various scales. (M)

Imrie-Risley Miniatures Inc, PO Box 84, Bank Plaza Sta, Merrick, Long Island, NY.
Stockists and makers of high repute of chiefly 54 mm models. Also retail ready-mixed paints in correct shades, books on the hobby, fixatives, brushes and other accessories. (M)

Merite-Monogram Models Inc, Morton Grove, Ill.

This firm has made the first nine of a promised series in constant 54 mm size metal model soldiers in kit form. The various pieces have a locking feature and display fineness of detail in casting as well as being specially packaged. (M)

Scruby, Jack, 2044 South Linwood, Visalia, Calif.

Another well-known and reputable maker of metal military miniatures, specialising in wargame figures in 20 mm, 25 mm, 1 inch and 30 mm scales of all periods, ancient to modern. (M)

Soldier Shop, The, 1013 Madison Avenue, New York, 10021.

This emporium of militaria is under the supervision of another internationally known modeller of repute, Peter Blum. Retails military miniatures by best of world's makers, as well as books and prints on uniforms and military subjects generally. (M)

Superior Models Inc, 2600 Philadelphia Pike, Claymont, Delaware.

A new firm of modellers specialising in guns and gun crews in 54 mm scale, in kit form. Illustrations of their model German 88 mm shows accurate reproduction down to the minutest detail. (M)

Appendix Seven

SOME SOCIETIES, ASSOCIATIONS, ETC, OF INTEREST TO MODEL SOLDIER COLLECTORS

MOST COLLECTORS will wish to belong to at least one fraternal association connected with their interest. Many societies and associations exist to cater for most needs, some more cultural and learned than others, some more commercial in their approach to the hobby. The average collector should, I suggest, belong to at least two—one being of the 'learned' nature and another which enables him to keep informed of market conditions regarding toys and models. (Replies based on a questionnaire circulated in July 1968.)

Name and address	Main activity	Meetings	Journal
UK and Ireland			
Royal United Service Institution, Whitehall, London SW1.	The senior independent body for defence studies in UK. Eligibility of membership restricted.	Seasonal lecture series in London.	A high-quality quarterly.
Society for Army Historical Research, c/o Library, Old War Office Building, Whitehall, London SW1.	All British and Imperial military matters before 1900.	Annual General in London.	Quarterly—contains queries and replies, and also very useful museum supplements.
British Model Soldier Society, Mr H. Middleton, 169 Queens Rd, Cheadle Hulme, Cheadle, Cheshire. (NB: A very helpful, friendly and lively group.)	General study of hobby; fosters many local displays, competitions and exhibitions.	Monthly in Manchester.	Occasional newsletters.

Miniature AFV Collectors Association (GB), Mr G. E. G. Williams, 15 Berwich Avenue, Heaton Mersey, Stockport, Cheshire.	Study of armoured vehicle warfare and fostering modelling of AFVs, etc.	Periodic in different areas.	Bi-monthly.
Irish Model Soldiers Group, Mr F. Glenn Thompson, 6 Greenlea Park, Terenune, Dublin 6, Ireland.	As for BMSS, above.	Monthly in Dublin.	—
Scottish Model Soldier Society, 80 Braid Road, Edinburgh.	—	Monthly.	—
The Sealed Knot (Society of Cavaliers), Brigadier P. Young, DSO, MC, Lovel End, Windsor Forest, Berks.	Study of British Civil War, especially Royalist Forces.	—	
International Society of Military Collectors, 188 Piccadilly, London W1.	'Tradition' publication.	Every month in London.	'Tradition'.
Society Napoleonic, Mr R. Leighton, 49 Brampton Grove, Kenton, Middlesex.	Research and publications mainly concerning uniforms, weapons and tactics of forces of 1790–1815. Also wargames.	Monthly in London.	Quarterly.
Outside UK and Ireland			
France—Soc de Collectionneurs de Figurines Historiques, Madame Simone Gayda, 38 Rue de Lubeck, Paris 16eme.	The premier society covering the hobby in France. Has international membership.	Normally monthly in Paris.	A high-quality bulletin profusely illustrated (written in French).
USA—Military Historical Society, Mr Peter Blum, PO Box 39, Times Sq, New York.	General study and furtherance of military miniatures in US.	Bi-monthly.	'Adjutants Call'.
Australia—Military Historical Society of Australia, 262 Tucker Rd, Ormond East SE 14, Victoria.	General study.	—	'La Sabretache'.
Belgium—Soc Belge des Coll de Figurines, 75 Rue de Prince Royal, Brussels 5.	General study.	—	'La Figurine'.

Germany—Deutsche Gesselschaft der Freunde und Sammler Kultarhistorischer, Hannovesche Neustadt 26, Burgdorf/Hamburg.	Useful society from which to obtain information regarding figure production in Germany.	—	'Die Zinnfigar'.
Italy—Unione Nazionale Collezionnista d'Italie, (Signor M. Gasparinette), Via Lattanzio, 15a Rome.	The only Italian society known to the author.	—	'La Voce del Collezionista'.
Spain—Agrrupacion de Miniaturistas Milvares, Senor M. Almirall Fuste, Avenida Jose Antonio 595, Cupala de Coliseum, Barcelona.	Senor Almirall is the only important model manufacturer in Spain.	—	'La Boletin'.
Switzerland—Figarina Helvetica Dr E. Diefenbacher, Via Bellavista, 17 6977, Ruvigliana.	The only society in Switzerland known to the author.	—	—

Appendix Eight

SOME GRAMOPHONE RECORDS OF MILITARY MUSIC

contributed by

JOHN FOWLES

'*A good march should make even a man with a wooden leg step out*' (Sousa)

THE PRESENT-DAY MILITARY BAND repertoire is more than adequately covered with records of all the well-known bands in programmes of marches, etc, plus trooping the colour, tattoos and changing of the guard. Choice from these must be left to individual taste and preference. Early military music has, however, been rather neglected by the record companies, except in Germany and France, and this appendix may serve to introduce some unfamiliar material to a wider audience.

When collecting individual marches, particularly regimental marches by regiments now disbanded, 78 RPM records still perform a useful service and enable the collector to be more selective and avoid the endless duplication of the more popular marches generally included on most LP records for commercial reasons.

(*Note: Stereo numbers, where available, given first; where only one number is given, the record was only produced in mono.*) *Of necessity, some of the titles are given in abbreviated form.*

Early Military Music

Music by Farnaby, Gabrieli, Harding, Locke, etc.
London Gabrieli Brass Ensemble.
Pye GGC 4072/GSGC 14072 (UK).
Music by Brade, Bonelli, Pezel, Reiche, etc.
Philadelphia Brass Ensemble.
CBS BRG 72525/SBRG 72525 (UK).

The Royal Brass Music of King James I

Brass Ensemble. Thurston Dart.
L'Oiseau Lyre, OL 50189/SOL 60019 (UK).

Military Music of Three Centuries

(by Bishop, Haydn, Pezel).
London Bach Ensemble. Trevor Sharpe.
Saga, Pan 6209/Span 6209 (UK).

The Art of the Trumpeter

(by Altenburg, M.A. Charpentier, Torelli, etc.)
Tarr Consortium Muskum Lehan.
HMV, HQM 1049/HQS 1049 (UK).
Handel. Music for the Royal Fireworks.
Wind Ensemble, Mackerras.
Pye GGC 4003/GSGC 14003 (UK).

FRENCH

Anthology of French March Music

Musique Des Gardiens De La Paix Dondeyne.
Music Guild, MG 145–6/MS 145–6 (AM).
Music of the Grande Ecurie Versailles.
(Lully Philidor L'aine) Dir Paillard.
Erato, STU 70410 (FR).

Military Fanfares, Marches and Choruses from the time of Napoleon

Musique Des Gardiens De La Paix, Dondeyne.
Nonesuch H 1075/H 71075 (UK).
Berlioz. Grande Symphonie Funebre Et Triumphale.
Musique Des Gardiens De La Paix Dondeyne.
World Record Club. T251/ST251 (UK).

GERMAN

Historical Marches, 1685–1823

Blaser Des Heeresmusikkorps 6 Hamburg. Schade.
Telefunken SLT 43104—B (GER).

Historical Marches, Fanfares, etc, 1600–1820

Das Stabsmusikkorps Der Bundeswehr. Diesenroth.
Ariola 705881U/705891U (AUS).
Der Grobe Zapfenstreich/Historical Marches.
Musikkorps 11 Panzer-Grenadiers DN. Friess.
Polydor 237.301 ST (GER).
Battle Music. Biber, Mozart, Neubauer, etc.
Angelicum Orchestra of Milan. Jenkins.
Nonesuch H1146/71146 (AM).
Haydn/Mozart. Divertimenti, etc.
Vienna State Opera Orc. Salzburg Wind Ensemble.
Dover HCR 5223. (M) (AM).
Beethoven Wind Music.
London Baroque Ensemble. Haas.
Pye GGC 4038/GSGC 14038 (UK)

AMERICAN

Sousa Marches

Goldman Band. R. Franko Goldman.
Decca DL 8807/DL 78807 (AM).

American Marches, etc, 1778–1897

Goldman Band. R. Franko Goldman.
Capitol SP 8631 (S) (AM).

Miscellaneous

Scots Guards Corps of Drums of the 2nd Battalion.
Marches.
Philips STL 5421/TL 5421.

Central Band of the Royal Air Force.
Music for ceremonial occasions.
HMV CSD 1615/CLP1892.

Band of the Royal Marines Beating the Retreat. Ceremony of the tattoo.
HMV CSD 1397/CLP 1492.

Band of the Royal Military School of Music (Kneller Hall).
Regimental Marches of the British Army
Columbia SX 1104.

Band of the Grenadier Guards Trooping the Colour.
Decca ACL 1032 (Mono only).
Decca PFS 4037/LK4562.

Searchlight Tatto (White City).
1955–1958
HMV ENC 150.
1959
HMV DLP 1207 (10″).

Edinburgh Military Tattoo.
1965 Waverley SZLP 2063/ZLP 2062.
1966 Waverley SZLP 2080/ZLP 2080.
1967 Waverley SZLP 2095/ZLP 2095.
1968 Waverley SZLP 4109/ZLP 4109.